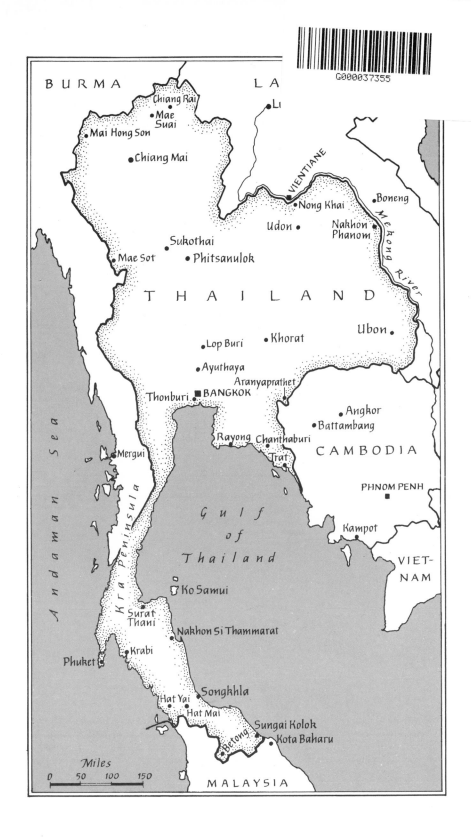

Thailand
The Last Domino

Also by Richard West

HURRICANE IN NICARAGUA

Thailand
The Last Domino

CULTURAL AND POLITICAL TRAVELS

RICHARD WEST

MICHAEL JOSEPH
London

MICHAEL JOSEPH LTD

Published by the Penguin Group
27 Wrights Lane, London W8 5TZ, England
Viking Penguin, a division of Penguin Books USA Inc.
375 Hudson Street, New York, New York 10014, USA
Penguin Books Australia Ltd, Ringwood, Victoria, Australia
Penguin Books Canada Ltd, 2801 John Street, Markham, Ontario, Canada L3R 1B4
Penguin Books (NZ) Ltd, 182–190 Wairau Road, Auckland 10, New Zealand

Penguin Books Ltd, Registered Offices: Harmondsworth, Middlesex, England

First published in Great Britain 1991

Copyright © Richard West 1991

Printed in England by Clays Ltd, St Ives plc
Filmset in Monophoto 11/13 pt Photina

A CIP catalogue record for this book is available from the British Library
ISBN 0 7181 3277 7

The moral right of the author has been asserted

Contents

Preface

The Kingdom of Thailand, which used to be known as Siam, has welcomed foreigners since the thirteenth century, when Sukothai was the capital and by the end of the seventeenth century was entertaining missions from Europe, including an Embassy from King Louis XIV of France. Although Siam was often at war with neighbouring Burma, Laos, Cambodia and Vietnam, she took care not to provoke or quarrel with the various European intruders in Southeast Asia. Thanks to her graceful diplomacy and her own internal stability, Siam was the only territory in the region to keep her independence.

Although Thailand was occupied by the Japanese in the Second World War and technically fought the Allies, she soon re-emerged as a friend of the West against the new enemy, communism. Thailand provided US Air Force bases during the Vietnam War and even sent troops to fight there. Some Americans had predicted that if Vietnam went communist, the neighbouring countries like Thailand would fall like a row of dominoes. But when Saigon was captured in 1975, the Domino Theory proved to be wrong. As hundreds of thousands of refugees poured into Thailand from Vietnam, Laos and Cambodia, the Thais were united in detestation of communism. With a booming economy, based on the wealth of her rice fields, Thailand became one of the most stable and prosperous countries in Asia. Millions of tourists have found that the Thais maintain their ancient tradition of welcoming and delighting visitors. The description of Sukothai in the thirteenth century still holds good for the modern country whose capital now is Bangkok: 'In the water there are fish, in the field there is rice ... Whoever wants to play, so plays.

Whoever wants to laugh, so laughs. Whoever wants to sing, so sings ...'

Because it is so attractive to tourists, Thailand is one of the best known countries in the world. Most travellers in this region, from Japan in the north to Australasia in the south, find some occasion to stop at Bangkok. Although most of the tourists now are from Western Europe, the Americans too remember Thailand where millions of them took their leave during the Vietnam War. Australians and New Zealanders often stop in Bangkok on their way to and from Europe. Most people who visit Thailand fall in love with the country and its smiling people.

But knowing and loving Thailand do not amount to an understanding. The charm and courtesy of the Thais are joined with an evasiveness, amounting to duplicity, which they employed on the Europeans during the nineteenth century, the Japanese during the Second World War, more recently on the Americans and on the Chinese. The longer you know the Thais, the less you feel that you understand them.

Throughout their history, the Thais have been in the habit of borrowing or adapting foreign fashions, from China, Japan, various countries in Europe and lastly from the United States. But the Thais can just as readily drop these fashions, whether for top hats, jazz or socialism. Underneath they remain Thais. Three things in the Thai national character have remained immutable; their love of the Buddhist religion, the King and the family.

Even when he has understood this, the inquiring foreigner still finds himself puzzled by certain questions about this country, questions for which there is no clear answer. Here is a sample: How did Thailand stay as an absolute monarchy until 1932? Has Thailand ever become a real democracy? Is Thailand ruled by the armed forces? Why have the communists never made any progress? Is Bangkok really a Chinese city? Are the Chinese accepted? Why did Thailand close American bases in 1975 and then make an alliance with Communist China? Why does Thailand support the Cambodian Communists, or Khmers Rouges, against Vietnam? Why was Siam renamed Thailand? Why do some people want the old name back? Does Thailand really try to suppress the heroin trade? Have the Thais been Americanized? Lastly, the most difficult question of all: why do so many Thai women go into prostitution?

The Thai evasiveness comes out in the Press and in books on the country, although there is no real censorship. The excellent

Bangkok Post, for example, has an unrivalled coverage of events in Burma, Vietnam and Cambodia, but is oddly oblique when writing of Thailand. You have to know how to read between the lines. An article on deforestation may be a roundabout attack on a Chinese businessman. An article on the army may be a critical reference to the Crown Prince. A debate on whether the country needs an anti-communism law, may be a coded condemnation of the regime in Singapore or Malaysia.

There are a few good history books on certain aspects of life in Thailand, for example the Chinese minority, but there are no good general histories of political life in the last fifty years. It is perhaps characteristic of the Thais that by far the best guides to understanding the country are three very good novels, one set in the Royal Court one hundred years ago, one in the north-east and one in Bangkok's Chinatown. All three books told me more about their respective subjects than I had learned in months or years of inquiry which usually lead to bland and evasive answers.

In writing this book, I have roamed through Thailand, visiting most of the places where tourists go and more where foreigners seldom venture. But this is not intended to be a guidebook. There are few remote or exotic places in modern Thailand. You can travel easily and in comfort by air, rail, bus or car, staying at pleasant hotels and eating clean and delicious food. Unless you are most unlucky, you will not encounter difficulty or hazard. Because the appearance of Thailand is so well known to millions of visitors, I shall not attempt the kind of pen-pictures written by earlier travellers in the East. My purpose is to describe not what tourists see but what they do not see, the enigmatic Thailand. I have set out to write the book I had always wanted to read on Thailand, but never found, the book which answered some of my questions.

More than most countries, Thailand has to be studied with constant reference to its neighbours, in this case Burma, Malaysia, Laos, Cambodia, China and Vietnam. To grasp the full significance of the fact that Thailand was never colonized, you have to compare it with countries that were. The fate of Thailand during the Second World War has to be understood in the context of all Indo-China and the Malay peninsula. The long insurgency in the South of Thailand has always been led by the Communist party of Malaysia. Above all, Thailand is still deeply involved in the endless Vietnam War, which now is fought in Cambodia. There are three Cambodian armies based in Thailand as well as hundreds of thousands of refugees. Artillery fire has taken a steady toll of Thais, both military and civilians. The Vietnam War is seen by the Thais as almost as much of a menace as during the 1960s. It preoccupies, even obsesses, the Bangkok newspapers. It is certain to interest any intelligent visitor.

When I first went to Thailand in 1963, I was on my way to the then peaceful kingdom of Cambodia. During the next twelve years, I generally stayed in Thailand either before or after visiting Vietnam, where I wrote two books, *Sketches from Vietnam* (1968) and *Victory in Vietnam* (1974), which also included chapters on Cambodia and Laos. To an extent, *Thailand: The Last Domino* is a sequel. It tells how the battlefield shifted from Vietnam to Thailand's border with Cambodia. It seeks to explain how Thailand avoided full-scale war and a communist revolution. Nevertheless, there is still political tension and sometimes shooting along the borders with all four of Thailand's immediate neighbours. This explains why so much of this book is concerned with the outer fringes of Thailand rather than with the central plains. Such concentration upon the borders would seem inappropriate in a book on, for instance, France, but it is vital to understanding Thailand.

Because of the arguments over the Vietnam War and more recent events in Cambodia, Thailand is now involved in the ideological arguments of the West. The friends of Vietnam and enemies of the United States, denounce Thailand's support for the Khmer Rouge in Cambodia. On this matter, I also support the Vietnamese position but do not go on from there to condemn Thailand, which has its reasons for fearing Vietnam. As far as anyone is to blame for the horrors afflicting Cambodia, it is the Khmers themselves, whether red or blue. When writing about the unpleasant aspects of life in Thailand, like prostitution and cutting down trees, I have tried to explain them rather than strike moral attitudes.

On questions of politics, I am opposed to both Left and Right, or socialism and nationalism. On the other hand, I favour the three institutions, religion, the family and the monarchy, which are the basis of Thai society.

London, September 1990

PART ONE

The North

CHAPTER ONE

This Land of Sukhothai

Although most visitors come into Thailand at Bangkok airport, the wise ones do not stay long in Bangkok. It is noisy, ugly, crowded with traffic and, if you have jet lag, lowering to the spirit. It is also a poor introduction to Thailand. In most of the world's great capital cities, however destroyed by war, or congested by traffic, or overshadowed by high-rise buildings, you get a sense of the country's history. Westminster Abbey, St Paul's and the Houses of Parliament help to make London a living museum of the past. Athens, Rome, Paris, Berlin and Washington are all, in their different ways, monumental. Old and New Delhi, created by the Moguls and British respectively, are starting points for a journey in search of India.

Bangkok tells you nothing at all of Thailand. You see the Thai script in cinema posters and neon signs; the waitresses in expensive hotels wear Thai sarongs; you may even meet some Thais among the Chinese and Laotians. If you visit the Palace and other buildings of Royal Bangkok, you may find them interesting and even attractive, but they are not old, and few are distinctively Thai. Even the nineteenth-century artefacts somehow foreshadow Hollywood. At some time during your stay, you are likely to be in a traffic jam beside the Democracy Monument and you are almost sure to be in a traffic jam near the Victory Monument, but you will not discover why or whether Thailand became a democracy, or what was the battle that ended in victory.

Although Bangkok is the capital of the present Chakri dynasty, which founded the city in 1782, the history of the country starts to make sense only when you consider the earlier Thai kingdoms. It is not a long history either by Asian or European standards. The Thais and their kindred people the Shans and Laotians came to

Siam from southern China at roughly the same time as the
Normans came to Britain. The Shans moved into eastern Burma,
the Laotians into their present territory, east of the Mekong River,
while the Thais moved south down the Chao Phraya Valley, which
had previously been under the rule of Cambodia and was probably
occupied by a people similar to Cambodians. Small Thai kingdoms
appeared at Chiang Rai and Chiang Mai in the north; during the
thirteenth century they built a magnificent kingdom at Sukhothai; then moved further south to Lop Buri and Ayutthaya,
which fell to the Burmese in 1767.

In the centre and north you see as well as the ancient monuments, the flourishing heartland of modern Thailand, rich from
the abundant rice, and strong in its devotion to monarchy and
religion. In the north especially, you also see some of the sadder
aspects of life in Thailand: the deforestation, the drug traffic and its
resulting lawlessness. In plotting this journey through central and
northern Thailand, I have tried to weave a historic thread through
the pattern of modern society. Thus I start at Lop Buri, a centre of
that Khmer civilization which existed before the Thais; then go on
to Sukhothai, the first and most splendid of Thailand's kingdoms;
then up to Chiang Rai and the Burmese border; a stay in Chiang
Mai, an enchanting city; then back to Bangkok, including a stop
at Ayutthaya, the last great kingdom before the Chakri dynasty
and the rise of Bangkok.

Getting out of Bangkok is a great deal harder than getting out of
Manchester, which, as I learned after a year in that city, means
getting drunk. During the daylight hours and till long after dark, a
journey always begins with a wait in a traffic jam. This part of the
journey is also expensive. The taxi fare from the New Trocadero
Hotel to Bangkok's Northern Bus Terminal usually costs more
than the air-conditioned bus from the Terminal to Chiang Mai. It
is not so hard to get to Hualumphong Railway Station and anyway
it is much more pleasant to travel by train. The question is whether
to travel by night or day.

The night trains to Chiang Mai, to the south, and to two different
parts of the north-east are all delightful. You leave in the late
afternoon and are out in the countryside when darkness falls. In
the Express trains you eat in a restaurant car, while in Rapid
trains the attendant brings the meals and the beer to your seat,
where a table is placed between you and the person opposite. Later
the seats become the lower berth to a bunk which pulls away from

the wall. You draw the curtains, undress and enjoy a good sleep, or you may be offered a girl from the railway entertainment department.

All this is in second class. The Express trains also provide private, air-conditioned compartments, still at about a fifth of the price you would pay for a second-class seat on one of the rotten trains of British Rail. Needless to say, there are no strikes, no queues for the buffet car, no vandals, no football hooligans, no rapists, no 'steamers' and no yobboes refusing to turn down their ghetto-blasters. The contrast with England is startling, even before you board the train at Hualumphong Station. There are no alcoholics sleeping rough on the floor, no rent boys touting for custom, no drug addicts 'shooting up' in the take-your-own-photograph booths. It is here in the railway station, waiting to leave Bangkok that I feel most poignantly how much I love Thailand and how much I no longer love England.

Because I was wanting to break the journey and anyway like to look out at the countryside, I took the Rapid train leaving Bangkok at 6.40 a.m. Before six in the morning, even the streets of Bangkok are empty and what is more, free of fumes, so that the trip by three-wheel scooter was almost refreshing. It is always worthwhile boarding a train early, to get a seat on the side that is out of the sun, that is, when travelling north, to sit on the left side in the morning and on the right side in the afternoon. All Thais know this, and also make sure that the nearest fan is working.

The railway tracks in Thailand are not, as in Europe, raised on embankments and fenced off from the countryside. They are more like tramlines running along the fields and villages and the streets of suburban cities. Although this means moving at fairly slow speed, for fear of hitting an elephant or a water buffalo, it also means that you get a close-up view of Thailand. Any journey from Bangkok starts with an amble through shanty-towns, then out past the airport into the rice land.

By the time you reach Lop Buri, eighty-five miles to the north, the train is moving through an immense plain of rice fields, brilliantly green with the summer rain, and studded with trees where the farmers can rest and eat their snacks in the shade. The kitchen attendants bring round plates of fried rice and egg, to which you can add bits of food from the free-lance vendors: grilled chicken on sticks, sugar cane, rice cakes and bunches of small green bananas. At every station, boys and girls rush on to the train to sell ice cream or sachets of fresh water, and as the train gets up speed, they play a game of chicken to see who leaps off last. They never appear to hurt themselves in a fall.

In contrast to other old cities in Asia, the ruins of Lop Buri are part of the modern town, so that a Hindu temple actually serves as a traffic island. This and the very tall TV aerials give an air of anachronism that I find pleasing rather than untoward. It reminded me of the laundry hanging out of the flats in Diocletian's Palace in Split, Yugoslavia. The most magnificent of the shrines at Lop Buri, the twelfth-century Wat Sri Ratana Mahathat, stands right in front of you as you leave the station. It was built by the Khmers at about the same time and in much the same style as the vast city of Angkor in northern Cambodia. Since at the time of writing the various Khmer factions show no sign of a compromise and may be bracing themselves for a further war, those who would like to see Angkor, still must content themselves with the Khmer remains at places like Lop Buri.

Another of these is the Phra Prang Suan Yot, or Three Pagodas, its sandstone and laterite *prang* representing the Hindu trio of Brahma, Vishnu and Shiva. The Three Pagodas also appear on the back of the old 500 baht note. Behind the Three Pagodas on the other side of the railway track is a shrine to Kali, the Hindu goddess of death, known generally as the Monkey Temple, because it is overrun by Samae monkeys. It is said that the locals revere these animals because they bury their dead; or at least no one has found a dead monkey. I have not been fond of these creatures since one of them put a paw through its cage in the Harrod's pet department and pulled out some of my hair, when I was six years old. The Lop Buri monkeys are just as aggressive. Fifty yards from the temple, a large menacing brute with its fangs bared, rushed at a small girl and snatched the plastic bag she was holding. When the monkey found that the bag contained no food and only a bunch of jasmine, it beat its fist on the ground and chattered with rage. Monkeys infest the railway track, the traffic roundabout and even the awnings of nearby shops.

The Lop Buri people laugh at the monkeys. It is a friendly and easy-going town. Cars slow down for you crossing the road, rather than picking up speed, as they do in Bangkok. As I strolled past Wat Sri Ratana Mahathat, a pedicab driver fell in beside me and asked if I wanted a ride. No thanks, I said, I liked walking. 'Yes, exercise, that's good for you,' was his tolerant answer. He pedalled beside me, happy to try out his English, then showed me the testimonial, written for him by one of his English clients. 'Khao will show you all the temples and is good company for a drink in the evening,' it said, or words to that effect.

In the market I was approached by a middle-aged gentleman with a sturdy bearing and clipped, grey moustache. I was not surprised to hear he had been in the services:

> I did fourteen and a half years in the Marines, protecting this country against Vietnam. This is a military town, Lop Buri, Thailand's army base. At the weekend market, more than half the shoppers are from army families. If there's ever a military take-over, how do you say, a *coup d'état*, it would have to have the permission of Lop Buri and its six or seven divisions. You see, now that Thailand's becoming an NIC, we have to be strong to defend ourselves.

An NIC or 'newly industrialized country' is one piece of socio-economic jargon you hear only too often in Thailand. It is popular with the capitalists who want to do down agriculture and plunder natural resources in order to make the cars and gadgets that Thailand can quite well buy from Japan.

The military man was eager to show me the sights of the town, in return for the chance to practise his English. He showed me the Palace and other buildings from Lop Buri's second term as a city of greatness. This was the reign of King Narai of Ayutthaya, during the seventeenth century. The Dutch had blockaded the mouth of the Chao Phraya River, so Narai had thought it expedient to remove upstream. Louis XIV had sent a Minister to the Court of Ayutthaya, who in turn provided an architect for Lop Buri. The Palace, the French minister's residence and a Roman Catholic chapel were built in a curious mixture of Thai, Persian and Louis Quatorze styles. One of these French mansions was home to the Greek trader-adventurer, Constantine Phaulkon, who basked in King Narai's favour. This did not survive the king's death. The military gentleman told me with suitable gestures as well as words, how Phaulkon was taken outside the city, obliged to kneel, then beaten to death with a sandalwood club. Other accounts say that his death was more cruel.

The military gentleman took me back to his house to give me some printed notes on Lop Buri's history. I saw on a blackboard in his front room two English phrases: 'There is a balance of payments deficit . . . It's not the size of the rabbit, but the magic of the wand.' As I read this, he tittered: 'An American friend told me that saying. This was after an American lady would not go with me because she said Thai men were too small.'

The Thai obsession with sex is found even in old-fashioned towns like Lop Buri, far from the Patpong Road. The rooms in the Asia Hotel here are fitted with condom dispensers. Yet at the public swimming pool, the women bathers have to wear full costumes and caps. Both these pieces of information I learned from Frank Kusy's contribution to *Thailand and Burma* in the Cadogan Guides Series. Some sort of guidebook is absolutely essential if you are travelling on your own, and you should choose one with care. There is nothing in this or any other part of the world to match the *South American Handbook*, which tells you everything from the politics of El Salvador to which hotels have thieves and malodorous dogs in Nicaragua.

Travellers should avoid any guidebook with photographs or fancy descriptive writing: they can see the place for themselves. In choosing hotels and places to eat, the traveller wants something between a guidebook for businessmen on expenses and those written for indigent backpackers, though in the latter category I can recommend *South-east Asia on a Shoestring*. At the time of writing, however, Mr Kusy's guide is the best. The book includes a section on Burma, which adds unnecessary weight, and the maps are inaccurate and not to scale. (What is the point of a map that is not to scale?) It also seems that Mr Kusy has a passion for cakes and pastry, which his readers may not share. But most of the places he recommends are adequate; he knows that a cheaper hotel or guest house may be more comfortable than the one offering luxuries; he is also a good guide to the character of a town. He was charmed by Lop Buri as by Sukhothai, where I stopped for some days on the journey north.

Between Lop Buri and Phitsanulok, where I got off the train and changed to a bus for Sukhothai, the central plain looked still more lush and fecund. Rice from this good earth is the wealth of Thailand, which should be remembered by those who would rather turn Thailand into an NIC. It is customary in the West to think of the Asian peasants as an oppressed and joyless people. Partly we get this idea from India, with its atrocious climate and desiccated soil. But this part of Thailand, like Burma and South Vietnam, is blessed by nature and rich not only in rice but vegetables, fruit, fish, pigs, oxen, chicken and ducks. Unlike the neighbouring countries of Indo-China, Thailand did not have a taxation system that forced the farmers into the hands of the money-lenders. Until this century, the Thais were obliged to do so many months of work each year for the king, in a system similar to the old French corvée. But since this duty fell in the idle months after the rice harvest, the corvée did not interfere with work in the fields, and it did not involve money indebtedness. There was much to be said for the feudal system, as for the absolute monarchy, under a wise and virtuous king.

One of the first and greatest kings in Siam was Ramkhamhaeng, who ruled in Sukhothai from the thirteenth into the fourteenth century. Sukhothai, meaning Dawn of Happiness, had been founded in 1238 as the first Thai kingdom independent of Angkor. During his forty-year reign, King Ramkhamhaeng established suzerainty over most of the present Thailand. He brought merchants and artisans from China, and Buddhist monks from Ceylon. He invented the present Thai alphabet, which was used to write in stone the principles of his economic and legal system:

> In the time of Father King Ramkhamhaeng this land of Sukhothai is good. In the water there are fish, in the field there is rice. The ruler does not levy a tax on the people who travel along the road together. Whoever wants to trade in elephants, so trades. Whoever wants to trade in horses, so trades. Whoever wants to trade in silver and gold, so trades. When common people of the realm, nobles or princes, are in dispute, the king sifts the dispute and decides in honesty . . . Over there, at the gateway, a bell is hung. If any people of the realm seek audience of the King, having anguish in their stomach, or grievance at heart, there is no obstacle. Ring the bell hanging there. Hearing the call, Father King Ramkhamhaeng will sift the case honestly . . . Whoever wants to play, so plays. Whoever wants to laugh, so laughs. Whoever wants to sing, so sings. It is as if this city of Sukhothai would burst from the clamour . . .

It has to be said that some modern historians challenge the school textbook version of Sukhothai. Professor Srisaka Vallibhotama of Silpakhorn University casts doubt on the theory that Sukhothai was seized from the Khmers in the thirteenth century by Thais, newly arrived from China. He says that it probably grew from trade between various ethnic groups. A lecturer in political science, Chai-anan Samutrawanich questions the truth of the famous inscription, 'In the water there are fish, in the fields there is rice'. He says (in the *Nation*, 8 February 1990) that in fact the soil was so arid that rulers and residents of the city had to build irrigation systems in order to farm the land. He argues that King Ramkhamhaeng was less important than his successors, adding, 'The interpretation of Sukhothai history has long been used as state propaganda to serve past governments when they needed to strengthen the concept of a unified nation, or to be exact, a nation state.' This is perhaps a guarded reference to a tendency by the ethnic Thais to play down the historic importance of other ethnic groups such as the Chinese, the Cambodians and the Laotians.

The remains of the old city stand about eight miles from modern Sukhothai, which is a friendly and most agreeable place. The hotel where I stayed, costing £2 a night for a room with fan, was occupied mostly by West European university students on long vacation. The bright young Frenchwoman whom I had seen on the train and wondered what she and her husband did for a living, was now engrossed in the stock market news of the *Bangkok Post*, so Sukhothai is also attracting the yuppy tribe. King Ramkhamhaeng would approve of their free market principles.

Between the hotel and the river there is a small park full of flowers, as well as swings, slides and roundabouts for the youngsters. A grinning girl of about eighteen came up, introduced herself and started to practise her English and teach me Thai. As she prattled about her family and how she was leaving home to be a hairdresser, I pondered upon the innocence of this country. A girl of that age in England who went up and chatted to strange men would risk getting raped and probably strangled into the bargain. In most parts of England, an adult on his own is not even allowed by law to enter a children's playground on the assumption that he is a child molester.

The old city of Sukhothai filled me with an intense delight each morning I spent there. In fact, I cannot ever remember having enjoyed any sights so much as these *wats, chedis* and statues of Buddha. A major part of the joy comes from the setting in what is now called Sukhothai Historic Park. The word park fills us with dread because we have so debased it by the creation of 'theme parks' or 'heritage parks', for example the Rhonddha Heritage Park, whose aim is to recreate a complete 1920s style Rhonddha mining village, complete with a working mine, a pub ... and a choral centre. But here the word park is used in its proper sense of nature modified by man, or something between a garden and a wilderness. There are many trees but not so many that they obscure the views of the temples. There are moats, canals, lakes and ponds, and flowers growing wild and in beds. Like all the best parks, this has patches of wilderness, even creeping over the ruins, as at Angkor. This immense, beautiful park is alive with the noise of birds, insects and animals, though thankfully there are not many dogs, which sometimes in Thailand are savage and rabid.

The renovation of Sukhothai was finished in 1989 after ten years' work under the sponsorship of the Thai Royal Family, which is behind most good things in this country. Indeed the Royal Family here has done what the British Royal Family does for the parks in London, that is keeping them out of the clutches of the politicians. At Sukhothai, the renovators have refaced and virtually rebuilt the temples. Some say they preferred them in ruins. I cannot agree. All the buildings here are solid and monolithic, so there was no need for structural alterations, as there would be for a building with a roofed interior space. We know what the temples looked like when they were built, so why not restore them? The work respects the original, unlike the embellishments made to some of our English churches by the Victorians.

Although Sukhothai is spread over forty square miles, the three temples I liked most were all within strolling distance from the main gate. Of those monuments that you have to visit by car or bicycle, the masterpiece is the Buddha at Wat Sri Chum, hidden away in a drab *mondop*, a brick enclosure. The figure is large, measuring ten yards from knee to knee, but it is not the size that exerts such wonder and fascination. Nor is it the colouring, for apart from some gilt on the fingers, it is grey, with patches of white and moss green, giving a fishy and underwater appearance. The mouth of the Buddha is neither smiling nor stern, yet something about the eyes and set of the jaw convey an immense authority. I can quite accept the tale that the sight of this awesome Buddha halted a Burmese army in terror.

The three wat near to the main gate include a trio of *prang* in the Khmer style, similar to the Three Pagodas in Lop Buri. But whereas the Lop Buri temple is sandwiched between the railway track and the main road, Wat Sri Sawai is ringed by a lotus pond and a number of flowerbeds. A quite different style is seen in the

Wat Sra Sri, a circular, concave spire which was no doubt built by
the monks from Ceylon. Near this temple there is a curious, black
life-sized statue of a 'walking monk', a genre invented at Sukhothai,
which shows the man in an unmistakably mincing and limp-
wristed posture, more commonly seen among Anglican clergymen
of the High Church persuasion.

The finest of all these temples is Wat Mahathat, consisting of
ninety-eight small chedi surrounding a large central chedi with
lotus-bud prang and a frieze round the base of walking monks,
though they are not camping it up like the black fellow. Present-
day monks have garbed some of the Buddha figures, the chedi and
sacred *bo* trees with saffron sashes of muslin or some fine cotton.
These add flashes of colour and serve to remind us that here are
shrines of a living religion. The atmosphere is very different from
Angkor which, in spite of its grandeur and beauty, gives no sense
of human or even ghostly life, and is somehow both sinister and
totalitarian. In Sukhothai you get a sense of the continuity of
worship, as you do in our English churches built in the same
thirteenth century; you sense that the Thais who lived here, seven
hundred years ago, were much the same as those living in modern
Sukhothai. 'Whoever wants to play, so plays. Whoever wants to
laugh, so laughs. Whoever wants to sing, so sings.'

Although the Kingdom of Sukhothai lasted a mere 150 years, it
had in that time created a Thai civilization quite distinct from the
Khmer domain of Lop Buri. And when, in the fourteenth century,
the Thais moved their kingdom south to Ayutthaya, they quickly
entered what is considered their Golden Age, the fifteenth century,
an epoch of war and woe in Europe.

Each morning, after a stroll round all three of the major wat, I
take a seat under a sacred *bo* tree in Wat Mahathat, to hear the
song of the birds and the breezes rattling the leaves, and to watch
the lizards scampering over the masonry, or a white cat stalking
some prey along Buddha's forearm. It is a place of enchantment
and utter peace. It is a place to be on your own, for the small talk
of tourists, even of friends and loved ones, breaks the spell of these
Buddhist temples. The Thais themselves respect the enjoyment of
silence. Although friendly and extrovert, they know when you
want to be on your own.

CHAPTER TWO

The Golden Triangle

At the height of the glory of Sukhothai, another kingdom came into existence far to the north, at Chiang Rai. King Mengrai had come from southern China and ruled for a time in what is now Laos, before crossing the Mekong River to present-day Thailand. There was not at that time, or even today, a clear-cut distinction between the Laotians and the Thais. The people in north-east Thailand call themselves Lao and speak the same language as those over the river in Laos. Until quite recently, Bangkok people gave the name Lao to those in the north as well as the north-east. The people of Laos, before the communists, called their kingdom *Lan San*, 'one million elephants', and King Mengrai called his kingdom *Lan Na*, one million rice-fields. Lan Na is still the word used for the north of Thailand. Although King Mengrai soon moved his capital to Chiang Mai, the major city of *Lan Na* today, Chiang Rai is the most important town close to the northern border.

There are still border skirmishes with Burma, and more serious ones with Laos, which in 1988 launched an artillery barrage and shot down a Thai military plane. But most of the trouble round here has little to do with the aspirations and quarrels of politicians in Bangkok, Rangoon and Vientiane; much to do with the hill tribespeople. The race and origin of the people found all over the uplands of Indo-China remain a puzzle to anthropologists. The Montagnards, as the French called them in Vietnam, were thought by some to have Polynesian ancestry. The Mongs of Laos are thought to come from Mongolia because of their name and their chubby moon faces. Whatever name you call any particular tribe arouses the ire of experts, who say it is incorrect and insulting. The lowland Thais, Burmese and Vietnamese all have their opprobious term for the hill people, meaning something like savage.

The highlanders in their turn distrust the men of the plain. In South Vietnam, the Montagnards looked first to the French and then to the American forces to save them from the rapacious Vietnamese. The Americans, who were startled and delighted to find people who liked them, got on famously with the Montagnards and joined in their parties of rice-wine drinking and animal sacrifice. In Laos as well, the hill people sided with the Americans, afterwards paying the price. In Burma, the Karens, a Christian people, fought with the British against the Japanese, and still resist the Rangoon forces who hold little authority in the mountains. Another force of disruption has been the Kuomintang or Chinese Nationalist Army (KMT), which came here in 1945. The United States wanted to use them to clear up the Japanese and to keep law and order. The KMT pillaged Vietnam and Laos, then moved into the borderland between Burma and Thailand, where they still remain, as a law unto themselves. When Laos went communist in 1975, thousands of tribespeople crossed the Mekong to Thailand where they naturally settled in their own kind of habitat in the hills. Burmese tribespeople came into Thailand from the other direction, fleeing the government troops, the Kuomintang or just the bankrupt economy.

This mountainous region of Thailand, Burma and Laos is also suitable to the growing of *papaver somniferum*, the opium poppy, and hence has become notorious as the Golden Triangle. The tourist touts of northern Thailand have given the name to a tiny patch of land at the junction of the three countries but Golden Triangle really means any place where opium grows. There have been countless articles, thrillers and documentary films on drugs and the Golden Triangle, of which the classic account is Alfred W. McCoy's *The Politics of Heroin in South-East Asia*, but here I shall mention only some aspects affecting Thailand.

It is wrong to think that the Thais have ever taken a tolerant view of drug abuse. The kings down to the nineteenth century condemned the use of opium on the grounds that the craving led people to steal. Smoking the drug as well as the failure to inform on those who smoked it was punishable by flogging. The Buddhists condemned all forms of intoxication. The common people believed that a man who died of opium smoking became a *prade*, a form of malevolent spirit as tall as the sugar palm tree, and with a long neck:

It was always hungry because its mouth was so tiny it could hardly eat anything, and yet somehow it had a long tongue hanging out and its body odour was so repellent that the *prade* itself suffered from it. On its head was a *chakra*, a sharp-edged discus which gradually cut the *prade*'s long neck causing a profusion of blood to flow; yet when the neck had been completely cut, the whole thing would grow again thus giving the *prade* years of repeated torment. The *prade*, which could be male or female, heralded its approach with a blood-curdling shriek, and its misery could only be ended by much merit being made on its behalf by intimate living relatives. (From *Lords of Life* by Prince Chula Chakrabongse.)

It was the British who first 'pushed' opium to Southeast Asia. The merchants of the East India Company encouraged the growing of opium poppies in Upper Bengal and other suitable regions, sending it back to England for use as a medicine. De Quincey and Coleridge are the best known of the many who became opium addicts. It was not till the 1840s, however, that East India merchants tried to enter the market in China, where opium was already a popular vice. The successful efforts to force its sale, not as a medicine but as a narcotic, led to the Opium Wars and ultimately to the growth and wealth of Hong Kong.

At about the same time, the British were trying to enter the Siamese market. Although King Mongkut did not want to allow the use of the drug by Thais, he did not object to it in the Chinese community, many of whom were already smokers. Indeed, he granted a 'farm' or monopoly of the opium sales to a Chinese syndicate, on condition that they did not sell the drug to Thais. Any Thai who broke this rule was made to wear the Chinese queue, or pigtail, and also to pay the Chinese tax. The Chinese farms for opium, liquor and gambling, continued into the present century, accounting for 40 to 50 per cent of the national revenue.

The French in their Indo-China colonies also paid half of their costs through a state opium monopoly. Visitors to Saigon in the 1930s complained that the whole city reeked of the drug, and that cycle drivers steered you to opium dens with the same persistence that Bangkok drivers now steer you to massage parlours. Many Vietnamese as well as French and Chinese became opium addicts. In South Vietnam, in the 1950s, the Diem regime closed down the opium dens and made it illegal even to own a pipe, although

Diem's secret police were engaged in selling the drug. After Diem's overthrow in November 1963, the CIA helped the military rulers of South Vietnam to finance themselves by selling opium flown down from Laos on military planes. Soon most of this opium was refined into heroin.

The availability in South Vietnam of heroin, marijuana, speed and various kinds of 'uppers' and 'downers' soon affected the US servicemen, especially the conscript troops who found a release in drugs from their fear and homesickness. In the second half of the 1960s, when there were 600,000 Americans serving in South Vietnam at any one time, the United States itself was undergoing a 'permissive revolution' with regard to drugs as well as to sex. It was the age of the film *Easy Rider*, the Woodstock Festival and the hippies of California. The US servicemen stationed in Thailand, or visiting here for 'R & R', introduced drugs to Bangkok and Pattaya.

The drug habit spread to the Vietnamese and, later, the Thais. When the American forces left Vietnam in 1973, the drug traders lowered the price and purity of the heroin to find new addicts among the locals, especially among the prostitutes and young soldiers. Even in April 1975, as communist troops surrounded Saigon, tens of thousands of desperate addicts were 'shooting up' the remaining heroin, or if they could not get it, sleeping pills or even aspirin. The Vietnamese and now the Thais have a great belief in the power of the needle to give some extra charge to the drug. Of 300,000 known drug addicts in Thailand, more than half take heroin intravenously. This is why AIDS in the country is largely an addicts' disease. Official statistics say that 80 per cent of carriers of the virus are drug addicts, and 10 per cent prostitutes, but the figures do not show whether the prostitutes are also takers of intravenous drugs.

We in the West must shoulder the blame for Thailand's epidemic of drug abuse, and now the fatal disease of AIDS. First Britain, then France and more recently the United States, pushed opium or its derivatives in Southeast Asia. Then, in a fit of permissiveness in the 1960s, the West abandoned its old religious prohibitions and taboos against everything from pornography, to drug abuse and sodomy. Tolerance of such mild drugs as marijuana led to the present epidemic of cocaine, crack and heroin, while legalization of 'gay' behaviour led, with frightening speed, to the AIDS epidemic.

Libertarians argue that AIDS and a drug epidemic are not too high a price to pay for greater freedom and toleration. What they should not do is to blame the drug epidemic in the United States and Europe on countries like Thailand from which the drugs come. In August 1989, President Bush announced a $7.9 billion campaign against drugs, which 27 per cent of Americans saw as the major problem facing their country. The United States financed an armed offensive by the Colombian government against the cocaine barons of Medellín, 'the extradictables'. The public in the United States and countries in Europe were calling for drastic prison terms or even capital punishment for the traffickers in drugs, but not, it appears, a return to the practice of jailing those who smoke, sniff or inject them. By making war on the cocaine barons, President Bush appears to accept the fallacy that the supply of drugs creates a demand, whereas all the evidence shows that demand creates the supply. When there was little demand for drugs in the USA, because people were frightened of going to prison, there was at the same time little supply, no Mexican marijuana plantations, no Medellín drug barons and no Golden Triangle. In their rage against the suppliers of drugs, the Americans seem to forget that cocaine and opium used to be valued as the basis for pain-killing drugs in hospitals.

The hypocrisy of the United States and the West European countries, is seen at its most unsavoury here in Thailand. The United States Government dare not offend its own heroin addicts or rich cocaine sniffers, but it has bullied the Thais into persecuting and jailing thousands of drug takers, most of them gormless, young Westerners who had been smoking marijuana. The United States, which during the Vietnam War encouraged the hill tribespeople of Laos to grow and export opium, now harries the very same people who try to grow opium here. Scores of agents of the US Drug Enforcement Agency, who might be employed at home arresting the heroin users, are here in Northern Thailand chasing the heroin traders. And all in vain. For although opium production in Thailand itself has fallen over the last decade from 200 to 20 tons, the shortfall will more than be met by smuggling over the frontier from Burma and Laos. The processed opium can then be smuggled down Thailand's excellent roads for shipment by sea or air from Bangkok.

If there is any glamour about the heroin trade, you certainly do not see it in Chiang Rai, an ugly and boring town, which explains why the tourist touts have tried to create a spurious glamour up by the Burma and Laos frontiers, in what they describe as the Golden Triangle. They have even succeeded in making a tourist attraction of Thailand's northernmost town, Mae Sai, where a small river divides it from Burma. The town consists of one long street lined with shops selling fake Burmese jade, garish folk-weave bags and misshapen hill-tribe carvings, though not, I am glad to say, the copulating elephants that the Montagnards in Vietnam produced for sale in Saigon. At the frontier post by the river, three cheeky girls in hill-tribe costume demanded I take their picture. 'You take photo, fifty baht, you take photo.' 'No take photo. No have camera.' 'You no have camera but you have mon-nee. You give fifty baht.' A kick in the pants more likely.

Drab and depressing though it may look, the Golden Triangle seems to be back in business. In August 1989, the American assistant secretary of state for international narcotics matters, Melvin Levitsky, told a US House Committee on drug abuse, 'Good weather conditions are expected to produce a large harvest throughout the Golden Triangle.' General Chavalit Yodmani, secretary-general of Thailand's Narcotics Control Board, said he expected the opium grown in the Golden Triangle to rise from 1,500 to 2,400 tons. Most of the increase would come from over in Burma where the political troubles over the last year had meant that troops were diverted from drug suppression to quelling revolt in the towns. The Burmese authorities had not the means to prevent the September planting of opium. The rise in production would put the Golden Triangle back ahead of the 'Golden Crescent', formed by Iran, Afghanistan and Pakistan, as the world's greatest supplier of heroin.

One of the reasons for the revival has been the end of the US programme of spraying poison on opium crops in north-eastern Burma. Strangely enough this cut-back was part of American sanctions against the Burmese government for its brutal repression of demonstrations in 1988. The troubles in Burma have also affected efforts to save the forests in this part of the world. Northern Thailand once rivalled Burma in the production of teak, the strong and magnificent wood that was treasured all over the world for its use in furniture, and here in the East for building houses. In Northern Thailand, as in Burma, most of the 'teak wallahs' were British, who prided themselves on careful felling, replanting and conservation. There is still in Chiang Mai, what is claimed as the world's only all-teak squash court, and bookshops sell copies of Reginald Campbell's *Teak Wallah*, first published in 1933.

After the Second World War, the British did not recover their teak concessions in northern Thailand. Japanese logging companies took the place of the teak wallahs; tractors replaced elephants at removing the fallen trees; young trees and even saplings were cut and not replaced. The majestic wood that had once provided the dance floors in P&O liners was now often turned into plastic. By the 1980s, most of the forests of teak and other timber had vanished, with catastrophic effects on the climate, soil and drainage system. The farmers, backed by ecologists from the city, railed in vain against the loggers until November 1988, when floods due to logging devastated the opposite, southernmost end of Thailand. In January 1989, the government brought in a national logging ban.

Just as the Thai heroin merchants made up for cuts in local production by imports from Burma, so did the Thai loggers. The Burmese government, which had long resisted demands from foreign loggers, now desperately needs hard currency. The various rebel armies near to the Thai border also discovered that trees, like jade and opium, could be exported for cash and arms. Communist Laos has also taken to opium growing and timber felling in order to pay for her socialist system. Soil erosion from tree felling in Laos is now so serious that the river runs red, 'from the blood of the forest' as one European said to me.

Most men of good will want to stamp out the heroin trade. Most men of good will want to preserve the forests. Unhappily, it appears that the aim of the first group comes into conflict with that of the second. The policies of the Drug Enforcement Agency wreck the work of the forest conservationists. That is the sombre truth conveyed by the Buddhist monk Phra Acharn Pongsak Techadhammo, who travels north Thailand preaching his conservationist message. Twenty years ago, Phra Acharn's pleadings fell on deaf ears. When he told the villagers to look on the forest as home and a second parent, they laughed at him. Yes, the trees were valuable all right, but only if they were sold to a logging company. But over the years, the villagers came to see that the monk was right. The whole of this mountainous region is one of the major catchment zones for the Chao Phraya River, which enters the sea just south of Bangkok. The forests in the lowland valleys were first to be felled by concessionary loggers, leaving only the mountains green. Illegal logging continued on mountain ridges. 'To make matters worse,' said Phra Acharn Pongsak, 'the hill tribespeople slash and burn the mountains from the top down, while the lowland farmers do it from the bottom up.'

The deforestation worsened dramatically in 1975 with a massive invasion of hill tribespeople from Laos, fleeing the communists. The attempts by the authorities to stop these people from growing their usual crop, which was opium, led to the ruin of most of the mountain ridges. The monk explained:

> For opium-growing, each Hmong family needed only one *rai* of land. And they cultivated only once a year in the rainy season. But when the cash crop programmes sponsored by foreign agencies and the Thai authorities came, the hill tribes needed to clear five times as much land to grow cabbages and potatoes. Worse, the rains brought the residue of chemical pesticides and fertilizers down the streams, endangering the livelihood of the lowland farmers.

The villagers in the Mae Sot valley who, twenty years ago, scoffed at the conservationist message, found that their brooks had all run dry. They could see no reason for this until Phra Acharn Pongsak took them into the hills. Nine-tenths of the once thick forest had been cut down for the hill tribes' cabbage plantations. The villagers in that year, 1986, resolved to protect the remaining fifty *rai* of watershed forest. Defying the Hmong and their govern- ment backers, the Mae Sot farmers set up a wire fence round this woodland. Guards were posted day and night. The Mae Sot vil- lagers got their way and have since replanted much of the upland forest. 'I feel sorry for the hill tribespeople,' said Phra Acharn Pongsak. 'They were caught in the middle, pressured both by the authorities and by the lowland farmers. But if the forests are destroyed, all parties including the hill tribes will be affected. They just have to move out of the rain catchment areas.'

Twenty years ago, the conservationist agitation by Phra Acharn Pongsak met with the disapproval of farmers, government agencies and most of his fellow monks. In the last three years, the inhabi- tants of the Mae Sot valley have spread the extent of forest from fifty *rai* to thousands of *rai* in the whole of their district. The government has awarded the monk a decoration and, what is more, reversed its programme for teaching the hill tribes to grow potatoes and cabbages. Phra Acharn Pongsak claims that his work accords with Buddhist teaching:

> Buddhism is essentially a conservationist religion. In the Lord

Buddha's time, the forests were the monks' abode. The Lord Buddha also told the monks to live simply and close to nature . . . Buddhism teaches the inter-relatedness of all things. Nothing stands in isolation. So it is with forest conservation. Without land security and self-sufficiency, we cannot expect villagers to stop encroaching on forests for their own short-term survival . . . The villagers must feel that the forest is theirs before starting to protect it. The present forestry policy, however, does not create the feeling, which makes conservation costly and, more often than not, ineffective . . . There are more than 300,000 monks across the country, and the authorities should make use of their roles as community leaders to restore the forest.

I have quoted these views at length partly because they are cogent and I agree with them; partly because they show how the Buddhist monks, with the King, are taking the lead in Thai public life.

CHAPTER THREE

The Road to Nirvana

After two days at Chiang Rai, including a trip to the Burmese border, I was happy to get on a bus to Chiang Mai, famous for roses and beautiful women, the city I like best in Thailand. So do most foreigners who come to Thailand for something more than a suntan. So do many Thais. Since it lies at a mere thousand feet above sea level, Chiang Mai hardly counts as a hill station, though some have tried to give it that label. But because of its northern latitude and relative freedom from air pollution, Chiang Mai's climate is always better than Bangkok's, and sometimes delightful. Most visitors will not feel the need for an air-conditioner, except in April and May, and even then only if they are living in a modern, concrete house. A fan is sufficient during the summer rainy season, while round about Christmas you may need a sweater and woollen socks.

Whereas Lop Buri and Sukhothai are modern towns, distinct from the relics of former civilizations, Chiang Mai has remained the northern or Lan Na capital since it was founded in 1296 by King Mengrai. During the subsequent five hundred years it was on occasions seized by Burma and sometimes paid tribute to Kings of Ayutthaya, but it never ceased to regard itself as the capital of Lan Na. It is not as old a city as, for instance, York or Edinburgh but it is just as proud of the past. Parts of the old wall and many wat survive but few domestic houses because they were always built of wood. There are still some fine wooden mansions, especially inside the old walled city, while the factories and the high-rise buildings are in the new suburbs. The craze for condominiums which, like the craze for condoms, has come from the United States, is spoiling Chiang Mai. So are the motor taxis that are replacing the pedal *samlor*.

The Top North Guest House stands in a narrow lane in the south-east part of the walled city, fifty yards from the moat. There is a kind of Swiss-Chinese chalet housing the restaurant, a swimming pool and rows of bedrooms at £5 a night. Dogs and children play in the lane outside; there is loud birdsong at dawn and, later on in the day, the surge and swell of a Puccini opera from the house of a neighbour. The outpourings of Mimi and Tosca sound especially clear as I take a shower in the bathroom next to the neighbour's window.

After a stroll down the lane and stopping to watch the fishermen by the moat, I tried to get my bearings from the map supplied by the Top North Guest House. This carried the usual warning not to leave valuables in the bedroom and also two unusual warnings: 'If possible when you go on tour or walking, try to avoid go in alone, should go in groups better . . . If you get molested by gangsters, try to remember their appearances, car's color, brand, model and plate number. . . .' Chiang Mai, and indeed the whole of Thailand, is not as peaceful as you might guess from the friendliness of the people. Passengers on overnight buses are quite often drugged and robbed. Highwaymen in pick-up trucks occasionally hold up motorists at gunpoint. Two years ago, bandits shot at a boatload of tourists on the Chiang Rai River, killing an Englishwoman.

Much of the violence goes with crime but here in the North there is trouble to do with the heroin trade and the discontent of the hill tribespeople. An old friend, Peter Duval-Smith, had nastier scrapes in northern Thailand, getting a bullet through his car door, than ever he did in Vietnam, where he died. Some of the Thai men here in Chiang Mai wear pistols under their shirts, but it is not wise to stare or let it be seen that you have noticed. You also see men sitting alone with a bottle of Thai whisky, which generally means they are working up to a tempest of rage.

When I first came to Chiang Mai, more than twenty years ago, I was writing an article on the beauty contests for which the North is famous. The contestants were lovely but vapid, and lacking the laughter which makes even the plainest Thai girls enchanting. Nothing they said now sticks in the memory, but I keenly remember the words of one of the female promoters. This fearsome old bag had somehow got it into her head that the photographer and I were acting against her interests, and were possibly in the pay of some rival promoter. 'If you write bad things about my girl,' she snarled at me, 'I cut you up and put the bits in a box and send it to London.'

On the bus coming down from Chiang Rai, they had shown the video of a melodrama in which a grim and bespectacled lady attacked and practically beat to death two different men who had offended her. Although she was smaller than them, and armed only with what looked like a cosh, she left them both groaning and spitting blood. Presumably this was some feminist statement. At dinner in the Top North Guest House, we saw a video on the plight of transsexuals, in full frontal nudity, and then when a diner complained, a film re-enactment of what looked like the Manson murders, with much stabbing of pregnant women; at which point I cancelled my order and went to eat elsewhere.

Chiang Mai was one of the haunts of a mass murderer still more frightening, because he was much more clever than Manson. This was the Vietnamese-Indian Charles Sobhraj, who made a career of befriending, then robbing and killing travellers. The *thuggees*, our thugs, who had done the same thing in the 1820s, claimed to be worshippers of Kali, the goddess of death, and in the same way, Sobhraj was a student of Freud and Nietzsche, and tried to explain away his crimes as a protest against the French legal system, or US intervention in Vietnam.

Although Sobhraj was ready to rob all and sundry, he preyed especially on that phenomenon of the Vietnam era, the hippy or travelling generation, naïve and drug-fuddled, their long hair trailing over their unkempt blouses, who sought in their own phrase to 'drop out' of this wicked world. Although opposed to the Vietnam War, the hippies were not a political movement. They did not join in riots at Berkeley, Berlin or Paris, but in gatherings such as the Woodstock Festival of music where they indulged in marijuana and group sex. In their ignorance and their innocence, the hippies resembled the Children's Crusade of the thirteenth century and, like them, made their way to the East. The 'hippy trail' led from Ibiza in Spain to Greece, Turkey, Afghanistan, India, Nepal and Thailand; hot, cheap countries, with freely-available marijuana and, in the last three at any rate, some kind of religion that did not unduly tax the brain.

Since most of the hippies were staying for months in Asia they had more money and travellers cheques than their shabby appearance suggested. Many were well-to-do young men and women, making a last fling before starting a job. Others were couriers for drug dealers. All had passports which could be stolen and sold or used to provide an alias. Although Sobhraj was an expert cracksman, forger and pickpocket, he liked to entrap his victims by first befriending and then drugging them. Most of the hippies were chronically ill with stomach troubles acquired in countries like Turkey and India. As Sobhraj himself said scornfully, 'Their resistance is low from smoking hashish. Then they get sick and go down with dysentery. After a few months on the road, diarrhoea is just about their only topic of conversation.' Sobhraj would offer to cure their sickness, dropping a sleeping pill into the medicine. Often he first gave his victims a laxative in order to get them into his power.

During his eight months in Thailand, ending in March 1976, Sobhraj combined murder with dealing in precious stones. This was not just profitable in itself, but helped him to meet and befriend his prey. His Bangkok flat offered a welcome to all sorts of travellers, charmed and impressed by Sobhraj's strong personality and delightful manners. When he had drugged and robbed his victims, he sometimes let them escape but more often took them out to the countryside or Pattaya Beach, where he killed them and burned the bodies. His one recorded trip to Chiang Mai was a rather unusual venture, involving a brutal but never detected murder, and also a victim who lived to tell the tale.

In an interview given in prison in Delhi, Sobhraj claimed he was acting in 1975 for a Hong Kong heroin ring that wanted to wipe out amateurs, small-time men and the young hippy travellers who, for a few thousand dollars, would carry consignments of drugs from the source to the market. He said that Hong Kong gave him the names of some of these drug runners, as well as their Bangkok hotel and probable date of arrival. One of these was a middle-aged Frenchman, André Breugnot, due to arrive at the Royal Hotel, before leaving for Chiang Mai to pay off suppliers. In early September, 1975, Sobhraj started to hang around the Royal until he spotted a lone, elderly European. By dropping some words of French, his own first language, Sobhraj got into conversation and mentioned that he was soon to go to Chiang Mai; whereupon Breugnot said he was coming here in his business as an antique dealer.

Sobhraj and his French Canadian mistress offered Breugnot a lift. They dropped him off at the Chiang Inn, near to the Night Bazaar, and gave him a mild dose of laxative. That same day, at a restaurant near the Top North Guest House, Sobhraj and his girl befriended a young and impressionable French bank clerk, called Dominique. After dinner, Dominique had a bad attack of diarrhoea,

for which his new friends gave him some medicine. He regained
consciousness in Sobhraj's Bangkok flat, where he stayed two
months before suspecting his host.

With Dominique installed in Bangkok and able to serve as an
alibi, Sobhraj returned by plane to Chiang Mai to finish his business
with Breugnot. His account of what took place in the Chiang Inn,
appears in *The Life and Crimes of Charles Sobhraj* by Richard Neville
and Julie Clarke:

> Breugnot was so surprised when I suddenly appeared at the door
> and told him that we had business to discuss. 'What do you come
> to Chiang Mai for?' I asked him, 'as a tourist or on business?' At
> first he denied everything and I continued to question him. Later I
> gave him a Japanese slap on the side of the head and he fell to the
> floor ... 'What do you want from me?' He was shaking. 'Your
> names in Bangkok,' I said. Later I made him take a Mogadon and
> waited for it to take effect. I didn't want to leave any marks. I
> showed him a gun. 'Either you speak up André, or I work on you.'

The terrified Frenchman spilled out details of his drug business,
and gave the names of some couriers who would arrive in Bangkok. Whereupon Sobhraj forced him to take more tablets.

> When the guy passed out I undressed him, and I put all his clothes
> neatly on the bed. I carried Breugnot to the bathroom – he was fat
> and heavy – and put him in the tub and turned on the tap. I laid a
> pipe near him on a stool by the bath and propped a newspaper, half
> in the water and half on the outside of the tub. I left some sleeping
> tablets on the sink. One thing, I didn't touch his passport or wallet.
> I held André Breugnot's head under water until he was dead.

Richard Neville, whose taped interviews furnish much of this gruesome but thrilling book, is inclined to think that Sobhraj invented
the tale of a Hong Kong syndicate. The hapless André Breugnot
may have been just what he said he was, an antique dealer. We
have only Sobhraj's word for what transpired. However, the files
of the French Embassy in Bangkok, show that André Breugnot,
aged fifty-six, was found dead in a hotel room in Chiang Mai on
21 September 1975. The maid had discovered the body in the
bath. Local police said there was no trace of foul play.

Richard Neville writes, in a personal epilogue to the book he co-
authored, 'I had come to Delhi [where Sobhraj was in gaol] with a
crude idea of Charles as a child of colonialism, revenging himself

on the counter-culture. Instead I was dazzled by a brilliant psychopath.' The admission is all the more poignant since Neville himself had once been a major voice of that counter-culture, the founder of *Oz* magazine, accused at an Old Bailey trial of corrupting public morals, as well as the author of *Play Power*, a 'tour of the international underground'. *The Life and Crimes of Charles Sobhraj* was a harsh reminder that play power, counter-culture, dropping out and doing one's own thing, were no protection against the power of evil. For every Little Red Riding Hood, there is a Big Bad Wolf.

Here in Thailand, as in the United States itself, there is now a revulsion against the permissive ideas of the 1960s. Toleration of marijuana is seen to have led to the present epidemic of heroin, crack and cocaine. The 'sexual revolution' is now held responsible for the mighty increase in broken marriage, abortion, rape, child abuse, sodomy and, as a result of sodomy, AIDS. On the twentieth anniversary of the Woodstock Festival, the Thai newspapers published bitter comments, such as this reader's letter: 'There was nothing then, nor now, amusing, wonderful, cool or worthy of respect about acid, hash, communal sex, nudity, or the massive garbage heaps so kindly left by Woodstock crowds for others to pick up.'

Many of those who took the hippy trail professed to be followers of some Eastern religion, generally of a mystical or contemplative nature, which did not demand either discipline or intellectual effort. Quack gurus, shamans and maharishis – the Eastern equivalent of the TV hot gospellers – erected their shrines for the shaggy pilgrims, at places like Goa and Katmandu, where there was also a ready supply of dope to induce mystical ecstasy. Some of these teachers so far adapted Western practices as to include the cults of Freud and other shamans of central Europe, like group confession and self-abasement, auto-analysis and of course communal sex. After the Beatles came East to see their guru, quackery took on an extra dimension; some of the maharishis shifted their business to Europe or the United States, to be nearer the market.

One young woman victim of Charles Sobhraj expressed the confusion of those who sought an Eastern religious experience. Having complained to friends that she was 'not getting f...ed enough in California', she told her family that she was 'into Buddhism', and wanted to go to Katmandu to begin a life of contemplation. Nothing bad could happen to her in Bangkok, she told her grandmother, because the Thais were also a Buddhist people. She was washed up, drugged and drowned on Pattaya beach. Reading about this sad young woman, I thought of the Ogden Nash poem, 'The Seven Spiritual Ages of Mrs Marmaduke Moore', a rich American lady who moved from cult to cult. The concluding lines are:

> For when a woman's over-sexed
> God knows what God is coming next.

Perhaps because the Thais are a Buddhist people who take their religion seriously, this country does not attract the Mrs Marmaduke Moores. Although Thailand produces weird and flamboyant monks, they appeal only to Thais. A few *farang* or Westerners come to Thailand in search of religious knowledge. Some claim to be Buddhist. But none whom I know has dared to shave his head and put on the saffron robes of a monk, any more than a Thai in Europe would dare to dress as a Christian priest. In India, you see Europeans as well as the locals wearing the uniform of a religious sect, while even in London or Sydney, you notice the shaven-headed and acne-scarred followers of the Hare Krishna. Such behaviour in Thailand would be condemned as a scandal and blasphemy.

Those foreigners who wish, may get an interview with a Buddhist sage. The author of one recent travel book went to visit a monk in the forest near here, but had to admit this was only a weekend search for wisdom. It often surprises me that the Westerners searching for truth in Buddhism, have taken no interest in the teachings of Jesus Christ. Why come all the way to Chiang Mai before going first to the local church?

Those who reject the faith in which they were born and brought up, are not likely to find another in travel abroad. All religions, even those which claim to be universal, are modified and restricted by variations of race, culture, nationality, language and climate, so that in very hot countries like India, worship tends towards contemplation. The Jews, from whom Jesus and his apostles sprang, did not themselves accept the new faith. Christianity triumphed in Europe and its American settlements, while Islam spread as far as its conquering armies, but neither converted the older civilizations of India and China. Even within a great religion, one sees variations from region to region. Christianity in Europe is roughly divided between the Orthodox of the East, the Roman Catholics of the

South and the Protestants of the North. Even within Britain, one sees the distinctive national characteristics appear in the Church of England, the Presbyterian Church of Scotland and Welsh Non-conformism. Ireland is still sorely divided between the Catholic Celts and Calvinist Saxons.

Although Thai Buddhism is neither exclusive nor bigoted, it is nevertheless the purest expression of national pride and tradition. The monks adhere to the older and more austere *Theravada* school, also known as *Hinayana*, or 'Lesser Vehicle', which looks on enlightenment as a personal search, achieved by self-denial and meditation. The monks are in constant communication with co-religionists in the other *Hinayana* countries such as Ceylon. Thai Buddhism also has elements of the later and less demanding *Mahayana* school, the 'Greater Vehicle', which sees enlightenment as a collective pursuit. Thai worship also includes many rites of the Hindu religion, from which Buddhism broke away 2,500 years ago. There are old Hindu temples in Lop Buri and Sukhothai, and brand new Hindu shrines in Bangkok, like the one in front of the Erawan Hotel. Hindu priests are called in to bless a new house, shop, restaurant or massage parlour.

Most Thais, like most people everywhere, combine their formal faith with belief in a spirit world. Only the most ascetic monks aspire to the rigid self-abnegation demanded by Buddha, just as only a few devout Christians live in the poverty, chastity and devotion, demanded by Jesus. The mass of Thais, like the rest of us, compromise with the world, the flesh and the devil. In time of trouble, such as drought, a flood or a loved one's illness, they may invoke spirits, rather as Christians turn to a favourite saint or the Virgin Mary.

Buddhism guides the Thais in birth, marriage and death, in war and peace, education, government and law. It is inextricably joined with the monarchy and the family, the other great institutions of Thai society. The Buddhist religion as much as the language defines what it is to be Thai. The very strength of their own Buddhist conviction permits the Thais to be tolerant of the religion of others. King Narai allowed the French to build a Roman Catholic chapel at Lop Buri in the seventeenth century. He granted the same religious tolerance to the Muslims. The present Chakri dynasty not only permitted but welcomed Christian missionaries, provided, of course, that they stuck to religion and did not dabble in politics. The Muslim Malays in southern Thailand are almost as patriotic as Buddhist Thais.

Tolerance does not extend to assaults on religion. There are frequent prosecutions for blasphemy as when the police recently charged the *Asian Wall Street Journal* for the suggestion that the Buddhist Patriarch erred in blessing an aeroplane. In the same week, a prosecution was brought against a Bangkok satirical magazine, whose front cover showed a male model dressed as a monk, but holding a Walkman machine and a copy of *Playboy*. Thailand was one of the three non-Muslim states, albeit with a Muslim minority, which banned Salman Rushdie's *Satanic Verses*. The other two countries were India and South Africa. Those who respect their own religion, tend to respect the religion of others.

Chiang Mai is especially rich in Buddhist wats, dating back to the thirteenth century, and some of them older than buildings in other parts of the country that tourists admire because they are now in ruins. I love to visit the wats, as much for the calm and silence as for the ornamentation. The temple courtyards give at least the illusion of coolness after the street outside. The first time I was in Chiang Mai coincided with one of the local festivals and there were services going on all day and much of the night. Outsiders are welcome to come in and kneel or sit on the floor, and hear the chanting. At one wat, I remember with pleasure, the congregation were smoking cheroots and cigarettes, which in fact were on sale inside the temple. Although only a very occasional smoker, I much enjoyed a cheroot in that atmosphere of heat, tobacco and incense. It also reminded me of Kipling's Supi-yaw-lat in 'Mandalay':

> An' I seed her first a-smokin' of a whackin' white cheroot,
> An' a-wastin' Christian kisses on an 'eathen idol's foot.
>> Bloomin' idol made o' mud –
>> Wot they call the Great Gawd Budd –
> Plucky lot she cared for idols when I kissed 'er where she stood!

The cheroots and cigarettes are made from tobacco grown around Chiang Mai. After my smoke in the temple, I met some of the foreign tobacco experts who had been brought in to help. Almost all of them came from what was then still called Rhodesia, but now is Zimbabwe. They used to congregate in a bar-cum-restaurant called The Pub, although it was quite unlike other such places in Thailand, which tend to consist of a girly bar, with a dartboard and a rosette of Liverpool Football Club. The Pub was a fine old teak house under the management of a courteous and quiet-spoken lepidopterist and his Thai wife.

The Rhodesians took me to see the tobacco plantations and then to a cigarette factory, where Thai girls giggled away through the heat and dust. Remembering that the opera *Carmen* starts with a strike of the girl cigarette workers in old Seville, I asked if they had any union trouble. No, said the Rhodesians, the girls all got their jobs through making a deal with the men trade union officials. I can imagine what sort of deal. One Rhodesian surprised me by saying how lazy the Thais were, compared to the Africans 'One of my blecks at home can do the work of a half dozen Thais.' I had come halfway round the world to hear a white Rhodesian praising the industry of the blacks. The Rhodesians said that the Thai and American governments welcomed the growth of the tobacco industry because it offered another alternative to the growing of opium. They said that Thai smokers feared no risk to their health and even insisted on high-tar tobacco.

But all that was ten years ago. The American anti-smoking lobby, triumphant in the United States, has now converted even the Southeast Asians. Cigarette advertising is now banned in Thailand. Smoking is banned on Thai Airways domestic flights and all buses. On one of the minibuses on which I travelled, I saw a No Smoking sticker, probably from the United States, which still has me puzzled. It shows a grinning girl on her back, and naked except for her high-heeled shoes and an Uncle Sam top-hat. Between her arms and her thighs she is clutching, with every sign of enjoyment, a man-sized cigarette with a crimson tip, from which is erupting a plume of smoke. It does not require a Sigmund Freud to interpret the symbolism. But why should a sticker intended to stop people smoking, convey the message that having a cigarette is like having an orgasm, which most people enjoy?

While one group of Americans are warning the Thais against tobacco, another group want them to smoke American cigarettes. This I learned from the business news of the *Nation* (23 August 1989):

> Prodded by the big tobacco companies, US trade officials are trying to pry open Asian markets to American cigarettes in a controversial strategy that is being likened to a modern-day opium war. Washington is currently mulling whether to level sanctions against

Thailand, which bans imports of foreign cigarettes and all cigarette advertising.

The Thais have affirmed their ban, although larger countries like South Korea and even Japan, have caved in to US demands.

The anti-smoking lobby in the United States now claims that the US cigarette companies want to make addicts of Asian women and young people. At present, in Thailand, only about 3 per cent of the woman are smokers, compared to almost 50 per cent of the men. Young Thai men smoke less than their elders. A Thai official claims that after Taiwan dropped its quota on foreign cigarettes, in late 1986, the company R. J. Reynolds sponsored three concerts featuring a Hong Kong rock star, for which the price of admission was five empty packets of Winston cigarettes. The article in the *Nation* drew this comparison with the Opium War:

> The nineteenth-century conflict between Britain and China broke out after the Chinese tried to ban British sales of opium to Canton and Macau. In arguments similar to the ones heard today from US cigarette manufacturers, British merchants said the Chinese were already producing their own opium and it was not up to British traders to safeguard the morals of Chinese citizens.

There is yet another twist to this sorry tale of hypocrisy. Those in the West who now want to penalize smoking tobacco are just the same sort of people, and often the same people, as those who wanted to legalize drugs, just as those who demand more public money for AIDS victims are just the same kind who wanted to legalize sodomy.

In *Views from Abroad: The Spectator Book of Travel Writing*, I found one curious outcome of that happy time I spent in The Pub. It comes in an account by Auberon Waugh of how he had gone to Thailand to smoke some opium:

> The explanation for my presence in Chiang Mai dates back to a conversation of two years ago with Richard West, the celebrated traveller, philosopher and visionary, in a Soho pub. I had just returned from a visit to Bangkok and was feeling generally sick of England. He said the only place to go was Chiang Mai. When pressed to explain its advantages over Bangkok, the one thing he could think of was that it had an English pub. He looked benignly around the bar where we stood, with its dingy, furtive inhabitants,

its revolting beer, its abiding smell of stale cigarettes and cat's piss and the permanent, haunting presence of Jeffrey Bernard. Oh yes, he said, and there were also the most beautiful girls in the world and opium dens.

In his search for a pipe of opium, Auberon Waugh went first to The Pub, which he found was a 'strange and marvellous institution, not at all like the model which inspired it'. But when Waugh explained his purpose in coming to Chiang Mai, he met with a hostile reception:

> The Pub, which is in fact an elegant, well-appointed restaurant . . . admits Americans too. Several of the overpaid boy scouts who work for the US Drug Enforcement Agency use it as their local. And it was an American who reacted most violently. Was I aware that I would almost certainly be shopped, if not shot, by the traffickers, he asked. The penalty for opium possession was thirty years, he said. Did I know that their gaols provided no food for prisoners, and there was no longer a British consulate in Chiang Mai to look after them?

Since my name is now certainly on the files of the DEA, in connection with Auberon Waugh and opium dens, and because one of the Rhodies had taken exception to something I wrote and threatened to knock my block off, I thought it prudent not to revisit The Pub, which is anyway now rather grand and was recently cited by *Newsweek* as 'one of the world's best bars'. But as it so happened, I found within fifty yards of the Top North Guest House what I decided was one of the best bars, if not in the world, at least in Thailand. Oddly enough, it has most of the virtues and few of the faults of the Coach and Horses in Soho, which Auberon Waugh was referring to in the passage I quoted.

The Chada bar is simply a wooden booth at the corner of Moon Maung Road and Soi or Lane number 2. On two sides of the booth is a bar with space for a dozen customers. Inside the booth are the landlady Chada, sometimes helped by her student daughter, a fridge for the beer and a number of vats of homemade honey whisky. Chada makes this out of a mixture of rice spirit, honey and various herbs designed to cure physical ailments. The different preparations include No. 1, to relax tendons, tensions, muscular pains; No. 2, long life, kidney inflammation, chase air in intestine; No. 7, Fine Dragon, to foster brain, heart, kidney, to add efficiency in sex; and No. 14, Morning Flower, exhausted, dizzy, hangover.

Although I could not always distinguish between these honey whiskies, they brought on a pleasant glow, and left me with less of a headache than did the Mekong whisky. However, I generally drank the Singha beer, which at Chada's is not quite so expensive as at an indoor bar. Chada herself is a handsome and energetic lady whose aim is to entertain customers and, in the case of farang, to teach us the customs and charms of Chiang Mai. She even offered to come with me to a local restaurant, specializing in northern food, to make sure that I got the right kind of Burmese pork curry and Nam Prik Ong, which is pork minced with tomato, garlic and ginger.

The regulars at the Chada bar include most of the types you would find at the Cambridge Circus end of the Coach and Horses. There is an off-duty detective, calming his nerves in Mekong whisky. There is a fiery and beautiful lady from Laos, manageress of a girlie bar near the Night Market, who comes to the Chada for honey whisky, and after a few cups, starts to complain of her parted American husband, his lack of sexual attention to her, his excess sexual attention to other women, although she describes these things in less delicate language. An American Vietnam veteran talks of his tax problems, the payment for articles in the *Bangkok Post*, and his work as props adviser to Vietnam films such as *Apocalypse Now!* and *The Deer Hunter*. The latter reminded me of a bar I had seen in Bangkok called The Beer Hunter.

There is a Swiss intellectual, who worked for some years as a cook in the south of Thailand, and likes to talk about Jung and Eric Fromm. Like most Europeans who live here, he is obsessed by deforestation and the replacement of local trees by harmful species like rubber and eucalyptus, or Oy-calyptus, as he pronounces it. He is saddened and angry at talk of Thailand becoming a NIC, and he says that the building boom in this region is tempting the farmers away from their land to waste their lives in cities like Chiang Mai.

When the Swiss stays too long in the Chada bar, his beautiful Thai wife comes to fetch him, and may be persuaded to take a soft drink. She has worked in the film business and is most instructive on what kind of film, or novel for that matter, appeals to the Thai women's taste. They cannot abide pornography and stick to romantic conceptions of love. This goes for literature also. Like almost every Thai that I meet, she gives me the name and address of a friend or relative I should visit, if ever I go to such and such town on my travels.

The Chada bar has its share of bores, on subjects like what is wrong with the English cricket team. An elderly Australian complains of the health scares: 'I used to love chicken claw soup when I was a boy in New South Wales, but now they say it's a health hazard.' Just as the regulars in the Coach and Horses debate the virtues of Oliver Cromwell, Dickens or Margaret Thatcher, so here they discuss the Asian figures of controversy, like General Douglas MacArthur, Prince Norodom Sihanouk and the Thai politician and author, Kukrit Pramoj. There was sardonic merriment on the day when Thailand's Finance Minister announced his annual award of honours to those in the country who paid the largest amount of individual income tax. Although the minister might himself have been a candidate for a prize – he is certainly rich enough – the honours this year went to the two bosses of Singha Brewery, which certainly ought to have made a profit in view of its near monopoly power and very high prices.

Some farangs who go to the Chada bar in the evening, begin at the nearby Library Service, a second-hand book exchange, which also serves breakfast. This establishment is especially vital since new books in Thailand are just as expensive as beer. The Australian Serb who runs the Library Service is also the driving spirit behind the Chiang Mai Motorcycling Touring Club and gets in the latest biking journals. As a life-long meccanophobe, I suppose I am prejudiced, but I find motor bikes more than usually undesirable in a place like northern Thailand, where the countryside used to be not only beautiful but serene. The forests, the fields, the villages, even Chiang Mai itself were once pleasantly quiet, a Buddhist quality.

The tourist touts are also promoting a craze for trekking, on foot or sometimes on elephant back, to see the villages of the hill tribespeople. The trek agents vie with each other in offering trips to smaller and more remote tribes such as the Lawa, Lisu, Panglong, Ex and Lahu, as well as to the more familiar Karen, Shan, Mong and KMT, the remnants of Chiang Kai Shek's Nationalist Chinese Army. Those trekkers who notch up their tally of tribes, remind me of bird-watchers in England, the 'twitchers' as they are called, who turn up in multitudes to get a glimpse of a rare waxwing or warbler. Most of these treks end up in what is really a shopping centre for folk-weave clothes, carvings and gems, followed by one furtive pipe of adulterated opium.

When I first came to Chiang Mai in the 1960s, tourists were not

actually banned but discouraged from going to see the hill tribes.
It was considered insulting to turn these people into a tourist
exhibit. The one or two villages that had geared themselves to the
tourist trade were already in danger of losing their tribal identity
and tradition. Now, these unfortunate tribespeople, driven from
Laos by Communism, from Burma by civil war, are harried in
Thailand by the United States Drug Enforcement Agency and,
more recently, by the forest conservationists. They are forced to
turn to the tourist trade as a means of earning a livelihood.

The tourist trade has also degraded the elephants. These magnificent beasts were once employed in hauling the trunks and logs of
trees in the days when North Thailand still had teak forests. The
elephant now is a menial beast of burden. I once saw one towering
over the traffic in Phloenchit Road, in the heart of Bangkok, with
a pile of plastic buckets heaped on its back. This sight would have
saddened King Rama I who founded Bangkok in 1782. He loved
elephants so much that he wanted to build a causeway over the
swamp to allow them into the city but his advisers warned him
that this would lay him open to a Burmese attack. When, five
years later, Rama I led an invasion of Burma over the mountains,
his favourite elephant sickened and he himself took the job of
nursing it and persuading it to eat. In that campaign, the paths
were so steep that the elephants had to ascend by coiling their
trunks around trees and hauling their bodies forward. Many
were killed in falls from cliffs.

Rama IV, whose life was caricatured in *The King and I*, wrote a
treatise on white elephants, which should 'possess a beautiful
snore'. Although these beasts, really a dull pink, were objects of
veneration, they were not regarded as gods or kings, as some
foreigners thought. White elephants could be punished, as an
Englishman saw: 'A keeper pricked the foot of one in our presence,
with a sharp iron until blood came, although his majesty's only
offence was stealing a bunch of bananas, or rather snatching it
before he had received permission.'

The elephants here were better treated than in neighbouring
countries. In Burma, at what is now Mandalay, a British diplomat
in the 1830s witnessed the unsuccessful staging of elephant fights:
'The elephant is not a courageous animal, nor is it pugnacious.
After a rencontre which does not last above a few seconds, one of
the parties is sure to run away.' At Saigon, the same English
diplomat witnessed a series of combats between elephants and a

tiger, which was not only tethered about the loins but had its mouth sewn up and its claws extracted. No less than forty-six elephants, all males of great size, were brought to attack the tiger. Before it was tossed to death, the tiger managed to spring on the head of one of the elephants, whose rider was then and there punished with one hundred lashes.

Only decadent kings or princes tried to pervert the elephant into behaviour like fighting. The wisdom and usefulness of the beast were widely acknowledged as well by European visitors. 'In my judgement there is not a beast so intellective as are the elephants, nor of more understanding in the world,' wrote the Venetian Caesar Frederick, 'for he will do all things that his keeper sayth, so that he lacketh nothing but human speech.' Quoting this in *The Making of Burma*, Dorothy Woodman writes that this sixteenth-century traveller was 'an early edition of Elephant Bill'.

Elephant Bill by Lieutenant-Colonel J. H. Williams was first published in 1946 and ranks with the very greatest of animal books, like Sir Percy Fitzpatrick's *Jock of the Bushveld*, and still deserves to be read not only for fun but for the insights into a now endangered species. Although Williams had worked in Burma, what he wrote of the elephants and the teak wallahs applied as much to northern Thailand, where most of the logging was run by British companies. Colonel Williams was not one of those animal lovers who hate the human race. He got on well with the Burmese, 'those cheerful Irishmen of the East'; he loved and was loved by his wife; he even enjoyed weekends and leave in Rangoon or one of the hill stations. Indeed I get the impression that most of the British, except for gloomy George Orwell, were happy in Burma during the 1920s and 1930s.

Colonel Williams corrects some of the legends that have attached to elephants. They can forget, though they will long remember a kindness like medical treatment. They are not frightened of mice but they loathe dogs, even puppies. The training of elephants, even of those who are born in the wild, need not involve any serious cruelty; scarcely more discipline than is needed by human children. Elephants have a life style exactly matching the human, so that the beast may grow up alongside its *oozie*, or driver, and grow old in friendship and understanding. Elephants fall in love like human beings, but when the female has given birth, she takes as companion and helper another female or 'auntie'. Together they guard the calf against the tiger, which tries to drive off mother and 'auntie' in a stampede:

To do this he will first attack the mother, springing on her back and stampeding her; then he returns to attack the 'auntie', who defends the calf, knowing that in a few moments the mother will return. On many occasions I have had to dress the lacerated wounds of tiger-claws on the backs of both a mother elephant and her friend.

Colonel Williams used to sit up all night to discover when elephants sleep, and for how long. 'The time is never the same, but it is always at that eerie hour when even the insects stop their serenades.' A Cornishman, Colonel Williams was sensitive as a Burmese *oozie* to jungle spirits and ghosts. 'Savage elephants are as rare as really wicked men', he said, 'but they sometimes have fits of temper'. He tells how a young European assistant, home on leave, tried to impress his mother and sister by giving commands to an elephant at the London Zoo:

> 'Shall I make her sit down?' he said, then shouted 'Hmit!', like a Burmese *oozie*. The elephant merely swished her tail. 'Hmit! Hmit! Hmit!' At last the elephant condescended to notice him ... With lightning swiftness, she seized a lump of her dung the size of a cottage loaf and slung it at the young assistant. It missed him, but it knocked a feather out of his mother's hat and exploded against a wall behind them.

Employed by a teak company, Colonel Williams was able to gain an understanding of elephants that went much deeper than that of scientists or television directors who study a species for only a few years, or months. When the Japanese invaded in 1942, Williams used elephants to carry a group of women and children out of Burma over the mountains to India, at an altitude higher than Hannibal reached when crossing the Alps. The journey included a stretch on a ledge that was narrower than the width of an elephant, overlooking a precipice. Colonel Williams, who suffered from vertigo, led the party on all fours with his eyes shut, but not one human or elephant fell. Later, Williams employed his beasts on building bridges for Slim's 14th Army. The jungle guerrilla leader, Brigadier Orde Wingate, also used elephants, which had the advantage over motor transport of silence, and of mobility in the dense jungle. However, the Japanese used elephants too, and scores of animals perished when dive-bombed and machine-gunned by Allied planes, a task the pilots hated.

CHAPTER FOUR

The Frontier

In Chiang Mai, I heard much of a town called Mae Hong Son, in the north-west mountains, near to the border with Burma. Some called it a Shangri La; others a Wild West town of desperadoes. Some of the travel agencies claimed that round Mae Hong Son, the tourist could meet the last, genuine tribespeople unspoilt by tourism. Motor bikers could find there a still, tranquil countryside, free of mechanical civilization. In other words, Mae Hong Son was the latest place to be trampled over and vulgarized by Westerners. Mae Hong Son had featured in one of the books I had read which glamorize the traffic in drugs and precious stones, and even the endless fighting between the hill tribes, such as the Karen, and the Burmese Army. These things hold no glamour for me. I had disliked Mae Suai, up on the northernmost frontier. The traffic in drugs is a bleak and murderous business, as we know from the story of Charles Sobhraj. The traffic in precious stones is almost as nasty, as I had seen in a weekend visit to Chanthaburi and Trat in eastern Thailand. The Cambodian Communists, known as the Khmer Rouge, have muscled in on the racket, earning themselves the nickname of Khmer Ruby.

My guidebook, *Thailand and Burma*, offered me three more reasons for not going to Mae Hong Son. The flights from Chiang Mai are infrequent and heavily booked, the alternative being an eight-hour bus ride, 'Landslides, floods, yawning chasms, hairpin bends and bulldozers shoving wreckage down the mountain are all part of the fun.' Not for me. Mae Hong Son is highly malarial. The region also has packs of savage and rabid dogs. It sounded like a place to avoid at all costs.

What brought me to Mae Hong Son was an article in the *Far Eastern Economic Review*. This is a fine weekly commentary on business, politics, literature and the arts, combining features of *The Economist*, *Time* or *Newsweek* and the *Spectator*, with which the *Review* has friendly relations. Published and edited in Hong Kong, the *Review* has staff correspondents throughout East Asia, Australasia and the Indian subcontinent. Because of their independent stance, the *Review* correspondents have often come into conflict with the regimes about which they write. Pakistan imprisoned one of their correspondents; President Lee Kuan Yew was so enraged by a critical article that he banned the *Review* and took it to court for libel. The *Review* is often at odds with China, South Korea and other countries fearful of criticism.

Although Thailand has more Press freedom than most countries in Southeast Asia, journalists work under certain restraints that are matters of tact and taboo rather than outright censorship. The King and the Buddhist religion are sacrosanct. The punishments for *lèse-majesté* apply to other and less beloved members of the Royal Family, such as the Crown Prince. Journalists may criticize and even berate the prime minister and the head of the army, but it is prudent to do this in an oblique, or even metaphorical fashion. The exposure of crime may also be hazardous for the Bangkok journalist, as shown by the many who die in mysterious circumstances. Foreign journalists who annoy the Thai Government may have trouble extending their work permits, so most papers send in an outsider to write on an emotive issue. The *Review* sent in Hamish McDonald to write the articles which appeared on 22 February 1990, under the heading 'Partners in Plunder', on how Thailand was helping Burma to sell that country's teak forests. It also revealed how the Burmese dictator Ne Win was using the profits from teak and other timber to crush the democracy movement, as well as putting an end to insurgency by the hill tribes like the Karens.

This 'Partnership in Plunder' stems from two tragic events in 1988, the one in Burma, the other in southern Thailand. In Burma, from March to September that year, a series of demonstrations started by Rangoon students threatened the long and brutal reign of General Ne Win. He held on to power by a massacre far worse than the one that occurred in Peking in June the following year. Many foreign countries, like the United States, suspended aid in protest at the repression. By the end of 1988, General Ne Win was starved of money to buy not merely foreign equipment but arms and ammunition to keep going the war against the rebellious townspeople and hill tribes. Like Ceausescu in Rumania at the same time, Ne Win found himself under siege. In November 1988, in southern Thailand, a series of floods drowned 350 people. The felling of trees for timber, mining, rubber plantations and tourist facilities had in the past thirty years diminished the forest cover to the extent that a fortnight of heavy rains flowed off the bare hillside, sending water, soil and refuse into the valleys and blocking the natural drainage system. In response to a wave of popular anger Thailand imposed a total ban on logging. The ban delighted the general public, especially the farmers, but vexed the loggers, who are a combination of businessmen, mostly ethnic Chinese, and senior officers in the army and the police.

On the one side of the frontier was Thailand, a country with plenty of cash but a shortage of trees; on the other was Burma, a country with plenty of trees but no cash. There were men in both countries ready and eager to talk business. On 14 December 1988, General Chavalit Yongchaiyudh, then Thailand's army commander, flew to Rangoon with eighty staff and journalists for a lunch with his Burmese opposite number, General Saw Maung. This was the first major foreign visit to Burma since the September massacres, and therefore a cause of dismay to the Burmese opposition, many of whom were now refugees in Thailand.

Little about this visit appeared in the Bangkok Press. The one journalist who explained some of its implications was savagely beaten up with a spanner. The basis of the deal was that Burma would cede to Thailand logging rights in the forests near to the frontier. In return, Thailand would help the Burmese Army to crush the revolt in the border region, also to send back students and other refugees from the massacres of September.

In February 1989, the Burmese Government Timber Corporation announced the granting of twenty concessions along the border, with total exports of 160,000 tonnes of teak logs and 500,000 tonnes of other wood. The Corporation reckoned that this would bring Burma US $112 million, enough to buy arms and ammunition for many a month. The Burmese Timber Corporation also announced: 'In furtherance of the friendly and cordial relations existing between the two countries, Timber Corporation enters into contracts with Thai firms which are recommended by the Thai authorities concerned.' Not surprisingly, these 'Thai authorities concerned' awarded concessions to businessmen who support the ruling Thai Chart Party and its ally the Social Action

Party. One major concessionary was the Union Par Company, which is just under fifty per cent owned by the businessman Preecha Navawongse, whose son married General Chavalit's daughter. Preecha had also been involved with Chaovalit in the purchase of Chinese armoured cars for the Thai Army. The Union Par timber concession is just over the Burmese border from Mae Hong Son, which is why I eventually came here, in March 1990.

Most of my dread of Mae Hong Son proved to be baseless. There was no problem in getting a flight from Chiang Mai, perhaps because the tourist season was over. Although I complained that my hotel bedroom had no mesh or netting against mosquitoes, the management proved to be right when they said there were no mosquitoes around. On my first, quarter-mile walk into town, I kept looking around for a pack of aggressive dogs but saw nothing more dangerous than a wheezing chow. A foreigner said there were no bad dogs in Mae Hong Son. 'If you meet one,' he went on, 'remember the story about the Thai woman who knelt and prayed for forgiveness before the dog which was attacking her. She thought it must be the spirit of someone she wronged in a previous existence.' Later I checked with *Thailand and Burma* and found it was Pai, rather than Mae Hong Son, that was infamous for its dogs.

In fact, I took a great liking to Mae Hong Son, a lackadaisical and friendly place, in character like the West of Ireland. The tourist advertisements boded ill: 'Sightseeing with Shan villages, Red Karen and wonderful long-kneck Karen ... Come and see unspoilt life by motor bike and jeep ... We are bring you to touch spirit of hill tribes. Back to nature with us! Thank you.' In practice, most of the few sightseers were elderly Europeans sitting in buses. The individual travellers seemed to be much more interested in beer and conversation than wonderful long-kneck Karens. Anyway, the Karens and other tribespeople wear their traditional clothes in town, and have not yet been taught to regard themselves as a tourist exhibit.

At the crossroads with the traffic lights, I found a wooden café with parasol lampshades, and antlers and skins adorning the walls. Snake sandwiches are the speciality and worth eating once, but sensible people stick with the Chinese noodle soup. Here, I fell into conversation with Bob, an American merchant navy officer with a Chinese wife, who had been here most of the winter. With him was Heinz, who spends seven months of the year selling cars in West Germany, and the other five here in Thailand. His mother-in-law runs a gambling saloon in Chiang Mai. The hot weather was here in force; the fans were broken; the waiter obligingly put our bottles of beer into individual ice buckets, then slumped down beside us to chat. Bob, Heinz, the waiter and, eventually myself as well, gazed curiously at the smart house over the road, from which there emerged a succession of beautiful women. Was it a new and exclusive brothel? A secret intelligence agency? The HQ of an opium ring? Or maybe the Mae Hong Son branch of the Union Par Timber Company, busy across the Burmese frontier?

Later in the afternoon, we moved to the second-hand bookshop kept by Richard, a likeable but cantankerous Ulsterman. He had first come to the East as a hippy, drifting and listless, 'just as stupid as the rest of them'. He returned to Bangkok as a university lecturer, then went to seed, recuperated, and came up here with his Thai wife. He gave me a hard time: 'I hate journalists who come to Thailand and write about heroin and prostitution and don't understand it. Don't even speak the language. I hate you.' I do not think he did but he wanted to needle me. At one point he went to the tape player and put on some Irish political songs. 'The Sash My Father Wore' blared out above the sound of the tropical forest. When I told him I was a Unionist and liked The Sash, he turned it off again, and started to rail against Margaret Thatcher. Then he became morose: 'How can we sit here, drinking beer, when Thai peasants are earning thirty-five baht a day'. It was one of the questions that Levin and other Russian landowners asked in *Anna Karenina*, which I was reading here in Mae Hong Son. We started to talk about Tolstoy; Bob worried about his visa and Heinz slept.

During my short stay in Mae Hong Son, I noticed a certain movement of troops in combat gear. Were they helping the Burmese Army against the Karens and other guerrillas, who range at will through this border country? Bangkok rumour says that General Ne Win and General Chavalit are not only 'Partners in Plunder' but partners in the suppression of democratic opposition. Not wanting to risk a spanner attack or arrest as a foreign spy, I did not inquire too closely into these matters. However, from reading the *Bangkok Post*, I learned there was trouble over the border from Mae Hong Son, involving the Union Par timber concern in which General Chavalit has a family interest. A report datelined Mae Hong Son in the issue of 1 March 1990, said that:

Fourteen Burmese troops were killed and a number of others were wounded when Karen rebels ambushed a Burmese force opposite Tambon Plang Moo in Muang District. Meanwhile two Thai logging workers escaped from a Burmese forestry camp seized by Rangoon troops last week. One hundred and fifty Thai workers were arrested and ninety are being detained. All the arrested men work for Sajjatham Co., a sub-contractor of the Union Par Co., which was granted a concession to fell trees in Burma. The report said Burmese soldiers seized seven tractors, seven trucks, twenty-four working elephants, two shotguns, two pistols and an M16 assault rifle during the raid.

It seems that the 'Partners in Plunder' are falling out among themselves.

PART TWO

Bangkok

CHAPTER FIVE

Princes and Politicians

By the seventeenth century, the power and the independence of Lan Na, the northern kingdom at Chiang Mai, was under threat from the great kingdom of Ayutthaya, on the Chao Phraya River, fifty miles north of the present Bangkok. After 150 years at Sukhothai, the Thais had decided to make their capital at this more advantageous site on an island, formed at the confluence of the Chao Phraya and two tributaries. It was the ideal place to receive then rice and teak from the hinterland of the country, but it was not so close to the sea as to be vulnerable to a naval attack.

From the fifteenth century, the Kings of Ayutthaya had ruled or taken tribute from a region stretching as far as Vientiane in the north, Pegu in the north-west, and Angkor in the south-east, that is much of the present Laos, Burma and Cambodia. As the city grew, the authorities built a pattern of waterways and canals to receive the visiting ships from China, Japan and then France, Portugal, Holland and England. By the second half of the seventeenth century, during the reign of King Narai, the population was probably several hundred thousand.

A visitor in 1682 found

> seventeen hundred temples within Ayutthaya, with at least thirty thousand priests and more than four thousand images of Buddha, all of them gold or gilt ... the spires of the pagodas and temples were so gilded that in the sunshine they reflected the light so strongly that they disturbed the eyes, even from two or three miles away. The King of Siam was indeed one of the richest monarchs of the East.

This wealth aroused the cupidity of the foreign traders. The Dutch East India Company at one time blockaded Ayutthaya so that King

Narai thought it prudent to move to Lop Buri, where his palace still exists. The English East India Company fought to hold its monopoly of the trade at Mergui, which then belonged to Ayutthaya, but is now in Burma.

When King Narai sent a diplomatic mission to France, King Louis XIV replied by sending a Minister with several thousand troops and a Jesuit Abbé, charged with the mission of Christianizing the Thais. King Narai had also invited Moors, as they called Muslims, from Java. To complete this international jumble, a number of European freebooters, or interlopers, were hoping to make their fortunes here. Among these was the Englishman, Samuel White, whose wicked career is chronicled by Maurice Collis in *Siamese White*, an entertaining account of Ayutthaya. The most famous of these adventurers was Constantine Phaulkon, a Greek who became the chief minister to King Narai. Although Phaulkon was a man of some principle and was certainly loyal to Narai, his wealth made him enemies. The Moors and Persians distrusted him as a Christian; the English and Dutch as a Roman Catholic; and the French because he distrusted them. As soon as the King died, Phaulkon was taken away and murdered.

The death of Phaulkon in 1688 has been compared by some English writers with the tremendous events of that year in England. Siam, like England, had reasserted its own religion and customs against the assaults of France and the Papists. But Ayutthaya did not enjoy a Glorious Revolution, nor a Constitutional Monarchy, for which the Thais were obliged to wait until 1932. However, the Thais had resisted the first serious efforts by Europeans to gain some mastery over their territory and trade. The Thais had survived by playing off the Europeans against one another, as they would do with equal success during a more dangerous threat to their independence, two centuries later.

The conquest and sack of Ayutthaya, in 1767, was carried out by the ancient enemy, Burma. The victorious army massacred all but ten thousand of the inhabitants and burned down the magnificent temples, sparing only the thirteenth-century Wat Na Phra Mane, because, according to legend, a previous Burmese King had blown himself up there. The Buddha inside that wat is now almost the only relic in Ayutthaya that bears comparison with some of the splendour of Sukhothai, or even the modest charm of Lop Buri. Although modern Ayutthaya is a distinct, rather unpleasant town, there are modern buildings scattered among the ancient ruins.

Hundreds of thousands of tourists come here just because it is near Bangkok, but few, I imagine, would come here twice.

Walking among the desolation of Ayutthaya, made more unpleasant by the profusion of pye-dogs covered in sores, I found myself brooding over an old historical puzzle. How, less than twenty years after this great defeat, had the Thais managed to get back most of their empire, then started a new kingdom at Bangkok, which not only kept its independence but now has grown into a city of seven million?

Shortly before the fall of Ayutthaya, a young general called Taksin, of Chinese blood, had fled with a few hundred soldiers to Rayong, near the modern Pattaya beach resort. He rallied the Thai people, defeated the Burmese Army, and soon won back suzerainty over most of the former vassal states, including parts of Burma itself. In 1778, he founded a new capital further downstream at Thonburi, on the right bank of the Chao Phraya River, opposite Bangkok. Meanwhile, Taksin's favourite general, Chakri, went north to subdue the kingdoms of Vientiane, Luang Prabang and Chiang Mai.

However, Taksin had started to show those symptoms of rage and suspicion that go with megalomania. He flogged Buddhist monks and put some of his wives to death. A frightened minister sent a message to General Chakri urging him to return to Thonburi 'at the speed of his fastest elephants'. Chakri arrived and was hailed as the new king in April 1782. This was the start of the Chakri dynasty, which established its capital at Bangkok, and still rules there today.

Arriving at Bangkok central station, at six o'clock in the evening, I got off the train and heard solemn music blaring over the loud speakers. All the alighting passengers dropped their luggage, and stood at attention, stiff-backed and motionless. It was the Thai National Anthem, which I had heard in cinemas and on television. Whenever I hear it in public places, even when several verses are played, I notice that nobody starts to slouch, or talk or even move away as they used to in England, when cinemas still played God Save the Queen. Here, we stood to attention until the National Anthem was finished. Foreigners, just like Thais, are expected and even commanded to show respect for the King. A joking remark about the King or his portrait is likely to land a tourist in jail. The national slogan, *Mai pen rai*, 'it doesn't matter', stops well short of the Royal Family.

The King is also the key to an understanding of Thailand. Foreigners from republican countries like the United States, France, Germany or Italy, are inclined to look on the monarchy as a meaningless anachronism. Those from constitutional monarchies such as Britain, Spain, Holland, Belgium, Denmark, Norway and Sweden, look on the Thai Royal Family as the counterpart of their own. Both these perceptions are wide of the mark. Until very recently, 1932, Thai monarchs were absolute rulers, or 'Lords of Life' with much the same powers as a king in medieval Europe. Even after the Constitution which brought democracy and a parliament, the King retained his spiritual authority as the only person worthy to change the vestments of the Emerald Buddha, which stands in the temple beside the Palace.

The monarchy is the force that has kept this country independent. In politics as in the Buddhist religion, the King must pursue the Middle Way. The Chakri dynasty started in 1782, when various European powers were building their overseas empires, and for the next 150 years the Chakris fought off efforts at colonization by England, Holland and latterly France. After the Constitution of 1932, by which time colonization was on the decline, Thailand was faced by a new threat to her sovereignty, from the fascist and communist ideologues. The Germans were spreading through Europe; the Italians were building an empire in Africa; and in the East, fascist Japan was fighting to build her co-prosperity sphere, which briefly included Thailand during the Second World War. After the war, came a new military threat from communism, first in China, then in Malaya and now in Vietnam. Both fascism and communism had their supporters among the Thais but neither movement dared to contest the authority of the King.

Thai politics have produced a few likeable, even admirable, leaders from both the military and the popular faction, but none has a following even remotely comparable with that of the King, who is above faction. He is also above attack and even criticism. No Thai politician or journalist would dare to express the anti-monarchist sentiments that are quite acceptable in Britain or Spain. One could not print even the mildest joke or cartoon about the Thai Royal Family. Only Japan has a comparable monarchy.

The Chakri dynasty and Bangkok began in the same year, 1782. The palaces, wats, museums and works of art are now on the quiet edge of the city, as commerce and population have spread north and east, away from the Chao Phraya River. The best way to see the area is from the river, or by joining a guided tour of the main attractions such as the Grand Palace, the Temple of the Emerald Buddha, the Wat Po and the Wat Sudat. Royal Bangkok is mostly a jumble of kitsch, hokum and imitation, like Disneyland. Some of the buildings copy Europe, some copy Cambodia, Burma, Japan or India. Bigness comes before beauty, as if the creators were hoping to beat a record, or make their mark at a World Fair. The centrepiece is the Wat Arun, which began as a sixteenth-century temple but later was raised from fifteen to seventy-nine metres in height, and its surface covered with glazed Chinese porcelain. The Reclining Buddha in Wat Po is forty-six metres long and fifteen high, constructed of brick but surfaced in gold leaf. No building here has even a fraction of the interest of the meanest temple at Angkor; here there is even a concrete model of Angkor Wat. Most of the things are not what they seem to be. The Golden Mountain is really a hill of bricks, covered with artificial grottoes, stalactites and hermits. The Emerald Buddha, itself a part of the loot from a war against Laos, is found in a room of life-size gold figures of shrubs, lamps, vases and parasols, none of which would attract a second glance if made from some other material.

Most of the palaces and wats are strewn with huge Chinese statues of dogs, lions and mandarins, which were brought to Bangkok as ballast for the ships. Some of the mandarins appear as the congregation for one of Buddha's sermons. Among the bric-à-brac at the Vivanmek Palace are Thailand's first shower-bath and typewriter; also a porcelain pig. Royal Bangkok may appeal to lovers of kitsch and high camp but even as Asian pastiche, it is neither as interesting nor as old as George IV's Pavilion at Brighton. Compared with Angkor, the Shwe Dagon Pagoda in Rangoon or the temples at Pagan in central Burma, Royal Bangkok is absurd and, to me, dispiriting. But the dynasties that created the marvels of Burma, India and Cambodia are long since forgotten. Those that succeeded them were in turn overthrown by the Europeans, whose glory is also departed. The Chakris have given to Thailand something far more valuable than the most magnificent art and architecture. They have given the country peace, freedom and, above all, independence.

The founding of the Chakri dynasty came midway between two of the most momentous and, some would say baleful events in human history, the American Revolution of 1776 and the French Revolution of 1789, ushering in the twin evils of nationalism and socialism, which re-emerged in this century as fascism and communism, the Holocaust and the Gulag Archipelago. Thanks to the Chakris, Thailand has so far escaped both these modern abominations. The Thai body politic has not yet been poisoned by 'isms' and 'ocracies'.

The Chakri kings have never been bloodthirsty or vengeful; and Rama I may well have regretted the execution of Taksin – killed by a blow on the neck from a sandalwood club – and also of Praya Sanka, the man who deposed Taksin, and therefore acquired the stigma of treason.

With this unpleasantness out of the way, Rama I turned his mind to moving the court from Thonburi, on the west bank of the Chao Phraya River, over to Bangkok, 'the village of wild plum'. The east bank was even then subject to flooding, however it had the advantage of lying across the river from the traditional enemy, Burma. The chosen site of the palace was the Chinatown ruled by a rich merchant, to whom Rama I offered compensation to move his people to Sampang, where they still are. The Chinese then, as now, were a prosperous and contented minority. The previous king, Taksin, was half Chinese, while Rama I himself had some Chinese blood.

The palaces and temples of Bangkok were as far as possible built from the bricks of Ayutthaya; just as humbler Thais who wanted to move their home used to dismantle the beams, walls and roof of their house and take them by barge to be put together again on a new location. The building was done by conscript labour, similar to the French *corvée* system, by which the Thai peasantry worked one month in four for the king. Sir John Bowring, a British plenipotentiary in Bangkok, said that the slaves, as he called these serfs, were better treated than servants in England. Probably they were better treated than labourers in the English mines and mills; certainly they were better treated than Black plantation slaves in the United States. An earlier British envoy, John Crawfurd, who came to Bangkok in 1822, complained of the vanity of the Siamese: 'The lowest peasant considers himself superior to the proudest and most elevated subject of any other country.'

The Europeans marvelled that such proud people abased themselves to the kings, the 'Lords of Life'. An American naval officer, Edward Roberts, wrote in the 1830s: 'A people who are habitually crawling upon their knees and elbows and performing the "knock-head" ceremony, cannot be other than ungraceful and inelegant in their manners.' This habit still shocks Americans. I remember the look on the face of a New York feminist, when a Thai girl came shuffling in on her knees to bring her boss some coffee.

All power belonged to the King, as well as the gold, the palanquins, the coaches, the barges and rowing boats, palace buildings, weapons and arms of all kinds, and above all the rice fields and teak forests. The King laid down both the secular and religious law, as well as being its judge. Yet the Chakris, without exception, tried not to abuse this power. The people were law-abiding. The rather cantankerous Englishman, John Crawfurd, had to acknowledge: 'We walked for miles unarmed and unattended in the vicinity of Bangkok without receiving insult or offence from anyone, and never for a moment suspected danger to our person or property.' Yet law and order were not enforced by cruelty. The Chakri kings seldom imposed the severest penalties. For instance, the law said that Buddhist monks could suffer death for unchastity, but Rama II commuted this to imprisonment with hard labour, which consisted of cutting grass for the royal elephants.

Even Rama I was an author as well as a soldier; and most of the Chakris have shown a talent for arts and science. Rama II, who is said to have been a distinguished poet, also reformed the ballet, and gilded a Buddhist image each day of his reign. He asked John Crawfurd for help in designing clothes to dress a Napoleon doll. His successor Rama III (1824–51) was greedy, or 'hungry' as he preferred to call it, and often cut short councils of state in order to eat. Like all the Chakris, he was at the same time a devout Buddhist and tolerant of other faiths. However, in 1849 he rebuked the Catholic missionaries who had criticized his pious action in buying back animals from the slaughterhouse.

Rama IV (1851–68) is the man whose reign has been travestied in the book, film and musical of *The King and I*. These were loosely based on Anna Leonowens' *English Governess at the Siamese Court* and later *Romance of a Harem*, both of which were in turn loosely based on Mrs Leonowens' brief time of employment as teacher of English to some of the children of King Mongkut, or Rama IV.

It is true that Rama IV had eighty-two children from thirty-five wives, but this was a matter of state, rather than sexual licence. Since there was no aristocracy in the English sense, all power derived from the Royal Family; so that ambitious parents gave their daughters in matrimony to the King. Most of the Chakri kings had up to twelve children by one favourite wife and few children, if any, by minor wives. For example, Rama V (1868–1910) had seventy-seven children by ninety-two wives. 'As it is inconceivable that birth control was practised,' writes Prince Chula Chakrabongse in *Lords of Life*, a history of the Chakri dynasty, 'many of the wives would have had little or no marital relations.' It is a sad thought for admirers of Thai female beauty.

Prince Chula remarks that *The King and I* bears no more resemblance to life at the court of Siam than Gilbert and Sullivan's *The Mikado* does to nineteenth-century Japan. The real-life governess, Mrs Leonowens, was a plain and ill-natured widow lady, with much prurient fantasy and an eye to the sale of suggestive tittletattle. She never became the *éminence grise* of the Siamese court, or even, as she implied, its letter-writer, since Rama IV wrote almost as good English as she did. When she started to work for him, in 1862, he had already done the bulk of his work on domestic reform, and on establishing diplomatic relations with France and England.

Far from being enchanted with Anna, the King could not stand her, and certainly did not fancy her. He had spent twenty-seven years as a monk obeying the 227 rules of conduct, including abstinence from sex, alcohol, places of amusement and even from food after noon. He was a man learned in poetry, mathematics, astronomy and comparative religion. He was warmly admired by the foreigners in Siam.

In only one respect did the real Mongkut resemble the figure portrayed by Yul Brynner. He had a quick temper. However, he was not cruel and had been known to sit up all night rather than sign a death warrant. There is no likelihood in the story that he had a wife burnt alive for adultery.

It was Rama V who brought Thailand into this grim twentieth century. He abolished serfdom, encouraged education and medical services and sent his children to England, Russia and Prussia, though not to republican France. He was fond of astronomy, cooking, clocks and, towards the end of his life, motor cars. 'Best of all probably he liked to drive himself in his yellow electric car with one or two of his elder grandchildren,' according to Prince Chula, who himself is the author (besides his historical works) of *Wheels at Speed* and *Road Racing 1936*. Rama V's widow, Queen Saowabha, became an assiduous reader of *The Motor* and *Autocar*.

With the death of Rama V in 1910, the Chakri dynasty entered a troubled era, which lasted until the accession of the present king. Rama VI was a military man, pro-English and conscientious but he broke with Chakri tradition in his reluctance to marry even one wife, let alone eighty. Engagements were made and broken off; his one marriage ended in separation. His successor King Prajadhipok (1925–32), the first not to be given the name of Rama was, also in the words of Prince Chula, 'the first monarch of any country to have been a boy at Eton.' He was also the last of the Chakris to rule as an absolute monarch or 'Lord of Life'.

The Thais, more than most people, are fascinated by dates, anniversaries, and numerical coincidences, especially when these refer to births, marriages, deaths and royal affairs. Omens and prophecies have surrounded every dynasty in this part of the world; the British in Burma were dogged by the prophecy that their rule would last only a hundred years and that their expulsion would come from a non-Burmese people (that is, the Japanese). Nobody quite knows when it was first whispered that Rama I himself had said that his dynasty would last 150 years, or until 1932. But so it happened.

The tactful Prince Chula wrote of King Prajadhipok: 'Although he was by upbringing a soldier . . . the seventh King of the Chakris was more of a philosopher.' Perhaps Prince Chula intended to say that his royal relation, though righteous and highly principled, was insufficiently cunning and tough to stay as an absolute king in a world of demagogues and dictators. He cut the civil list in order to save on public expenditure but only made enemies of the bureaucratic class. In 1931, when the world was in the grip of Depression, King Prajadhipok kept his country on the gold standard, so that its rice became too expensive to sell to sterling countries like India and Malaya. One of the Royal Princes was sent to the neighbouring countries to study the crisis but when he came back had little to show for his work but films and snaps of himself at cocktail parties and tiger shoots.

There was grumbling at home but the real threat to the monarchy came from the Thais who had studied in Paris. Since the First World War and the downfall of monarchy in Russia, Austria and Germany, many young Thais had gone to study in France, where they picked up the ideas of the French and maybe even of the Russian Revolutions. Among them were two young men who, as friends or rivals, would dominate Thai political life for the next thirty years. The lawyer Pridi Panomyong and the army captain Luang Pibun Songgram, known as Pibun, plotted the *coup d'état* of 1932. Later Pridi and Pibun became the leaders of, respectively, the Left and the Right political groups or, to put it another way, the middle class and the army. During and after the Second World War they took opposite sides in what amounted to armed confrontation. Only in old age, when both men were living in separate exile, would they at least be reconciled, if never again friends. Pridi, the high-minded and rather priggish socialist lawyer, and Pibun, the extrovert, rascally army man, are names that should be remembered by students of modern Thai history.

The 150th anniversary of the Chakri kings fell on 6 April 1932. As the date approached, according to Prince Chula, 'superstitious pessimists were reminding one another of the alleged prophecy of Rama I that his line would only last for 150 years.' The anniversary celebrations passed off quietly, the King went down to the sea for a golfing holiday and it was not till 24 June that a *coup d'état* began, with tanks clattering into the Palace. It seems that seventy people knew of the plot, which was led by Pridi and Pibun.

A revolutionary People's Party issued bloodthirsty pamphlets attacking the King and the whole Chakri dynasty but public opinion in Bangkok was neutral or hostile to the rebellion. The countryside, then as now, was royalist, and quite indifferent to politicians. The King agreed to return to Bangkok to get the release of some royal hostages and he did not object to the new Assembly. After all, he had been brought up in England, which has enjoyed such things for hundred of years.

Democracy in the Thai fashion began with deputies waving guns at each other in the Chamber. Pridi and Pibun emerged as the leaders of two apparently opposite factions. Pridi, a constitutional lawyer, university lecturer and rather austere man of principle, represented the aspirations of middle-class, educated, professional and academic people. He was an advocate of land reform and socialism but not of extreme measures. In character, he appeared to be rather reserved, or haughty and proud. Political principles did not bother Pibun. He was ruthless but charming, especially to women. Jealous husbands were no doubt responsible for the two attempts on his life during the 1930s, one when he was leaving for a football match, the other when he was pulling up his trousers. Pibun was more seriously damaged by the suggestion that he had lined his pockets by selling crown land.

The 1930s were years of ideological polarization, when politicians tended to swing to communism or fascism. Although in these terms Pridi and Pibun were at opposite extremes, they also had much in common. For example their factions both tended to persecute the Chinese minority in Thailand: the Left because it was capitalist and exploitative of the peasants; the Right because the Chinese were foreign.

The American historian, David A. Wilson, says in his *Politics in Thailand*: 'In the years before the beginning of the Far Eastern War, Pibun and Pridi worked closely and enthusiastically in a policy which aimed to glorify the Thai nation, first at the expense of the Chinese minority within the country and subsequently at the expense of France in Indo-China.' After the Fall of France in 1940, but before the Japanese war at the end of 1941, the Thais forcibly won parts of Laos and Cambodia – only to lose them again in 1945.

The 'Lords of Life' had looked after the interests of everyone in Thailand. But by this time the monarchy was in exile. King Prajadhipok stuck it out as a constitutional monarch till 1935, when he abdicated and went to live in England. The succession fell to a young nephew, Ananda, who had been brought up in the United States, and spent the war in Switzerland. This was fortunate for the monarchy, which did not share the disgrace of the Japanese occupation from 1941 till 1945. But the return of Ananda after the war was followed by a dreadful and still inexplicable tragedy.

The violent death of King Ananda on 9 June 1946 was an event so harrowing to the people and so convulsive in its political consequences, that it is still taboo in this otherwise open and freedom-loving country. There has been only one full and objective attempt to discover what happened that day. The inquiry by Rayne Kruger, a South African author (who went on to write *Goodbye Dolly Grey*, a classic history of the Boer War) was made in the early 1950s when most of the people involved were still alive, which adds extra conviction to his book *The Devil's Discus*. The book is still banned in Thailand.

The death of the King gave rise to all kinds of ingenious conspiracy theories, one of which was accepted by the government and the police. Those who first discovered the body at once put forward the two most probable explanations, that Ananda had died either by accident or by suicide. Rayne Kruger plumps for the second of these. Had the government and the courts been willing to settle for accidental death (often a euphemism for suicide) the sad affair would have soon been forgotten. Instead, the government chose to regard Ananda's death as regicide by Left-wing revolutionaries and used this as a pretext to overthrow the Pridi government and bring back his military rival, Pibun. The new government justified its return to power by fabricating a plot to murder Ananda and executing three of the men who were claimed to have been accessories.

It has long been the practice of writers on Thailand to pass hurriedly by the subject of Ananda's death, because it is painful still to the Royal Family. I certainly do not intend to rake up all the sad and unpleasant details of what I believe was a private tragedy. But Ananda's death was turned by politicians like Pibun into a public matter as well. It resulted in this country being put into the hands of military politicians who ruled it for three decades by more or less arbitrary methods, and still rule it today, with the consent of Parliament.

I too had intended not to discuss Ananda's death. But I now find that it cannot be avoided. However, I shall keep the story as factual and brief as I can.

To recapitulate the position of Thailand in June 1946: Less than a year after the end of the war, the country had been forgiven for taking the side of Japan, under heavy duress. The wartime collaborator, Pibun, had spent a few months in prison but had now been released, since the Allies thought he had acted in Thailand's interests, rather than out of any real sympathy for Japan. His left-wing old friend and rival, Pridi, had acted as regent during the Royal Family's exile, and also, secretly, headed a Free Thai movement under the auspices of the US intelligence agency, the Office of Strategic Services (OSS), who gave him the code-name 'Ruth'. He was now Prime Minister and, as a former regent, the man with most influence on Ananda. The young King had returned to Bangkok from the wartime exile in Switzerland, in the company of his devoted mother, and of his younger brother, the present King Bhumibol.

The last days of Ananda were later portrayed as fraught with mystery and foreboding, but no one seems to have mentioned this at the time. He was getting ready to travel back to Switzerland where he had lived for most of his twenty-two years, and where he was going to complete his studies in Law at Geneva University. His few public engagements were not momentous. On 3 June, he paid a visit to Chinatown, where he was given a rapturous welcome; the Chinese rightly regarded him as their friend against the jealous politicians like Pridi and Pibun. On 6 June he attended the annual Oxford and Cambridge Dinner, which delighted the many Thais, both royal and commoner, who had studied at either of these universities. On 7 June, he met with the Prime Minister, Pridi, to discuss the membership of the Royal Council, which would be sitting in his absence. There may have been disagreement but there was no quarrel, as later would be alleged. On 8 June, King Ananda complained of a stomach upset and was found to be running a very slight temperature. He also suffered from Bangkok's hot season, understandably in a man brought up in the Alps. He took sleeping pills that night.

Early on 9 June, the Princess Mother, who lived in the northwest wing of the Palace, crossed to the east wing, housing the royal apartment, to bring Ananda some hot water, milk and brandy, to wash down a dose of castor oil. She said that she found him asleep, woke him and asked how he felt, to which he replied, 'good'. The Princess Mother left the King in the care of the two royal pages, experienced men in their forties, named Butr and Nai Chit. The first of these, Butr, said that at 8.30 a.m., as was his custom, he brought the King his orange juice and a newspaper. He saw the King go wordlessly to his bedroom, then lie on the bed with his knees drawn up, gazing forward. With his hand nearest to Butr, he waved a gesture of dismissal.

The other page, Nai Chit, arrived at the east wing that day two hours before he was due on duty, a fact that was later held against him. At about 9.20 a.m., both pages heard a report from the King's apartment. After taking a quick look inside, Nai Chit ran to the Princess Mother in the other wing and said, 'The King has shot himself!' She and Ananda's brother, the Royal Nanny, the Royal Physician and later a horrified group of courtiers and politicians, including Prime Minister Pridi, the Minister of the Interior and the Chief of Police, all came to witness the corpse of Ananda. They found the King lying prone with his arms stretched out over the covers and almost parallel with his body. His Colt 45, which he kept by his bedside, lay near his left hand. There was a bullet hole over the right eyebrow.

In the first hours of distress and anguish, most of those present seemed to assume that Ananda had shot himself. Prime minister Pridi was heard to exclaim in English, 'The King is a suicide!' This

was the view of the courtiers and the police chief, who found no
evidence of an intruder, and saw and examined the revolver. But
even in humble families, those near the deceased are reluctant to
accept suicide as the cause of death. Feelings of guilt, at not
having foreseen the disaster and offered appropriate comfort, joined
with grief. All who had known him, loved the King for his good
humour, kindness and sincerity.

The public men who had gathered beside the corpse were exercised by the question of how to explain the tragedy. Thailand is
not one of those countries where news of the death of the head of
state can simply be hushed up for weeks on end. The King's death
was promptly announced, causing nationwide grief and bewilderment. Some kind of announcement now had to be made as to the
cause of death, if only to halt the burgeoning rumours. But what
was the cause? Nobody knew then, or knows for certain now. At
last the Prime Minister, Pridi, and court officials managed to draft
a communiqué ending:

> An examination thereof [the body] was made by the Director-
> General of the Police Department and the Department of Medical
> Sciences, as the result of which it is concluded that the King must
> have played with his pistol, as he was fond of doing, resulting in an
> accident.

This explanation comforted those who refused to believe in a suicide. For politicians, like Pridi, it was the easy way out. Some of
the people involved continued to think it an accident. But reason
argues against this theory. For one thing, Ananda was an experienced pistol shot who would often practise at length in the Palace
gardens. There is also a technical matter. Anyone who has fired a
Colt 45 knows that it needs considerable pressure both on the
trigger and on the safety spring in the rear of the butt. If it is hard
to exert that pressure *firing forward*, it would be quite a feat to
exert it firing backwards, into one's own head by accident. It is
rare, if not impossible, for a Colt 45 to go off by accident, such as
dropping it on the floor.

Such technical matters were not discussed at the time. The
Press and the public did not accept the communiqué, just because
it sounded like a cover-up. They wanted someone to blame for the
death of the King. The Bangkok Press and politicians, like their
kind all over the world, believed the conspiracy theory of public
events. All kinds of rumours were whispered about and even got

into print. Some doctors who had examined the body told the Press that the bullet-wound at the back of the head was smaller than that in the front. Popular wisdom holds that the exit wound is larger. Therefore the King was shot from behind. The King's own doctor and others were later to prove by shooting at pigs and the bodies of dead men, that exit wounds are not necessarily larger than entrance wounds except when dum-dum bullets are used. But rumour was stronger than medical fact.

Prime Minister Pridi formed a commission of inquiry into the death of the King; but this merely enraged the conspiracy theorists, who thought that Pridi himself was involved in a plot. These rumour-mongers, opponents of Pridi, pointed out that two of Pridi's political friends had left the employ of the Palace in unusual circumstances. These were naval Lieutenant Vacharachai, and a minor politician called Chaleo. Both had indeed got jobs at the Palace, thanks to Pridi, and Vacharachai had certainly displeased the King. Many people in Thailand at this time really believed that Pridi wanted to transform Thailand into a left-wing republic. This was a time when communist movements were gaining strength in neighbouring countries like Burma, Malaya, China and Vietnam. On one occasion somebody, in the dark of a Bangkok cinema, shouted out, 'Pridi killed the King!' Such shouts and murmurs were heard and noted by Pridi's political rival, Field-Marshal Pibun. In March 1947, Pibun founded his 'Might is Right' party.

On the night of 7 November 1947, Pibun's supporters staged a successful *coup d'état*, with the proclaimed purpose of solving the mystery of the King's death. Aided by friends in the British Embassy, Pridi fled to Singapore, where he issued a statement denying any part in Ananda's death: 'I further declare that to the best of my knowledge and belief, no member of my present entourage was implicated in that unhappy event.' This was meant to exonerate Lieutenant Vacharachai, who had escaped with Pridi. It could not help the former Palace official Chaleo nor the royal pages, Nai Chit and Butr. On the night of the *coup d'état*, all three were arrested and later were charged with conspiring to murder King Ananda.

Although Field Marshal Pibun considered it prudent, at first, to rule through a front of respectable, monarchist politicians, Thailand was drifting into a period of corrupt and brutal oppression, symbolized by Pibun's chief of police, the infamous General Pao. Although Pao was not much use at catching genuine communist rebels out in the jungle, he was adept at framing innocent people by torture, blackmail and perjury. These were some of the methods used to indict the three supposed regicides, whose trial opened on 28 September 1948, nearly a year after their arrest.

The trial was held in a room of the Justice Ministry, close to and almost overlooked by the room in which Ananda was shot. The court consisted of four judges, presided over by the Chief Judge of the Criminal Court. The defence was conducted throughout by a criminal lawyer called Fak Nasongkhla, and later by the young barrister daughter of one of the three accused, Chaleo. It was not easy to practise law in the days of Police Chief General Pao. Two of the lawyers for the defence in the regicide case were murdered. The defence was further hampered by the fact that they could not openly suggest that King Ananda had taken his own life, which would sound like *lèse majesté*. They could only argue that the accused were not responsible for the King's death.

There were three groups of charges against the accused: First, that all three had treasonably plotted to kill the King. Second, that the two pages had actually killed the King or, alternatively, given 'aid and abetment' to the killer. Third, that Nai Chit alone had planted a ·45 pistol and cartridge case, which were not the ones actually used in the killing.

This last was part of some technical and sometimes obscure evidence brought by the prosecution, which we might look at first. The Director-General of the Science Department alleged that the ·45 produced by the page Nai Chit, just after the shooting, had not been fired for days, perhaps weeks. The prosecution further alleged that the ·45 bullet found in the mattress three days after the death was not the one that had killed Ananda but had been planted there as a substitute for the bullet fired from the assassin's weapon. It was further pointed out by the prosecution that what they called the 'planted' bullet was undented and unmarked, though tests carried out on cadavers showed that a bullet passing twice through the skull would be deformed.

Doctors brought by the prosecution said that the state of the corpse, with legs and arms outstretched, with eyes and mouth closed, indicated that no 'cadaveric spasm' had occurred, as would have followed violent muscular action such as pulling a trigger. The inference was that the King had been shot in his sleep. The prosecution explained that 'cadaveric spasm' occurs when the cerebral cortex is destroyed but the basal ganglia is left to continue contracting the muscles in use at the time of death. If both parts of the brain are destroyed, no spasm occurs, so the prosecution set up a gruesome demonstration in court; a glass tube was inserted into a model human brain to follow the path of the bullet through King Ananda's skull. The tube narrowly missed the ganglia.

Whether the judges, or even most brain surgeons, were quite convinced by this esoteric evidence, most people got the point of the prosecution's next line of argument: that the recoil of a ·45 could not possibly have thrown the weapon three feet away from the King's forehead to the vicinity of his left hand. If Ananda had shot himself, is it not common sense that the gun and his hand, or his hands if he had used both would be near his head, not drawn to the sides of his body?

Almost all the prosecution's technical evidence led to suggest that the King could not have killed himself. The only part that directly implicated one of the three accused was the far-fetched suggestion that Nai Chit had somehow 'planted' a different pistol and bullet, though it was not suggested how this could have been done.

Virtually all of the evidence against the accused consisted of hearsay or speculation. For instance, the Royal Nanny told the court: 'Of one thing she was positive. Ananda had been murdered. She did not believe that either Nai Chit or Butr was the killer – but they must know who he was, since they were sitting outside the door when the shot was fired.' A police officer told a long story of how a timber-merchant had been to a party before the assassination and had heard of a plot to kill the King involving, among others, Chaleo and Nai Chit. The same two, Chaleo and Nai Chit, had also been heard to predict at different times that the King would not be going to Europe – as though the conspirators to a murder would talk of their plan in advance.

The judges made an inspection of the Grand Palace and they decided that access for an intruder would have been easy. But who was this man? Here the prosecution, helped by Pao's police, came up with some less shadowy evidence. One of the royal gardeners had recognized Lieutenant Vacharachai somewhere behind the Palace shortly before the shot was fired, and after the shot a Palace servant said he had seen the Lieutenant hurrying down the steps; Lieutenant Vacharachai's chauffeur testified that he had driven him to a point near the Palace; and the Lieutenant's laundress remembered washing blood from his sleeve.

Since all four of these witnesses were humble folk with every
reason not to displease General Pao, their evidence does not mean
much. Moreover, the man they implicated was safe in exile and
most unlikely to come back to give evidence in his defence.

In March 1950, Ananda's younger brother Bhumibol returned
to Thailand from Switzerland for three solemn ceremonies. He lit
the pyre for the cremation of Ananda's body, prostrating himself
with grief. He was crowned King. Then he married the beautiful
Sirikit, the much loved Queen of Thailand until this day. Later that
year, King Bhumibol agreed to give evidence at the trial, for which
the judges, the counsels and the accused attended the Grand
Palace. The King said that his brother had been a very calm
person: 'When he used guns he was very careful in every way,
and even warned me that when playing with a pistol I should
make sure the breech was empty . . . The King never told me that
anything troubled him.'

In November 1950, Counsel Fak opened the case for the defence,
Apart from questioning some of the prosecution's scientific evidence, he did not dispute the fact of assassination or suggest who
else might be to blame. The three defendants took the stand.
Chaleo, the politician, blamed his enemies in the Democrat Party
for having spread rumours against him. He also said, on the
hearsay of a court official, that Ananda had been in dispute with
his mother. The page, Nai Chit, was asked why he had gone to the
Grand Palace two hours before he was due on duty. His explanation, too commonplace to be worth repeating, convinces us. Nai
Chit sounds an engaging character. He had six daughters and
loved practical jokes, also knitting. The other page, Butr, burst
into tears in the witness box, and said that in prison he had been
chained, beaten and kicked. He also came up with the statement
that on the evening before the shooting, Ananda had burned
about half-a-dozen sheets of paper in his bathroom. He gave other
evidence, which can be found in Rayne Kruger's book, suggesting
that the young King had formed an emotional attachment with a
young woman, of which his mother disapproved. Although Rayne
Kruger supports his story and even names the young woman, the
evidence is again only speculative.

When the defence closed on 9 May 1951, the court had listened
to 161 witnesses over a period of two and a half years. The judges
then conferred for four and a half months. On 27 September
1951, five years and three months after the death of Ananda, the

court declared that in view of the lack of marking on the bullet in the mattress and in view of the lack of 'cadaveral spasm' in the body: 'The court accordingly rules that the death of His late Majesty King Ananda Mahadol was brought about by assassination.' The court then went into a very long summing up of the evidence against the accused, concluding that Chaleo was innocent, Butr was innocent but Nai Chit guilty, though not the actual assassin. Nai Chit appealed against his conviction, while the prosecution appealed against the acquittal of the other two. A final appeal went to the Dikka, the highest court in the kingdom, which decided that all three men were guilty. At four in the morning, on 17 February 1955, almost nine years after the death of King Ananda, the three men were executed by firing squad.

Prince Chula's *Lords of Life*, which is otherwise so informative on the history of the Chakris, dismisses the aftermath of Ananda's death in one bald sentence: 'Some years later and after a long trial, two men, who were royal pages, were executed for the crime in connection with the King's death, and it was declared that other suspects had escaped.' Hardly an adequate treatment of the story. It is understandable that the Thais, with their love of the family, Buddhism and monarchy, should turn their backs on a subject so painful in all three respects. But those who died in front of a firing squad were also family men, Buddhists and quite possibly monarchists to the end. In fairness to them and the cause of truth, the sentence should now be reviewed.

The prosecution at no time offered serious evidence as to who committed the murder, or even that murder took place. The evidence against Lieutenant Vacharachai from the gardener, from his chauffeur and his laundress was never even tested in court. It was almost certainly trumped up by General Pao's police. On the other hand, the prosecution could not shake the evidence in his defence by Vacharachai's wife. Not only was there no evidence of a plot by Pridi to kill the King, there was no conceivable motive. Had Pridi really wanted to found a republic, why had he not done so before the King's return from Europe, when he, Pridi, was regent? Or why did he not wait till the end of June when the King was once more back in Swizterland?

It seems to me probable that King Ananda shot himself with his own gun. The evidence that so impressed the judges concerning the lack of dents in the bullet can be explained by the relative softness of living bone. The positioning of the corpse and the gun do not accord with suicide while lying down. But as Mr Kruger so forcefully argues, the positioning does accord with the King having shot himself while sitting up. This was the position in which he was last seen alive by the page, Butr. However, if this was the case, why did the bullet enter the mattress, and not the wall behind the bed? The pathetic Butr also supplied the evidence which, in Kruger's judgement, explains the King's motive. The papers which he was burning on the day before his death could well have been letters from a young woman.

Of course, such explanations are speculative. Nobody can pretend to know what was going on in Ananda's mind. He was off colour from his illness. The account of his behaviour on that morning suggests he was gloomy. He had been burning letters. And he had at his bedside the fatally tempting pistol. The suicide of the young Lord of Life was sad and shocking, but suicide had occurred before among the Chakris. As recently as 1935, Prince Oscar Anuventura, the President of the Regency Council, had taken his life because of the strain of the abdication crisis.

The tragedy of King Ananda brings to mind that other young Prince who toyed with the thought of suicide:

> O! that this too too solid flesh would melt,
> Thaw, and resolve itself into a dew;
> Or that the Everlasting had not fix'd
> His canon 'gainst self-slaughter!

After the *coup d'état* and the abdication during the 1930s, and then Ananda's death in 1946, there were some who predicted the end of the Chakri dynasty perhaps of the monarchy itself. The country seemed to be polarized between the increasingly left-wing stance of Pridi, who went into exile in Communist China, and military gangsters like Pibun. Thailand found itself part of the Cold War between the United States and the Soviet Union. The Cold War turned into a shooting war in Korea in 1950, by which time there was also guerrilla war in the nearby countries of Vietnam and Malaya. Yet Thailand never succumbed to extremist politics. In Buddhist fashion, she kept to the Middle Way and, forty years later, is prosperous, free and peaceful. The Chakri dynasty not only survived the Constitution but grew in strength. The present King is just as loved and revered as those who were Lords of Life.

Thailand today has reached a compromise, or Middle Way between the Pridi and Pibun factions, the ideologues and the generals. The politicians know that they cannot rule through the Bangkok mob and the university students. The generals know that they have to put up with a free-speaking Press and Parliament. In spite of the Constitution of 1932, the ultimate power in the country rests with the crown.

The survival and strength of the Thai Royal Family is largely due to the courage and steadfastness of King Bhumibol who has grown from a shy young man into a wise and confident ruler, with an unrivalled knowledge and understanding of his country. His health has not always been good. He lost the use of an eye in a car crash, which almost paralysed one side of his face. But physical pain has never prevented his ceaseless travel about the countryside, taking a special interest in agricultural development and irrigation schemes. He is an artist, a sailor, composer and musician, preferring the kind of jazz which was popular during his childhood in the United States. Foreign newspapers frequently publish items like this:

> King Bhumibol of Thailand is a keen jazzman who blows up a storm on clarinet and trumpet. So much so that he sat in with a band led by the legendary New Orleans trumpeter, Kid Sheik Cola, 79, during a jam session at his Bangkok palace. Afterwards a bemused Sheik said: 'It was strange for the musicians when the King, Queen and Princess were waited on by chamberlains crawling on their knees, but the King got right into it.' Indeed, he enjoyed himself so much that he presented Sheik with a French-made trumpet.

The King's compositions include 'Love Over Again' and 'HM Blues'.

Queen Sirikit is also much loved by the Thais, not least for her outspokenness. She has been known to startle interviewers, by putting questions in return. An English journalist was asked whether he thought Margaret Thatcher beautiful and why the trade unions were infiltrated by communists. Some of Queen Sirikit's most outspoken comments concerned her controversial son, the Crown Prince Vajiralongkorn, an army officer, educated at Mill Hill in England and the Australian Military Academy. He has a playboy reputation, which prompted the Queen to tell an American newspaper: 'My son is a little bit of a Don Juan so his family life is not so smooth. He is a student, he is a good boy and the Thai people like him very much.'

That last statement perhaps needs some qualification. The Bangkok students and some of the left-wing are less than enthusiastic
about the Crown Prince, although they refrain from attacking the
monarchy as an institution. The Royal Family has made it be
known that it might allow a change in the usual succession pro-
cedure to let a woman be monarch of Thailand. King Bhumibol and
Queen Sirikit have three daughters capable of ruling the country.
The eldest, Princess Ubolratana, who was her father's favourite,
cut herself out by renouncing her royal status to marry an American pilot. She lives in the USA as Mrs Jensen. The second daughter,
Sirindhorn, is a shy and conscientious woman, a student of Sanskrit, who often goes with her parents on their trips round the
country. She is a likely successor. The third daughter, Princess
Chulaporn, has a scientific job. She takes after her father as a jazz
musician, though naturally in a more modern style.

The 150th anniversary of the Chakri dynasty had been awaited
in rumour and dread. And sure enough, tanks clanked through
Bangkok. The 200th anniversary of the Chakri dynasty in 1982
came in a mood of thanksgiving and hope. It is true that tanks
still occasionally enter Bangkok when a disgruntled general or
junior officer tries his hand at a *coup d'état*. But most of the *coups
d'état* are bloodless as well as unsuccessful. The Chakris are no
longer under threat.

The festivities for the 200th anniversary of the Chakris, and of
Bangkok, were also my first experience of the Thai New Year, or
Songkran feast, which occurs in April, the hottest month of the
year. It is also the windiest month and therefore the time when
people indulge their passion for flying kites, in the parks and open
spaces of Royal Bangkok. It is not such a peaceful pastime as it
at first appears, since Thais like to 'fight' their kites against opponents, just as they love to stage fights between cocks, fish, dogs,
chameleons, buffaloes or indeed any creatures, large or small.
Watching the kites in Bangkok in 1982, reminded me of the kites I
saw over the river in Saigon, in April 1975, also a windy month.
There was something magnificent about those kites, soaring and
dipping over the city under siege.

The most startling feature of Thai New Year is constantly getting
splashed with water. Glasses, saucepans and buckets are employed
in the work of drenching all and sundry. In the coffee shop of the

Trocadero hotel, the waitresses squealed with joy as they took it in turns to empty buckets of water on to the fat Australian construction worker who had been grabbing them for the past few weeks. There is a certain amount of by-play in splashing the opposite sex, but it is all good natured. I have never heard of the Thais throwing dirty water, or even soot, as they do at the Indian Holi feast, or at certain Catholic processions in Central America.

On the first day of Songkran, I joined the staff of a local restaurant on what was in fact a kind of works outing, cruising around in a boat on the river and then the canals, lined with wooden houses, go-downs and gleaming pagodas. Even Bangkok seems beautiful from the water, even the Wat Arun and the area of the Royal Palace. Everyone on the boat drenched everyone else with cups or bowls of water poured down the back of the neck. When we got to the narrow canals, our boat was fair game for the locals who swam out to board us and empty buckets of water over us. Everyone in the party drank Thai whisky, sang and made jokes (of breathtaking obscenity, I was told) about everyone of the other sex.

Yet it was also a holy occasion, the Buddhist equivalent of our Christmas and Easter rolled into one. The boat stopped for prayers at one of the old pagodas. Frequently, those in the boat would pray in the local fashion with palms together, as someone poured water on them, invoking the name of Buddha. On these religious occasions, the water should really be pure and scented with petals, rather than the canal water. It washes away the sins of the past year.

The word 'Songkran' derives from a Sanskrit word for the passage of the sun into a new sign of the zodiac; and since the feast comes in April, the end of the dry season, it no doubt partakes of a supplication for rain. Although Thai Buddhism has other elements of Hinduism, Buddhism rules Thai life to an extent that foreigners often ignore. It is still the custom for young men to spend some months as a monk. Among the privations that go with monkhood is chastity, a rule it is hard to break since Thai women, even the prostitutes, will not make love with a monk. Generals or politicians who have disgraced themselves often go for a year to a monastery, a custom that others might do well to follow. It is pleasant to think of, say, Edward Heath or Neil Kinnock, with shaven head, saffron gown and a metal begging bowl.

Since this New Year was also the 200th anniversary of the

Chakris, I wanted to know the religious role of the King. This has been described by an Anglophile Thai as Defender of the Faiths, note the plural, for Thai kings have always tolerated and even financed the churches and missions of Islam and Christianity. This corresponds to their feeling of obligation to non-Thai subjects, like the Chinese, Laotians and Malays.

In spite of their freedom, the foreign missionaries made few converts. A representative in Bangkok of the China Inland Mission complained long ago that Buddhism was deeply ingrained 'and most of the natives found it difficult to accept a faith whose confession of sin and other doctrine appeared in no way different.' The British Protestant missionaries in the first eighteen years of their work, till 1846, made not one convert. Their American colleagues converted only Chinese servants. A French Catholic bishop about the same time, said that the Thais found his faith 'too difficult and troublesome a road to heaven.'

But Thai religion has not been lax. One of the first acts of the first Chakri, Rama I, was to unfrock 128 profligate monks 'for drinking intoxicants, wandering out at nights to see entertainments, rubbing shoulders with women, engaging in loose talk . . . boarding Chinese junks in order to obtain financial objects of merchandise.' An old Thai prior warned an English visitor in the 1820s not to drink wine, 'for that the punishment of that crime in another existence was to have a stream of melted copper perpetually poured down the throat.'

An editorial in the Bangkok *Nation* (13 April 1982) noted the fate of another Buddhist nation nearby: 'We don't know whether the people of Kampuchea [Cambodia] would be celebrating Songkran today or not but certainly the spirit of national cohesiveness and identity would be sorely missed in that country invaded by Vietnam.' Another neighbouring Buddhist country, Laos, has also suffered the joyless oppression of communism. Many years ago, when Laos was still a free country, I noted the merriment when a Russian 'journalist', wearing a heavy serge suit, came to Vientiane at Songkran. Every time he was drenched with water, he went home and dried his suit to be promptly drenched again. I doubt whether Laotians these days dare to throw water over the communists.

Here, during the bicentennial celebrations, I understood the good fortune of Thailand at having escaped the hideous consequences of that other event in the late eighteenth century, the French Revolution, with its ideologues and disciples: Rousseau, Tom Paine, Robespierre, Napoleon, Hegel, Marx, Freud, Lenin, the Webbs, George Bernard Shaw, Trotsky, Stalin, Marie Stopes, Hitler, Goebbels, Marcuse, Mussolini, Castro and all the anonymous tribe of sociologists, feminists, abortionists, sex educationalists and believers in 'situation ethics'. They rejected God and tried to create a new mankind, without sin. The results of their teaching are to be seen in the hell of Cambodia.

CHAPTER SIX

The Domino Theory

The reign of King Bhumibol, which started with the calamity of his brother's death, has been on the whole a time of peace and prosperity, with Thailand holding on to its faith in religion, the monarchy and the family. The only aspect of Thailand which has changed out of all recognition during King Bhumibol's reign is Bangkok, the capital. Forty or even thirty years ago, Bangkok was a city of largely wooden houses beside the river or one of the *klongs*, the canals that earned it the title of 'Venice of the East'.

Even in 1963, when I first came to Bangkok, I caught the feel of the city which had enchanted earlier visitors. The heat, the ripe smells and the water everywhere gave a sense of fecundity, of nature flowering, spawning, exuberant. At the small hotel where I stayed, in a tranquil side-street called Patpong Road, enchanting girls in sarongs of iridescent silk, served me with curries and fiery soups of a kind I had never tasted. It was only a short stay, and even the joys of Bangkok were later eclipsed by the ecstasy of a journey to Cambodia; but I had seen Bangkok first. It was here that I fell in love with Indo-China.

Nostalgia cannot disguise the fact that, even in 1963, Bangkok was a bustling city of $1\frac{1}{2}$ million people, too many cars and little respect for antiquity. Nevertheless, there were still klongs, tree-lined roads and plenty of gardens. You could turn off even a major thoroughfare, like Silom Road, and find what were virtually country lanes, with pigs and chickens. I remember an evening with friends in an old teak house on the bank of the river, where it was possible to forget the noise and traffic.

On this first visit to Bangkok, I carried an introduction to Jim Thompson, an American who had re-established the Thai silk industry, and helped to make Thailand fashionable with discerning travellers. He was an early conservationist who had built for himself a fine teak house, instead of the air-conditioned boxes that were coming into fashion. I did not see him for the perhaps rather priggish reason that he was too much part of the tourist round. Afterwards I regretted this, for Thompson was a remarkable and mysterious man who disappeared from the face of the earth in 1967, a story that I shall later recount. The old Thailand he loved and tried to preserve has also vanished, at least in Bangkok.

The city's population over the last three decades, has been quadrupled to something like six million. It is forty times the size of the second city of Thailand, Chiang Mai. What began in 1782 as the new royal capital in a bend of the Chao Phraya River, has moved progressively eastward into the paddy fields and marshes. Roads like New Petchburi and Sukhumvit, which scarcely existed when I was first in Bangkok, now stretch for mile after mile of housing estate and traffic jam. Skyscrapers rise up and after a few years fall again to be replaced by others still more gigantic, of eighty or more storeys. The Erawan Hotel, which was the latest and most de luxe in 1963, has been torn down and replaced. The Ambassador, which justly calls itself a city within a city, is pulling down two of its towers to make room for a few more hundred rooms and dozens of restaurants. The dust from the building sites mingles with the petrol fumes in the poisonous smog that hangs over this sweltering city. The roar of the bulldozers and jack-drills adds to the cacophony of traffic and pop music.

The developers have paved or blocked almost all the old klongs which once provided Bangkok with its transport system and drainage. The huge weight of concrete is pushing the city down to meet the level of the sea, which itself is rising because of the 'greenhouse effect'. When the Chao Phraya River is full and the tides are high, Bangkok is flooded, the traffic is halted and many drown. The high-rise buildings, based upon deep foundations, stand as islands among the surrounding waters.

In a country where 'green' issues, above all deforestation, predominate in political life, Bangkok itself is a major worry. Imported oil is the life-blood of this megalopolis, superimposed on a farming country. The city fathers long since banned the samlors or bicycle-taxis, which get people around most provincial cities. The motor car and the frightful scooter command the streets.

Bangkok is also extravagant with its fuel. In the winter of 1973–4, when as a result of the Yom Kippur War the world was facing its first major fuel crisis, several countries in Europe banned the sale of petrol at weekends, the Dutch took to their bicycles, and a British Cabinet minister lectured us on how to shave in the dark. That winter, a few other Englishmen and I staying in Indo-China were offered the job of manager of an English bar-restaurant in Bangkok, a tempting post that included a flat, free meals and drink and the help of a half-dozen Thai waitresses. But how could one work in a place that boasted of being the only bar in Bangkok with both air conditioning and a log fire? Bangkok people have pulled down their cool wooden houses to live in concrete boxes dependent on air conditioning. They are also profligate in lifts, and neon advertisements. Most shops and offices have darkened windows so that as well as air conditioning, they need artificial light by day.

The physical change in Bangkok since I was first here, in 1963, is not as striking as what might be called the moral debasement. The city is notorious as the brothel of all the world. Two-thirds of the tourists who come in their millions each year are men on their own, of whom at least half are thought to have a sexual encounter. The prostitution is seen at its most blatant in Patpong Road, the tranquil side-street in which I stayed on my first visit. During the 1960s, when tens of thousands of US servicemen came here from Vietnam for 'R & R', meaning Rest and Recreation, Patpong Road become a centre for bars, massage parlours and 'live shows', in which girls perform tricks with their private parts. The red light district spilled into the next street, Patpong Two, followed by Patpong Three for homosexuals, and even a Patpong Four that caters for Japanese men, who seem to have their own esoteric sexual habits. Patpong is noisy, garish and rather ugly. Even when there is a girl popping ping-pong balls, there are two or three doing a go-go dance to the blare of thudding rock. The thump and grind which might be exciting in long limbed, full-breasted Anglo-Saxon or African girls, looks ridiculous in the graceful and delicate Thais. The crudity and the nakedness do not become them.

Foreign feminists and socialists blame the prostitution in Bangkok on economic pressures and a 'male-dominated' social system. For reasons that I shall mention later, I do not believe that poverty, at any rate, can begin to explain why prostitution flourishes here in Thailand, rather than in very poor countries like India. Like most people, I find some of the prostitution shameful and depressing. There is a massage parlour just off New Road, where prospective customers stare at the numbered girls through a one-way mirror, like diners choosing their lobster or trout from a tank. There are plenty of men, as well as women, who speak disdainfully of commercial sex. But I sometimes think that those who frankly purchase gratification are really more honest than those who get it by playing on the emotions of women who may be looking for love and marriage as well as sex.

The Patpong 'live shows' are coarse and demeaning but they are hardly new. Pope Alexander VI, the father of Cesare and Lucrezia Borgia, presided over a party in the Vatican at which prizes were given out to the men who copulated with most girls. The Papal Master of Ceremonies, John Burchard, reported that afterwards chestnuts were scattered on the floor, 'which the courtesans, crawling on hands and knees among the candelabra, picked up, while the Pope, Cesare and his sister looked on.' Today the masses enjoy the vices once enjoyed only by the few. There is nothing new about Patpong Road except its democracy.

Thai men have always been eager to pay for a courtesan, or a 'travelling wife', to use one of the many euphemisms. One day I fell into talk with a man who had recently come back from years in the United States, and was now once more enjoying Thai women. In the United States, he complained, 'When I went for a massage there, this big, muscular woman showed me a certificate of her degree in physiotherapy. The only massage was hitting me on the body, *crack, crack*. When I asked for sex afterwards, she said it would cost me $100 because I was coloured.' Understandably, he was glad to be home.

Some tourists, as well as the foreign residents, say that the spirit of Patpong now envelops the whole city. It is rare to find a bar outside one of the better hotels, where a man can enjoy a drink or a conversation without a girl approaching and putting a hand on his thigh. Foreign women alone, or with their husbands, are made uneasy or even unwelcome in many places, hence the old joke that tourists who come with their wives are made to pay corkage at Bangkok Airport. One English-language newspaper went as far as to say that Bangkok is one of the dullest cities in Asia, with little to do for family tourists except sit in their hotel rooms watching videos. Single men who are living in Bangkok complain that because of the prostitution, educated and well-bred Thai girls will not be seen with them in public. The fame of Patpong Road has indeed made Bangkok a much less interesting place for those who are not sexual tourists.

Thais from the rest of the country say they detest Bangkok, although many still come here in search of money or fame. The farang at their cocktail parties and dinners constantly harp on the manifold miseries of Bangkok life. There are very few centres of social life where you might meet people you know without an appointment. There are few clubs, such as the British left in Singapore and Hong Kong, and none of the French cafés, which still make Saigon the pleasantest city in Southeast Asia.

Because of the traffic problems, most Bangkok people endeavour to live and work and enjoy their social life in one specific district of Bangkok. To the west, in the bend of the river, is Royal Bangkok, with most of the government offices, army headquarters and the most senior university. This is also a gathering place for the backpacking 'travellers', as they call themselves, who are moving around the east on as little money as possible. They find here lodgings at two or three dollars a night, and plentiful 'bucket shop' travel agents. The tourists go there by day to see the palaces and temples but there is not much to do in the evening.

Moving east from Royal Bangkok, you pass through old Chinatown to the southern district dominated by two long parallel streets, Suriwongse and Silom Road. This region has most of the tourist hotels, including the Oriental, looking over the river, also Patpong Road and hundreds of shops for the women tourists. A still better region for shopping is Siam Plaza and Phloenchit Road to the north. To the east of this is the area roughly defined by Sukhumvit Road, which I now regard as the least awful place to stay. If you are asked out to dinner in Bangkok, the odds are that your hosts live in one of the *sois* or lanes off Sukhumvit Road. Although the thoroughfare is as noisy and garish as any, the sois are often surprisingly green, quiet and pleasant, with fine apartment blocks and houses with gardens, sometimes bordering on to a klong. Most of the shops, bars and restaurants in Sukhumvit Road cater for residents rather than tourists, and therefore are much more relaxed.

Perhaps on my first visit, at any rate during the 1960s, I heard people say that Bangkok was 'not really Thailand', and thought they referred to the frenzy of big city life. It seemed absurd to suggest that the seat of monarchy and government, of Parliament, law, the Press and cultural life was somehow unrepresentative of the nation. It was not till later that I understood how, in one very important respect, Bangkok is indeed not Thailand: the ethnic

Thais are here in a minority. The Thais are only one, though the largest ethnic group in a country that used to be called by the geographical term, Siam. Within Siam there were other ethnic groups of whom the most prominent were the Laotians, from the north-east, and people descended from Chinese immigrants.

There had been Chinese merchants in Bangkok even before the King of the Chakri dynasty made it the capital in 1782. Over the next two centuries, the Chinese became not only the businessmen of Bangkok but powerful in the professions, politics and government. If the Chinese are the Bangkok middle class, the humbler citizens are for the most part Laotians, fleeing the poverty of the arid north-east.

Since both the Chinese and Laotians talk of themselves as Thais, at least to a foreigner, the ethnic divisions are not at first apparent. But you soon learn to spot them, not least in the tourist trade. The restaurant managers, hotel reception clerks and the cashiers in the girlie bars, are almost without exception ethnic Chinese, just as the dishwashers, room maids and go-go dancers are likely to be from north-east Thailand. In later chapters I shall attempt to explain how these two ethnic groups, who are not strictly Thais, have come to predominate in the capital of Thailand.

Besides the Laotians and the Thai Chinese, there are hundreds of thousands of foreigners in Bangkok, a most cosmopolitan city. Japan is by now the main economic power, whose products have swamped the market with cars, computers and electronic gadgets as well as clothing. Yet the Japanese themselves are inconspicuous. They tend to keep to their own hotels, their own street in Patpong and even their own favourite golf courses. A few years ago, when the Bangkok students mounted a boycott of Japanese goods, they found it hard to discover a target for protest meetings, and therefore had to content themselves with singing the popular number, 'Made in Thailand'. Although the Japanese occupied Thailand during the Second World War, they treated the people as allies rather than subjects and did not incur the same hatred as elsewhere in Asia. The Thais regard them now with awe and some bewilderment; the Europeans are not the only ones who find Japanese inscrutable. A Thai once remarked to me that whereas the Japanese used to be short in height, the same as themselves, 'now they are tall, almost as tall as Americans, perhaps because of the beef steaks they eat.'

There is a large Indian community in the New Road area, close to the Oriental Hotel. Most started off in the textile business, especially in sewing materials, and now provide instant suits for tourists. There are Muslims and Sikhs, often employed as guards, but most are Hindus. They used to keep cows on the outside of town and sold the milk to dairies or in the street. Although the Thais, like the Chinese, seldom use milk in their cooking or tea, they make and consume large quantities of delicious ice cream. The Hindus in Thailand have one other peculiar function. Although the Thais are Buddhists, they cling to certain Hindu beliefs, particularly with regard to the household spirits. Hindu priests are normally asked to bless the shrines that are found in most Thai homes and businesses, even massage parlours. Some of these shrines, like the one outside the Erawan Hotel, have a sanctity and reputation greater than many temples.

The Indians are accepted but not the Arabs. A multitude of Thais go every year to work in the Gulf oil states, especially Saudi Arabia, where there were 200,000 last year. In turn, the Arabs come to Bangkok to enjoy the alcohol and the prostitutes that they cannot obtain in their own puritanical lands. The Arabs, especially, congregate in the lower end of Sukhumvit Road but in other parts of Bangkok they are made unwelcome. You see signs in Thai, English and Arabic, saying 'No Arabs'. The signs explain that the management does not want to offend the Islamic customs relating to women and alcohol. In private, the Thais call Arabs quarrelsome and complaining, especially when they have taken drink. The women accuse them of unpleasant sexual habits. A Saudi tourist recently died in a bomb explosion outside a sex hotel, which, incidentally, advertises in some of the British newspapers. In 1989 and early in 1990, four Saudi Arabian diplomats were murdered in Bangkok. The Thai police at first suggested that this was part of a feud with Islamic extremists. Public opinion believed that the murdered diplomats had refused to connive at a racket in selling work permits. After the latest murders, a Thai lady manager of a work placement agency told the Press that hundreds of Thais 'would be disappointed if they could not go to Saudi Arabia, after spending large sums of money.' She went on to say that 'most Thai workers want to work in Saudi Arabia because they love the country, although they may have the choice to go elsewhere.' Bunkum.

There are tens of thousands of Westerners in Bangkok, some of them resident, but most passing through, or on holiday. In proportion to population, Australians and New Zealanders are the most in evidence, since many of them on the way to or from Europe break the journey here. The Thai word 'farang' is said to derive either from 'Frank' or 'Français', perhaps from the time of the French mission sent by Louis XIV. During the late nineteenth century, the French in Laos and Cambodia demanded and seized some of the border regions of what was then Siam. After the fall of France in 1940, Thailand took the territory back and still has designs on it. Many Thais who were students in Paris during the 1920s took up ideas that were not only socialist but republican, inspiring the *coup d'état* of 1932 which changed Siam from an absolute to a constitutional monarchy. For both these reasons, the patriotic, royalist Thais regard France with coolness and suspicion.

Although Britain too, in the nineteenth century, had toyed with the hope of adding Siam to her Asian Empire, the mutual respect of the monarchies kept the peace. By the twentieth century, the Thai Royal Family and the upper classes sent their sons to English boarding schools and Oxford or Cambridge. British influence at the Thai universities means that the language is taught with an English rather than an American accent; the foreign bookshops get their stock from London rather than New York; the English-language newspapers write with a British flavour. There is a British Club and a host of British pubs, some of which are like their original. The recent British craze for snooker has spread to Bangkok, whose star player, Wattana, studied the game in England and still lives in Bradford.

To judge by impressions and by the newspapers on sale, by far the largest farang community are the Germans, whose restaurants with wurst and beer offer a change from too much spicy food. The fun-loving and cheerful Danes have long had a special affinity with this country, which did not prevent them cutting down most of the teak in the north-east. They run a charming hotel, the Mermaid, in Soi 8. The Swedes are here in great numbers but they are neither fun-loving nor cheerful.

In writing about farang in Bangkok, I have made no mention so far of Americans who, strange to say, are no longer much in evidence. During the 1960s, it was accepted wisdom with writers on Southeast Asia that Thailand was an American client state, and Bangkok itself was a sultry Los Angeles, or Chicago. From the 1950s, Thailand had been the most fiercely pro-American, anti-communist country in Southeast Asia, ruled by a series of larcenous generals. United States politicans vied with each other in praise of Thailand. After one visit, accompanied by his wife, President Lyndon Johnson said, in tribute to Bangkok's famous, erotic atmosphere: 'Last night I gave Lady Bird the biggest bang of her life'. The former Vice-President, soon to be President, Richard Nixon not only loved Thailand but worked here as legal advisor to Pepsi Cola in Southeast Asia. In spite of him, this branch of the Pepsi empire came under attack in Alfred W. McCoy's *The Politics of Heroin in Southeast Asia*, which said that the Pepsi plant in Laos was used as 'a cover for purchase of chemicals vital to the processing of heroin'.

During the Vietnam War, Thailand provided the US with air force bases and even despatched two divisions to fight. Thailand was also a centre for rest and recreation. Some of the GIs went to Hong Kong, Taiwan, or even as far as Sydney, where there were many girls eager to keep them company, and for free. But the great majority came to Bangkok, so that for eight years, the city was constantly host to thousands of randy young men, with plenty of money to spend, and all with the thought that they might not live to spend it. The War created Patpong Road and the beach resort at Pattaya, two-and-a-half hours' drive away.

The troops on R & R contributed to the general idea that Bangkok was Americanized. As well as the concrete, high-rise buildings and ever-increasing traffic, the Thais had taken to supermarkets, bowling alleys, Coca and Pepsi Cola and hamburgers. One of the Bangkok universities even boasted a faculty of public relations. The foreigners in Thailand, if not always the Thais themselves, took avidly to the latest Californian cults of radical politics, drug abuse, hippy living, heterosexual and homosexual promiscuity. With hindsight I think that American influence did not go deep in the Thais themselves; but people like me, who loathe the Californian life style, turned against Thailand. It seemed to have lost its identity, more than South Vietnam, where more than half-a-million GIs were stationed. This seemed especially true of the women.

In South Vietnam, there were, of course, bar girls and prostitutes, most of them countrywomen and refugees from the fighting, but none of them did their work in the smiling and almost light-hearted fashion of Thai girls. By Vietnamese law, the bar girls had to be modestly dressed and could not perform the go-go dancing, let alone 'live shows', which were a feature of Patpong. What one might call respectable girls, who lived with their family, would not go out with Americans. There were very few Vietnamese GI brides, proportionate to the number of Thai women who married American airmen.

Apart from the bar girls, few Vietnamese women, even those who spoke English, adapted to American ways. They preferred Vietnamese music, or old-fashioned tangos, to new American rock. I once saw the film of the Woodstock Festival in a Saigon cinema, where the audience hooted their scorn. When *Playboy* magazine wanted a special issue on Asian girls, showing them naked, the Vietnamese representative appeared in an *ao dai* and pantaloons, clothed from the neck to the ankles. And even this lady, the actress Kieu Chinh, told me that she was furious at appearing on the same page with naked women. Saigon remained an Asian city, with French rather than US overtones. From this I concluded, wrongly I think, that Bangkok and its women were Americanized.

With hindsight, I think that Thailand had merely adapted to the United States or, to use a favourite Siamese metaphor, bowed like a reed before the wind. However, this involvement with the United States in the long Cold War, is central to Thailand's history over the last four decades, and helps to explain the position today. It also introduces the everlasting problem of Thailand's relationship with the neighbouring warring countries of Laos, Cambodia and Vietnam.

Just as Thailand, alone among countries in Southeast Asia, avoided colonization during the nineteenth century, so Thailand was also alone in avoiding disaster during the Second World War. Although technically on the losing side, as an ally of Japan, Thailand quickly became one of the firmest friends of the winners, the United States. Moreover, the very Thai politicians who had been most pro-Japanese, became the most pro-American.

The two dominant factions in Thai political life were led on the left by Pridi Panomyong, the intellectual lawyer of largely Chinese ancestry, and on the right by Pibun Songgram, the bluff but cunning military man and assertive Thai nationalist. At the time of the outbreak of war in Europe, Pibun was Thailand's Prime Minister, Pridi the Minister of Finance, while the young King Ananda was living in semi-exile in Switzerland. Whereas Pridi supported the Western democracies (or the Soviet Union, as enemies later claimed), Pibun admired the Axis powers and had tried to make the Thais follow the Japanese in adopting Western clothes such as frock coats, top hats and gloves. When

Paris fell in 1940 and Japanese troops entered French Indo-China, Pibun annexed the western provinces of Cambodia.

When the Japanese attacked the United States and the British Empire, in December 1941, they entered Thailand in order to get at Malaya. Whether or not Pibun acquiesced at this breach of neutrality, he did not have either the power or the will to resist aggression, and Thailand became a reluctant Japanese ally, declaring war on Britain and the United States, although fortunately as it later turned out, the Thai Ambassador in Washington, Seni Pramoj, refused on principle to deliver the message. Another Thai who took the side of the Allies was Pridi, who stayed in Bangkok throughout the war as regent for the absent King. The fact that Pridi remained free, and even worked for the OSS is proof that Pibun was not a Japanese puppet. Nor, to his credit, did Pibun allow the Japanese to persecute their political enemies, such as the interned British and Americans. The Japanese Army's treatment of Allied prisoners-of-war on the Burma Railway was not under Thailand's jurisdiction.

After the fall of Japan in August 1945, British and Indian troops moved into Bangkok, where the American Office of Strategic Services (OSS) had set up an interim government. Seni Pramoj became Prime Minister and a signatory to the peace treaty. He quarrelled with the Allied Supreme Commander in Southeast Asia, Lord Louis Mountbatten, who had demanded, not unreasonably, that Thailand should provide the rice to feed destitute refugees in the region. An American writer, David van Praagh, suggests in a recent book (*Alone on the Sharp Edge: The Story of M.R. Seni Pramoj*) that Mountbatten hoped to make Thailand part of the British Empire, a theory that will astonish all those British Tories who blame Mountbatten for the loss of India.

The young King Ananda returned from abroad; Pridi became Prime Minister; Field Marshal Pibun was let out of prison. The Pridi government repealed the anti-communist law in order to win the support of the Soviet Union for Thailand's admission to the United Nations. It backed the rebel nationalists in Vietnam, Laos and Cambodia who sought to prevent the return of the former French colonialists. Here Pridi had the support of the OSS which still favoured the Vietnamese Communist Ho Chi Minh.

The course of Thailand's history changed when, on 9 June 1946, King Ananda was found in the Royal Palace, dead from a gun-shot wound. As we have seen in the last chapter, this led to the downfall of Pridi and the return of Pibun. Field Marshal Pibun who had ruled Thailand before and during the Second World War, was to stay in power until 1957, when he was forced out by a younger, right-wing general, and went off to live in exile, like his old friend and rival Pridi. Pibun was the only political leader on the Axis side in the Second World War who went on to become an ally of the United States. The reason for this was the Cold War and the threat of communist revolution in Southeast Asia. China itself went communist in 1949. A year later, North Korea invaded the South. In Indonesia, Nationalist and Communist guerrillas succeeded in driving out the Dutch. In the Philippines, a band of guerrillas called Huks, challenged the newly independent government. In Malaya, in 1948, the Communist party mounted attacks on rubber plantations and tin mines in what would later be called the Emergency. The French were embroiled in an ever more savage war against the Vietnamese communists, whom the Americans came to see as the gravest political danger in the area.

Throughout the 1950s, Thailand represented Western hopes in this part of the world. In 1952, Pibun reintroduced the anti-communist law and stepped up the harassment of real or suspect left-wing subversives and followers of the former Prime Minister, Pridi, now living in exile in Peking. The Police Chief General Pao directed a counter-insurgency war against the communist groups in the north, the north-east and the far south of the country. Through the Manila Pact of 1954, Thailand became the headquarters of a regional anti-communist league, the Southeast Asia Treaty Organization, or SEATO, whose other members were Britain, France, the Philippines and Pakistan, which then included its eastern part, now Bangladesh.

In that same year, 1954, President Dwight D. Eisenhower coined or popularized a famous metaphor on what might follow a communist victory in South Vietnam: 'You have a row of dominoes set up, you knock over the first one, and what will happen to the last one is the certainty that it will go over very quickly.' Two years later, in 1956, Senator John F. Kennedy told the 'Friends of Vietnam' that 'Burma, Thailand, India, Japan, the Philippines and obviously Laos and Cambodia are among those whose security would be threatened if the red tide of communism flowed into Vietnam.'

Even during the worst of the Cold War, when Stalin was still alive and millions were dying in the Gulag Archipelago, the Americans were aware that being an anti-communist was not the only qualification for being a friend of Western Democracy. Republicans like Eisenhower were as much embarrassed as Democrats by the dictatorial methods of Synghman Rhee in South Korea, Franco in Spain, Batista in Cuba and the Somozas in Nicaragua. With Stalin's death and a more open leadership in the Soviet Union, the West was still more anxious to foster liberal, progressive governments. There was much anxiety about South Vietnam where Ngo Dinh Diem, his brother Nhu and his termagant sister-in-law Madame Nhu, were exercising a brutal and vicious tyranny. In Thailand, Marshal Pibun had been replaced by the corrupt dictator, Sarit Thanarat, who collected business holdings and mistresses.

An earlier President of the United States, Woodrow Wilson, had once announced: 'I propose to teach the South American Republics to elect good men'. Forty years later, during the 1950s, the Americans tried to do the same in Southeast Asia. In his novel *The Quiet American*, Graham Greene made savage fun of the earnest and simple United States agent who came to Vietnam hoping to start a 'third force', opposed both to the communists and the French. A few years later, in 1958, two American authors, William J. Lederer and Eugene Burdick brought out a bestselling novel, *The Ugly American*, which also concerned the troubles of Southeast Asia. 'Written as fiction, based on fact,' *The Ugly American* drew on the experiences of Edward Lansdale, a US diplomat and intelligence agent, who had helped to save the Philippines for democracy. The fiction state of 'Sarkhan, a small country out towards Burma and Thailand', was probably meant to be South Vietnam, where Lansdale had helped to install President Diem.

President Kennedy, who came into office in 1960, believed in the message of books like *The Ugly American*. He established the Peace Corps and the Alliance for Progress in Latin America, both of which were designed to frustrate communism by doing away with the poverty and corruption which are its causes.

Although Kennedy's programme of peaceful change was valid for Latin America, the situation in Indo-China had reached a state of war. In Laos, three shadowy armies, of left, right and centre were stalking each other up in the mountains. In South Vietnam, especially the Mekong Delta region, communist troops were mounting constant assaults on pro-Government villages and on the troops despatched to defend them. The United States sent out liaison officers and observers who were becoming in effect combat commanders. During the first half of the 1960s American Air Force personnel in Thailand rose to over 50,000 as more and more planes were sent out on reconnaissance or on bombing attacks on North Vietnam. This escalation of military power was insufficient to save the regime of Diem, who had alienated not just communists but students and the Buddhist monks, some of whom burned themselves as a protest. In November 1963, Diem and his brother were overthrown and then killed in a *coup d'état* almost certainly planned in the US Embassy in Saigon. Three weeks later, President Kennedy was himself murdered in Dallas.

The bombing of North Vietnam and the fighting in South Vietnam increased till, in March 1965, some thousands of US Marines disembarked at Da Nang on the central coast. The war in Vietnam resulted in great economic and social advance in Thailand, especially Bangkok. Here are a few statistics: In 1960, 74 per cent of Thai households lived off agriculture. By 1970, this had fallen to 63 per cent. In 1960, seven million Thais had finished primary school, 275,000 had finished secondary school, and 95,000 had finished university. By 1970, all these figures were doubled. In 1957 there had been three tourist hotels in Bangkok. Ten years later, they had become almost innumerable. Thailand's progress to being a NIC, or New Industrial Country, an acronym that you hear very often these days, had started during the boom produced by the war in Korea. A decade later, a still more horrible war in Vietnam produced even bigger advantages. The new prosperity of Thailand as well as the rise in education and living standards meant that, even if South Vietnam fell to the communists, there was now little likelihood of the 'domino theory' taking effect. Paradoxically, the American aim of preventing communism by raising the living standards and hopes of ordinary Asian people had been achieved not, as President Kennedy had intended, by peaceful progress, but out of the profits of war.

There were so many American servicemen in Thailand, either as Air Force personnel or holidaymakers on R & R, that I sometimes felt the country was part of the US war effort. This impression was strongest during a week I spent in December 1968 at the Erawan Hotel, which Bob Hope and his troupe used as a base for their Vietnam concerts. Hope, the hotel and, by inference, the country all seemed to be equally involved.

President Johnson had not sought re-election and Hope's friend Nixon was waiting to take up office. He and Kissinger were preparing the disentanglement from Indo-China. The Thais were beginning to wonder whether in fact they should look around for another ally. The anxiety of the Thais increased when in 1970, Prince Sihanouk of Cambodia was overthrown by a *coup d'état* and South Vietnamese and American troops invaded Cambodia bringing this next door country into the war. In July 1970, Thailand's military leaders thought of invading Cambodia, not just to secure their frontier but to regain the territory which they still regarded as theirs. But to embark on this venture, they had to have the support of the Nixon government which was itself under heavy attack for its Cambodia policy, especially after the riot and shootings at Kent State University. The army commander, Praphas Charusathien, so far accepted the democratic conventions of this time that he took part in a student debate about Cambodia, arguing with Kukrit Pramoj. It was not rational argument that decided against invasion but loss of faith in US commitment to Indo-China. In November 1971, Praphas and other military leaders mounted a *coup d'état* and got rid of the constitution, Parliament, the Cabinet and other political parties. They claimed that China's entry to the United Nations would lead to a rise in communist insurgency. They put into question the loyalty of the Thai Chinese. But as so often in Thailand, things were not as they seemed. In the course of the 1970s, Thailand was moving away from alliance with the United States to alliance with China. At the same time, it was moving away from old style military rule to the present compromise, in which the army is answerable to Parliament, Press and public opinion.

In 1972, the United States withdrew most of its troops from South Vietnam and mounted a last, massive air attack on the North, to force them into a peace agreement. By 1973, South Vietnam was not only on its own but bound by the terms of the Paris Treaty to let the North keep part of its army actually in the South. The Cambodian Communist Party, the Khmer Rouge, now held most of that country outside Phnom Penh. Laos was rather more peacefully turning communist. Thailand was in an already nervous state when, in October 1973, the people of Bangkok rose in a vast demonstration in favour of more democracy. It was not, as the army afterwards claimed in order to justify their shooting and brutal repression, a left-wing revolution; rather a sign of impatience with dim and corrupt authoritarian rule.

Although afterwards some of the student radicals fled Bangkok to join the guerrillas out in the forest, the demonstrations had made their point. The army leaders knew that they could not again impose dictatorship. The King supported the popular wish for freedom. After a caretaker government, Seni Pramoj returned to the post of prime minister that he had first held almost thirty years earlier. Then in March 1975, after much party political wrangling, Seni's younger brother, Kukrit Pramoj, took up in earnest the role of an Asian prime minister that he had once played in a Hollywood movie, opposite to Marlon Brando. Kukrit's brief term in office saw a momentous change in Thailand's history.

Kukrit, whose name means 'bold supernatural power', was born in 1911, the fifth child of a royal prince of Persian as well as Thai and Chinese ancestry. After an education at Trent College and Queen's, Oxford, Kukrit returned to Bangkok and a job in the Finance Ministry. He served in the army, seeing action during the border war with France in 1941, then went into banking. After the Second World War, when his brother Seni became Prime Minister, Kukrit also went into politics, founding his own party and later his own very successful newspaper, *Siam Rath*. He wrote for it not just political squibs and satire, but serializations of his delightful novels on Thai life and history, including *Four Reigns* which I discuss in this chapter. Kukrit is a renowned director of Thai dancing and theatre. He is most famous of all for his wit. He is the country's most famous character, or card, a joker who also talks very good sense. Once, when invited out to dinner in one of the small streets near Silom Road, my host said to me not to bother with street names, which taxi drivers ignore, but simply to ask for Soi Kukrit, 'Kukrit Lane'.

Kukrit's appointment as premier came as a major sensation, presaging all sorts of excitement. He did not disappoint these expectations. Kukrit took it upon himself to perform three tasks. First, he wanted to guarantee the freedoms won by the demonstrations of 1973. Second, he wanted to end the discontent and rural poverty by pumping some of the wealth of Bangkok into the agricultural community. Third, he wanted to reconsider Thailand's foreign policy, especially with regard to Cambodia, Laos and Vietnam, now that all these countries seemed to be turning communist. All three of these tasks were aimed at making sure that Thailand did not become the next domino to fall. Kukrit's domestic policies were to a large extent those pursued by his brother before and after his premiership. His foreign policy changes were both more radical and more sudden.

Like almost all Thais, Kukrit fears and distrusts the Vietnamese. In an interview given in 1976, he spelled out these feelings to his questioner:

> *Do you think Vietnam will go on aiding insurgencies?*
> It will go on. It will go on aiding insurgencies in this country and others in Southeast Asia. That's normal work – that's routine.
> *What did Thailand learn from the Vietnam experience?*
> We have learned that Uncle Sam is impotent.
> *In these circumstances, or in any conflict?*
> Impotent in the full sense of the word. I don't know – ask the doctor.
> *Impotent, or just tired?*
> I think impotent. [But] impotency can be cured if you stop smoking and drinking . . . you asked me what we learned about the fall of Vietnam. That's what we learned. That's what I learned anyway.

Since the Thais felt threatened by Vietnam, and no longer believed that the United States could defend them, they looked to a new ally, Communist China. Soon after taking office in March 1975, Kukrit told the United States that Thailand would not renew the lease for the air force bases. In June 1975, Kukrit went to Peking.

With Chou En-lai, Kukrit worked out the basis of Thailand's new partnership with China in an alliance against Vietnam and her backer, the Soviet Union. At this time it still was not clear, at least to the Western world, that a rift had occurred between the Vietnamese communists and their Cambodian counterpart, nick-named the Khmer Rouge. Three years later, in December 1978, Vietnam felt obliged to invade her communist neighbour, where-upon China invaded Vietnam. Kukrit's mission to China sealed the pact which still underlies the never-ending misery of Cambodia. While Vietnam tries to support a Cambodian government friendly to Hanoi, China and Thailand support a coalition against Vietnam embracing both Sihanouk and the Khmer Rouge.

In return for backing China, Thailand received the latest Chinese weapons, as well as a promise to stop backing insurgencies. In seeking advice on how to defeat Thai communists, Kukrit went to the world's most famous guerrilla fighter, Mao Tse-tung. In one of the strangest cases of poacher turned game-keeper, Mao offered these maxims on anti-communist war:

First of all, don't issue any propaganda against them to tell the people they are bad. They won't listen to you . . .

Secondly, don't kill them all because they like being heroes . . . They'll come to get killed; they like to be killed.

Thirdly, don't send any soldiers against them because you'll be wasting time and a lot of money. The communists are in the jungle. If you send soldiers against them they will just run away.

Finally, the only thing to get rid of your communists, the only way to defeat them, is to see that your people are happy. See that they are well fed, that they have work to do, that they are satisfied with their work and their station. Then the communists cannot do anything.

This last piece of advice from Chairman Mao on how to prevent communist revolution is oddly similar to the theories advanced in books like *The Ugly American* and the Kennedy speeches supporting the Peace Corps and the Alliance for Progress.

Kukrit's policies aroused a strong and sometimes bloody response from right-wing militants, backed by the army and the police. Thugs calling themselves the Red Gaurs, after the fierce water buffalo, broke up meetings of students, strikers and peasants. In August 1975, a mob of policemen wearing civilian clothes invaded the house of the Prime Minister, Kukrit Pramoj, looting or smashing his priceless collection of Thai antiques. They funded a successful campaign to defeat Kukrit in his constituency in the election he had called for April 1976. Once more Seni Pramoj came back to replace his younger brother as Prime Minister. In spite of a prickly, jealous relationship the two men have broadly similar views, and Seni maintained Kukrit's policy on agricultural loans, guaranteed farm prices and land reform.

The radical Bangkok students kept up their raucous clamour against the army and the Americans. Many old-fashioned Thais including, so it is thought, the King, were feeling uneasy about the turbulent mood of the country. In September 1976, one of the former military strongmen, Thanom Kittikachorn, came back from exile to enter a Buddhist monastery. In October, the favourite month for riots and *coups d'état*, all hell broke loose at Thammasat University, in south-east Bangkok. A few days earlier, two students who had protested against the return of Thanom were hanged by a right-wing lynch mob. On 4 October, a group of their colleagues staged a mock hanging in front of the Press photographers. One of the five volunteers bore a marked facial likeness to Crown Prince Maha Vajiralongkorn, the only son of the King and the least popular member of the Royal Family. Artificial make-up by drama students still further increased the resemblance. When pictures of the 'hanging' appeared next day in two Bangkok newspapers, not just the generals but most Thais were enraged by this insult to the monarchy. The Prime Minister, Seni Pramoj, signed an authority for the police to investigate and arrest any students involved in the mock hanging.

Two days later, on 6 October 1976, a vast mob of Red Gaurs and other right-wing militants broke in to Thammasat University where, they believed, the communist students were armed and backed by Vietnamese infiltrators. Behind them came heavily armed units of the Bangkok Police and the border guards. In the mayhem that followed, four students were hanged or beaten to death and forty were killed by gunfire. The generals who had exploited the mock hanging in order to punish the students and so bring down the civilian government, summoned Seni Pramoj to army headquarters. With characteristic Thai good manners they offered him the consolation job of adviser, which he refused, then invited him to partake of a Chinese supper and finally pressed him to stay the night, for his own comfort and safety. Afterwards Seni lamented: 'In Thailand, they can stick a knife in your belly and say, "Sorry, we've just got to do this." They're very decent about it.'

This was not the last military *coup d'état*. In the following year, 1977, as usual in October, a new group of military officers moved against the civilian goverment ushered in by the late *coup*. However, this time, the officers represented the left, or democratic faction in Thai political life. There was another abortive *coup d'état* on April Fool's Day, 1981, and another in 1985. On this last occasion, the five people killed included Neil Davis, an Australian reporter and cameraman for NBC, whom I had known since the war in Vietnam and Cambodia. He was a good companion and, rather unusually for a journalist, most generous with his knowledge of Indo-China. He was one of the few people in Bangkok who might have made sense of the *coup* in which he was killed.

These last two *coup* attempts were significant not just because they failed but because the King went out of his way to show disapproval. He was and remains a friend and supporter of General Prem Tinsulanonda, who had become Prime Minister in 1980 and stayed in the post until 1988 when he stepped down, much to the chagrin of many Thais. Unlike most of the Thai military politicians from Pibun down to the present incumbent, Chatichai Choon-havan, Prem is taciturn, modest and dignified. He carried on with the policies of Seni and Kukrit Pramoj with regard to rural develop-ment, winning over insurgents, constitutional freedom and the alliance with China. The 1980s were for this country a time of continued growth and prosperity. Throughout the prime minister-ship of Prem and his successor Chatichai, there has always been a kind of alternative, parallel government under the army com-mander of the time. Sometimes these military men have challenged or seemed to challenge the power of the elected prime minister, himself always a former army officer. The latest in line of these army commanders is Chavalit Yongchaiyudh who in March 1990 went on to become the defence minister. A man of forthright views on every subject from AIDS to Cambodia, Chavalit sometimes sounds left-wing. When Kukrit Pramoj implied that Chavalit was a communist, two hundred militiamen in civilian clothes turned up at Kukrit's house in a demonstration reminiscent of 1975. Humbler journalists think twice before writing critical comments on Chava-lit's views or business connections.

Nobody would pretend that democracy is secure in Thailand, when there are men around like Chavalit or, dare one say so, the Crown Prince. But Thailand seems at the moment a happy, confi-dent and, above all independent country. It is no longer under the shadow of the United States or any other country. The Thais get on well with Americans who, like them, tend to be extrovert and pleasure-loving; but they are not in awe of them or obsessed with them as are, for example, the Filipinos. Because China is now an ally, this does not mean that Thailand is left-wing. Western isms and ideologies do not easily take root in what is essentially a religious country. The beliefs and ideals of the Thais were once well summed up, with characteristic wit and wisdom, by Kukrit Pramoj:

> There are certain institutions which a Thai respects ... They are his religion, which is mostly Buddhist, his King and his parents. If you say to a Thai that his politicians are rotten he will kiss you on both cheeks. If you tell him that he is a crook, he will deny it with great good humour and will not take offence. If you call his wife a bitch he will agree with you completely and ask you to have a

drink on that. but as for those three institutions which I have already mentioned, I would advise you to leave well alone . . . since according to police statistics, the percentage of premeditated murders in this country is very low; most murders are committed in sudden passion.

CHAPTER SEVEN

Chinatown

After five hours on a bus from Aranyaprathet, I found that Bangkok was for once almost free of traffic jams, although this was neither a weekend nor public holiday. It proved to be Chinese New Year. During the three day holiday, Bangkok virtually comes to a standstill. Most of the banks and shops are shut. Hotels operate on a skeleton staff. It took me an hour to make a plane reservation because the airline had only one clerk, an Indian.

Some Chinese families go for three days to Chiang Mai or Phuket but the great majority stay at home. They observe the new moon, perform their religious observances and hope to be cleansed of the sins of the past year. They give one another presents of money or gold. They feast on pork or duck, with modest amounts of brandy or wine for the men. For many Bangkok Chinese, these three days of the year are almost their only respite from work.

Their industry is the most famous quality of the Chinese abroad, although I am told that at home they are learning the habits of sloth that go with socialism. The Chinese are industrious not only as individuals but as a family. In any small restaurant in this country, most of which are run by Chinese, you notice small children sweeping the floor, washing the dishes or running errands, while grandpa and grandma keep the till or stir the noodles.

Nobody knows quite how many Chinese there are in Thailand. For centuries the Chinese men have married Thai women so that most of them are of mixed blood. The Chinese must by law take Thai names, though apparently some of these names sound odd, like the names the Jews had to take in Bismarck's Germany. All Chinese learn Thai and many can no longer speak their ancestral language. Although some Chinese have adopted Thai religion and customs, for example on burial, this is unusual, largely because it is rare for Chinese women to marry Thai men. Religious customs go through the male line.

Those who have studied the Chinese in Thailand think that they numbered about 1½million by 1949, when immigration virtually came to an end because of the communist takeover in China. Since then, it is fair to assume that the Chinese population has risen only because of the birth rate, which is lower among the Chinese than among the Thais, especially the north-east people who swell the population of Bangkok. We can therefore assume that Chinese in Bangkok make up about a fifth of the population, although they probably own four fifths of the wealth. The Chinese also control much of the wealth of the countryside, as rice millers, tobacco buyers and entrepreneurs in mining, forestry and fisheries. These last three businesses have brought the Chinese into conflict with those who worry about the environment.

Although the Chinese have no political party, they have always fought for the interests of their community. Since the Constitution of 1932, the Chinese have sometimes been attacked by Thai politicians, mostly the right-wing military men, but also by socialists, envious of their wealth. Today the Chinese are the basis of what might be called the Bangkok interest, which naturally favours cheap food and petrol. The Chinese are numerous at the Bangkok universities, and probably played a big part in the riots of 1973. The Chinese were prominent in the Communist party and other left-wing movements but they have taken pains never to seem anti-Royalist.

The role of the Chinese in Thailand is now of particular interest to Britain which may have to take in refugees from Hong Kong. Thailand is one of the few countries where Chinese immigration has been, on balance, beneficial and harmonious. The life of the Bangkok Chinese has also been the subject of a delightful novel, *Letters from Thailand*, which now is a set book for social studies courses at universities here. It is also instructive to see how Thailand's handling of the Chinese has differed so markedly from that of some of the neighbouring countries, like Vietnam and Malaysia. It helps us to understand Thailand's place in Southeast Asia, and its present good relations with Communist China.

Since the start of their recorded history, the Chinese have always been active in Southeast Asia, as military rulers in Vietnam and everywhere as traders in silk and ceramics. In the Bayon, one of the temples at Angkor, built in the thirteenth century, there is a carved Chinese junk with what are recognizably Chinese sailors.

The Chinese came to trade at Sukhothai. We know from the testimony of two Chinese in the fifteenth century that they were much impressed by the independence of Siamese women, and still more by their predilection for Chinese men. At about this time there appeared the first *lukjin*, or children born to Chinese men by Siamese mothers. At Ayutthaya, during the eighteenth century, there were not only Chinese traders but artisans, pig-breeders and actors. King Taksin, who moved the court to Thonburi after the sack of Ayutthaya, was half Chinese and the first of the Chakris also had Chinese blood, though it is not known quite how much.

The Chakris not only welcomed but actually sought Chinese immigrants, all of whom came from the south-east seaboard. At first, the Chinese arrived in junks or long boats, but after 1865, they started to come on steamships. By the end of the nineteenth century and for well into the twentieth, there was a net immigration of something like 15,000 a year, most of whom stayed in the Bangkok district. The Chinese provided the coolies who built the foundations, houses and roads that transformed Bangkok from a city on water to what it is now, a city on land.

Some of the Chinese stayed as coolies but many made good as traders or government servants, notably tax collectors. The Chakris granted them free immigration, the right to travel around the country, and also immunity from the corvée or forced labour. The Chakris gave to the Chinese 'farms' or monopolies for the sale of opium and alcohol, and also for running the lottery and the gambling dens. Thais were in theory forbidden to join the Chinese in indulging these vices.

The Chinese coolies were often addicted to opium which helped them to keep going as dockers or navvies. By 1890, there were 1,200 licensed opium shops in Bangkok, and the 'farms' used every device to hook more addicts. The Thais had no tradition of opium-smoking and seldom took to the habit while those who did were obliged to wear the pigtail and pay the triennial tax levied on all Chinese. The Thais at that time had not acquired their later fondness for alcohol but they did take to the Chinese gambling games. People could gamble freely for three days each at Chinese and Thai New Year but at other times they had to use the dens of the gambling 'farm'. The 'farmers' were also involved in the Chinese secret societies, enforcing their privilege through the use of toughs. For the purposes of the lottery, Bangkok was divided up into thirty-two districts, each with its manager from one of the secret societies.

The opium, alcohol, gambling and lottery 'farms', all in theory catering only for Chinese customers, provided Siam with 40 to 50 per cent of its total revenue during the second half of the nineteenth century. The Chakri rulers understandably looked on the Chinese as a valuable middle class between the Thai aristocracy and the peasants, whose status was near to serfdom. Since there were virtually no women immigrants, the Chinese men took Siamese wives to the satisfaction of both. The Siamese women considered the Chinese more considerate than the Thai men, who then as now had a macho and male chauvinist reputation. They had always run businesses and therefore were useful partners in trade, especially in dealing with Thai-speaking customers.

The Chinese lived happily with the Thais until the end of the nineteenth century when things started to go wrong. The Chinese were coming under the influence of the revolutionary nationalists in China itself, whose leader, Sun Yat-sen, despatched a delegation to Bangkok in 1907. The Chinese started to take an interest in politics. At the same time, a new generation of Thais had come to share the European obsession with what at the time was called the 'Yellow Peril'. Already the Anglo-Saxon countries had started to ban Chinese immigrants.

The British advisers in Siam encouraged this prejudice. One Warington Smyth, attached to the Mines department, wrote in 1895:

> Beyond the very high qualities of which he is undoubtedly possessed – qualities shared perhaps equally by the buffalo – I have no great admiration for the Chinese coolie. The Chinese are the Jews of Siam ... they have on the whole enjoyed an immunity from official interference which they have neither merited nor appreciated ... The toleration accorded to them by the Government is put down to fear; they bow and scrape before the authorities, but laugh behind their backs; and they could sack half Bangkok in a day.

Smyth congratulated the Siamese commissioner at Phuket for having adopted anti-Chinese policies, and he advised the government to suppress Chinese secret societies, as the British had done in Malaya.

The British adviser on education, J. G. D. Campbell, also

compared the Chinese to the Jews and thought that the Siamese had 'sold their birthright for a mess of pottage'. The French shared this British hostility to the Chinese. An article in *Revue Indo-Chine*, entitled *'Bangkok, colonie Chinoise, ou le secret du colosse jaune'*, portrayed the Chinese immigrants as part of a Chinese Imperial plan.

A Thai lawyer, educated in England, started a journal to air his Sinophobia, but this was suppressed by King Rama V, who thought the whole matter best left alone. The King wrote in 1907:

> It has always been my policy that the Chinese in Siam should have the same opportunities for labour and for profit as are possessed by my own countrymen. I regard them not as foreigners but as one of the component parts of the kingdom and sharing in its prosperity and advancement.

The tolerant Rama V died in 1910, the year of the Chinese general strike, which brought Bangkok to a standstill and badly damaged relations between the Thais and Chinese.

In 1909 the government had abolished the special capitation tax for the Chinese and forced them to pay the slightly higher tax levied on all Siamese. When this new tax was levied a second year running, some of the Chinese were angry. The secret societies, the people who ran the 'farms', were now in the position of British trade union leaders when governments threaten some vested interest. To show their power and to save their face, the secret societies ordered the general strike in Bangkok which started on 1 June 1910. They sent out gangs of thugs, what we would now call 'pickets', to burn or loot the premises of the strike breakers. All Chinese stopped work except those employed by foreign firms and domestic servants.

As a strike it had proved triumphant. Almost all Bangkok was closed and soon basic foods became scarce and very expensive. The city was not completely paralysed only because the power station and trams were run by Thais, as were a few food shops. The Thai police and army at last ended the strike with little violence but it had proved most damaging to the Chinese community. The Thais had been made to suffer inconvenience and they were also dramatically shown the almost monopoly power of the Chinese in Bangkok. By striking against a reasonable tax, the Chinese had reinforced the belief that they stayed in Thailand only to make money, without giving anything back in return.

Among the Thais enraged by the Chinese strike was the new

King Rama VI, who had studied in England and numbered Europeans among his close friends. He had already absorbed some of the myth of the 'Yellow Peril', and what he had seen in June 1910 reinforced this prejudice. At the time of the coronation in 1911, the Chinese community tried to placate the King with generous gifts and protestations of loyalty. It was no use. In 1914 there came out in Thailand a pamphlet, almost certainly written by Rama VI himself, entitled *The Jews of the East*, which accused the Chinese of being unassimilable, disloyal and ready to use any wickedness in pursuit of money. The Thai government brought in a Nationality Act saying that anyone born in the country was Thai. Several hundred thousand Chinese now in effect had dual nationality and therefore dual loyalty. The King also warned: 'If there should be another incident like the Chinese strike, I should not care to be responsible for the outcome.'

Throughout this century, the fate of the Thai-Chinese has depended as much on events in China as in Thailand. At first there was the agitation, led by Sun Yat-sen, to replace the Empire by a republic, like France or the United States. When the Emperor was deposed, the Republicans soon divided into a National party, the Kuo Min Tang, under the leadership of Chiang Kai-shek, and the Communists, under Mao Tse-tung. Both had to fight a number of regional warlords and, after 1931, a Japanese invasion. The confusion and trouble in China during the 1930s are known to most of us from Hollywood movies about Shanghai in which opium smugglers clash with white Russian princesses, in which secret agents with indescribably evil faces are found stabbed with daggers of an intricate oriental design and in which Marlene Dietrich, asked if she has a husband, drawls: 'It took more than one man to change my name to Shanghai Lily.'

For the Chinese, even for those who lived abroad, the politics of their country were tragic and anguishing. Among the Chinese in Thailand, there were in this period both Royalists and Republicans, both Nationalists and Communists, but all were united by enmity to Japan. Their increasing concern with events in China tended to make the Chinese more foreign in Thailand, especially after the *coup d'état* of 1932 and the introduction to Thailand of foreign ideas like democracy and nationalism.

The two friendly rivals, Pibun and Pridi, who dominated political life for the next quarter century, were both inclined to distrust the Chinese. Pibun, the military man, had a marked dislike of foreigners, intellectuals and commercial men – although he was fond of their money. It was Pibun, during his two terms in office, who forced the Chinese to enter the Thai education system and to take Thai surnames. Even before the war, in which Pibun served as a Japanese puppet, he took the side of Japan in her attack against China. Although he crushed demonstrations in favour of China, it should be said in Pibun's favour that even during the Japanese occupation, he did not encourage or even permit any actual persecution of ethnic Chinese.

The Thai-Chinese might well have expected more favourable treatment from Pridi, a man of liberal, left-wing principles who disapproved of the chauvinism of Pibun. Moreover, Pridi was at least three-quarters Chinese. In spite of this, Pridi was quite as harsh as Pibun in his attitude to the Chinese in Thailand. He seems to have swallowed the old socialist fallacy that the amount of wealth in a country is static: if the rich grow richer, the poor grow poorer. In particular, Pridi believed that the Chinese rice merchants and traders cheated the rural population and therefore wanted to nationalize the land and make the peasants sell their rice to the state which would also be their employer.

Mercifully for Thailand, Pridi was never able to put into practice his crackpot schemes of land collectivization. They would have proved as disastrous here as they did in the Soviet Union, China and Communist Vietnam. Nobody would have suffered more than the peasants themselves who did not have any grievances about ownership of their land, being much more concerned with natural problems like drought. Nor is there any evidence that the Thai peasants resented the Chinese traders setting up shop in the villages. On the contrary, the presence of traders saved on the cost of travel to buy and sell goods. The Chinese were not monopoly traders, often competing among themselves or with Vietnamese. There are still Chinese loan sharks in Thai cities, especially Bangkok, but out in the countryside they do not have a reputation for driving their customers into debt. The village attitude to the Chinese trader is well expressed in the novel *A Child of the North-east*, to which I referred in an earlier chapter. The anti-Chinese theories of men like Pridi were founded on books he had read in Paris, not on popular sentiment.

The fact that Pridi himself was Chinese, no doubt fuelled his hostility to the merchants. The Chinese sinophobe resembles the anti-semitic Jew in tending towards the political left. Jews like Marx and Trotsky, and half-Jews like Lenin, did not direct their anti-semitic feelings only at Jewish capitalists. They rejected the Hebrew religion and language and everything setting the Jews apart. Marx at least was a rabid Jew-baiter. The Chinese Left in Thailand did not go to such morbid extremes, but sometimes became very critical of their own community. This was especially true of those who entered the Thai professions such as the law, the civil service and the police.

When the war came and with it the Japanese occupation, Pridi was now on the side of the Allies. As well as acting as regent during the young King's absence in Switzerland, Pridi built up the Free Thai movement under his OSS code-name of 'Ruth'. In the confused political aftermath of the war, the KMT of Nationalist China sent their armies to Indo-China and even threatened the sovereignty of Siam, as it had been briefly renamed. Some pro-KMT newspapers denounced Siam for having declared war on the Allies – of which China was one – and even called for a KMT army of occupation. In November 1945, thousands of Thai-Chinese came out in the streets of Bangkok to voice their support for the KMT but British and Indian troops dispersed the riot with rifle fire, killing more than a hundred.

From 1945 until 1949, there was famine in China, as well as a civil war between Nationalists and Communists. Both things helped to produce a new wave of emigration to Thailand. This lasted until the Communists took the mainland and Chiang Kai-shek fled with his army to Formosa, soon to be named Taiwan. The majority of the Thai Chinese at first supported Mao Tse-tung until, in the 1950s, news started to trickle out of the massacre of the landlords and the collectivization of land. In the increasing polarization between the communist and the Western worlds, Thailand was now very much with the latter. Field Marshal Pibun and his police chief, General Pao, went into action against the Communists in Bangkok and the growing insurgency groups in the countryside.

Pridi, the politician whom Pibun blamed for the death of King Ananda, had gone into exile in Peking, where he stayed after the city fell to the Communists. From Peking, he continued to make broadcasts in Thai attacking the Pibun dictatorship. This added credence to Pibun's claim that the opposition to his rule came from the Chinese community in the land. General Pao was certainly close to the truth when he said that of Thailand's 12,000 guerrillas, only 2,000 were Thais. In the 1960s, during the Maoist

Cultural Revolution, some of the young Thai-Chinese proclaimed their faith in the 'Little Red Book'. In 1973 and again in 1976, there were university riots in Bangkok, followed by shootings in which hundreds were killed. After both massacres, scores of students fled the city to join one of the partisan groups in the forest. Since Thai universities have a high proportion of Chinese students, many of them were among the insurgents.

The 1980s saw the decline of the Thai-Chinese left. In China itself, after the death of Mao, there came a revulsion against everything for which he had stood. The flood of refugees from Laos, Vietnam and above all Cambodia, brought more disillusionment with the Marxist dream. In Thailand itself, the benign and tolerant rule of Prem Tinsulanonda won most of the communists back to civilian life.

Communist rule in China had severed, for thirty years at least, any contact between the homeland and the diaspora. During the early 1950s and once again during the 'Cultural Revolution', the Peking government mounted a terror campaign against anyone tainted with bourgeois or foreign ideas. The Chinese living abroad were singled out for abuse. Like Stalin, his idol, Mao Tse-tung understood that in order to hold a people in slavery, he needed to keep them in ignorance of the outside world, particularly of their own kinsmen abroad. It is only during the last ten years that China opened her doors to the Chinese from Thailand, Hong Kong and Taiwan. The sight of these prosperous, happy Chinese from free, capitalistic countries helped to produce the discontent and ill-fated demands for change, that came to a head in June 1989.

The sealing off of the mainland also affected the Chinese diaspora abroad. Since 1865 and the introduction of steamboat services, many Chinese living in Thailand paid regular visits home to see their relations, to find a bride, or finally to retire and be buried alongside their ancestors. Since Bangkok was only a few days' journey by boat, the Chinese had closer links with home than did the Europeans in America. The Thai-Chinese did not suffer from what the Australian Geoffrey Blainey has called in his masterly book, *The Tyranny of Distance*. But for thirty years, from 1950, they were quite as cut off from their homeland as though they lived on another planet. It is one of the themes of *Letters from Thailand*.

The book begins with a cod 'foreword' by Police General Sala Sintutawat. Two months previously, General Sala's men had acquired a collection of letters sent over the previous twenty years by a Chinese immigrant in Thailand, Tan Suang U, to his mother at home. Already in 1945, the local postman had failed to deliver the first of these letters, either because he had stolen the money inside or because he could not find the address. Moreover, he found the letter interesting, with its tales of starting a new life in Bangkok. The postman went on waylaying these letters and when he achieved promotion, made sure that they kept on coming to him. By the time of his defection to Thailand in 1965, this postman had risen to be the official censor for Shanghai region, while U had become a prominent Bangkok businessman. Police General Sala says that on finding the letters stolen by the defector, he had offered to give them back to their author, whose only reaction was grief that his mother had not received them.

This fanciful explanation on how the letters came to appear in Thailand serves to remind the reader that Tan Suang U has been effectively dead to his mother, the one person he really honours and loves and sees as a symbol of home and country. His mother had taught him, along with the Chinese language, the stern Confucian rules of survival in an impoverished countryside. Happiness meant seeing the rice grow and raising at least one son to manhood. Hard work and frugality were the two chief virtues.

The translator of *Letters from Thailand* is that same excellent Susan Fulop Kepner who did *A Child of the North-east*. Once again she has given a wise and witty introduction to what is a wise and witty book. She calls *Letters from Thailand* the best and most entertaining picture of life in urban Thailand in mid twentieth century: 'Years from now, Thais will be able to re-read the novel and say, "yes, that is just how it was . . . that's what people said and what they did in those days . . ."' In 1975, the Thai Ministry of Education made *Letters from Thailand* a set book for the teaching of social studies in this country, and wisely so, for a good novel is worth a shelf of sociology. Coming from England, I envy and admire this candid and witty approach to racial relations. In Thailand they have no laws against discrimination; no paid officials concerned with the matter; no scolding harangues against 'racism', a bogus concept in any case. The Thais and the Thai-Chinese accept and are even proud of their differences; they do not want to live in a 'multi-racial society', another bogus concept; they try to resolve their disputes through tolerance, humour and common sense. Susan Kepner explains that the comedy lies in the failure of

Thailand to live up to the expectations of Tan Suang U, the letter-writer and hero:

> His children would marry his colleagues', everyone would continue to prosper and the whole Chinese community in China would remain happily separate from its host culture, enjoying the benefits of its own cultural traditions, while reaping the profits to be easily won in the relatively lush economy of Thailand – and won all the easier because the Thai population was split between farmers in the countryside and aristocrats and their servants in Bangkok. Trade was open to all comers, and the Chinese near Tee-Chiu province came in droves until the population of Bangkok was fully one-half Chinese, as it remains today.

That had been U's expectation in 1945.

U gets his first lessons on Thailand even before his arrival. On board ship he is befriended and then 'adopted' by the purser, a widower who has lost his own wife and son. His 'father', a Chinese who has spent most of his life in Thailand, gives U some basic advice: Never to let on that he has not been to school; the Thais have more respect for diplomas than skill and like to see a bit of paper to say you have been to school for so many years. With this he can get a job without being able to count past five. With the older Chinese, this does not matter so much, but the younger ones who grew up in Thailand have started to think like Thais. He also tells U never to let slip that his mother worked as a servant. Thailand is full of people who would rather steal than be servants.

When the ship reaches Bangkok, U is surprised to see Chinese dock labourers. His 'father' explains that many are working as coolies to pay off their passage:

> The wise ones have made their sacrifices before they came out – not after ... And yet a few of them actually become millionaires from no better beginnings than this – hauling seventy-five kilo loads from ship to truck and back again under a broiling sun, sixteen hours a day.

Through his *sae* or clan organization, 'Father' finds U a job and a home with a merchant who imports Chinese food and sends it out to the retailers all over Bangkok; he also buys Thai goods to send back on the ship to China – this was in 1945, before the communist revolution. When U arrives, the store is busy with salesmen of teak and rice. The merchant has two daughters, the

beautiful Mui Eng who means to get U as her husband, and Ang
Bui, who is witty, mischievous and less respectful of Chinese tradition, including their colour prejudice: 'I'm as dark as a cup of old
tea but I don't care. I know I don't even look like a Chinese –
everyone says so . . . You should see the Thai farmers who come
in here sometimes. They're almost black from working in the
fields; I stay indoors all day, and look at me.' There are many dark
Chinese, U tries to assure her: 'Not lots . . . a few, and no dark
Chinese girl is thought to be pretty.'

The burden of all these letters is grumbling about the Thais,
above all their laziness. A drunken Thai abuses him with the usual
complaint against the *jek*, the Thai slang for Chinaman: 'Hey jek!
You like getting rich in Thailand. It ain't enough to charge double
what the food is worth . . . This guy gets interest on a lousy ten
baht besides . . . Hey jek! Why don't you go back to where you
came from?' But a Thai woman is pleased as punch when her
daughter marries a Chinaman; 'Good for you, daughter! Marry a
jek and you'll eat pork every day; you won't eat dried fish and
chase ducks round a pond all your life, like your poor mother.'

The book's comedy lies in seeing how U's Chinese friends and
relations, his wife and his sister-in-law, his children and even he
himself, are drifting away from the stern Chinese virtues of work
and thrift, and towards the local spirit of *mai pen rai* or 'it doesn't
matter'. Quite early on in the letters, a friend complains of his
daughter: 'She even wants us to rest on Sundays, like the Thais,
who have forgotten their own religious days to imitate the
foreigners; some of them even take off Saturdays.' According to U,
the Thais work 50 per cent and spend 110 per cent, while the
Chinese work 100 per cent and spend only 10 per cent.

As a Chinese traditionalist, U prays that his wife, Mui Eng, will
bear him sons, for nobody wants daughters, except for the rich
who have the money to dress them up and treat them like dolls.
To U's chagrin, his wife bears him three daughters and only one
son. When Mui Eng suggests contraception, her husband tells her
to stop talking filthiness. Children are strength, he says, to which
his wife replies with a Thai proverb that one child equals seven
years' poverty. U tells her:

> Sure, if you raise a child the way the Thais do. Treat him like a
> little god. Give him everything he wants. If a child is twenty and
> hasn't even begun to work – like some I've seen here – then one

child is a lifetime of poverty, not seven years. But my children will
be raised to work, and study, and grow up able to look after
themselves.

But in this too, he is disappointed.

He complains of the children talking Thai in the house and later
taking Thai names. He does not object to Thai citizenship but
works in vain to impress on his children the honour they owe to
the family and the sae. He especially dislikes Chinese who join
with the Thais in sneering against the jeks: 'Do they suppose they
escape this insulting word themselves? Or that a Thai respects a
man who can barely speak a hundred words of their language and
already seeks to disown the people to whom he belongs?'

U disapproves of the Thai fashion of Westernizing. He laughs at
the craze before the war for hats and gloves and kissing in public.
He is horrified by the 'Turkish Baths' which are springing up for
the US servicemen. When a farang tourist comes to his shop, he
rushes off to a medicine man to ask if the woman had brought bad
luck on his house. He remarks that although the farang are now
everywhere, even in Chinatown, one seldom observes a Japanese,
who have cornered the market in fabric and gadgets. He has
words of praise for the Indians in Bangkok, most of them dealers
in textiles and sewing supplies.

U's troubles begin when his children come to the age of marriage. The eldest daughter chooses a man of whom U approves,
being thrifty, strong as an ox and a good accountant. But U's son,
Weng Kim, is idle at work and comes home drunk every night.
Worse, he has taken up with a Thai prostitute. U pleads with his
son and even invites him to bring the girl to live in their home,
remarking that Thais are unfair to women of this kind. He asks
the prostitute where her family are: 'Starving on a rice farm up in
Udon. I saw my sister last month, and she looked about a hundred
years old. She's twenty-five, she's got eight kids, and do you think
she called me dirty names when I threw a hundred baht on her
kitchen table?' U understands this, but doubts if his wife will.

As it happens, U's wife is killed in a car accident. U sells his business
and goes to live on his own. Now, in 1965, with his fortune gone and
his family scattered, U has to face what in his philosophy is the final
shame and unhappiness: his favourite daughter becomes engaged to
a poor Thai schoolteacher. U's first reaction is to repeat once more his
maxims and warnings about the fecklessness of the Thais:

They import almost everything they need, and look what happens when they have a few years of famine. Thousands of peasants from the north-east descend on Bangkok to beg in the streets until the rains begin. And then they return to their farms to plant rice again, with never a thought for the next time.

U's ungraciousness to his future son-in-law is met with good humour and patience. The young man explains to the older that Thais love and respect their parents just as the Chinese do but show their feelings in different ways:

> You see, Thai parents let their sons depend on them. The Chinese and the farang don't understand why Thai parents encourage that, but they do it because they see dependence as a form of love. The Chinese raise their children in just the opposite way – your son knows that he must one day be willing to provide for you.

This high-minded young schoolteacher is in the habit of telling his class that the ideal man in today's world would combine the moral principles of the farang, the diligence of the Chinese, and the heart of the Thai: '. . . the love of peace, contentment with little, concern for others and a sense of moderation.' In fact, the Buddhist virtues.

At last U relents and goes to live with his daughter, though he cannot get used to the sight of his Thai son-in-law sharing the housework. (I found this a bit improbable, too.) He becomes friendly again with the sister-in-law, whom he had once reproached for accepting Thai ways. Perhaps it occurs to him now that she would have made a better wife; indeed they are thinking of marriage. At last U accepts that he failed his own son by sticking too rigidly to the Chinese virtues. He says about all his children:

> I could not shelter them from the thousands of daily experiences which made them another people, another race. There are so many of our people here, yet the Thais have won. And it was never a contest anyway, but I pretended it was for the sake of my selfish pride.

When *Letters from Thailand* first appeared, it roused much anger from Thais and Chinese, who both thought that their race was maligned. But then, on a second reading, most people had to acknowledge the truth of the satire and anyway could not resist the humour and good nature with which it was done. For even before the denouement and U's conversion to tolerance of the Thais, the reader has no doubt that the book is a plea for mutual tolerance. Yet it is never goody-goody.

Although the *Letters from Thailand* stop in 1965, they still give a true picture of Thai and Thai-Chinese relations. Political changes work on the side of harmony. The end of the Cultural Revolution and opening up of Communist China, make it less of a threat to neighbouring countries. China is now the diplomatic and military ally of Thailand so the Thai-Chinese can no longer be seen as a Fifth Column. The Thai-Chinese have large business investments in Communist China. The great unrest in China in June 1989, leading up to the massacre in Tiananmen Square had few repercussions among the Thai-Chinese, whose interest in the motherland is more cultural and commercial than it is ideological.

The Thai-Chinese are prominent in businesses harmful to the ecology, such as logging, fishing and mining for lead and tin. However they are often joined in these ventures with senior officers of the police and army, most of whom are ethnic Thais. Even the most fanatic 'Greens' in Thailand have not descended to Chinese-baiting.

Nevertheless one can say that during the twenty-five years since *Letters from Thailand*, the Chinese community here has been thriving and happy. Yet during that same time, in almost all other countries of Southeast Asia, the Chinese have been at odds and sometimes in bloody conflict with the majority population. Here once again, the success of Thailand can only be properly understood by comparison with the failure of the surrounding countries.

The Chinese in Singapore and in Hong Kong itself are not always hospitable to those of another race, even to those unwilling to live under communism. A poll taken in Hong Kong in 1989 found that more than 80 per cent believed that the Vietnamese Boat People should not even have the right to put ashore in the colony, let alone stay there. There are countless stories of how the Hong Kong Chinese mistreat and exploit the 50,000 Filipino women who work there as servants. The Thais who visit Hong Kong complain of the harsh reception they get from immigration officials. One Englishman who had gone there on holiday with his Thai girl friend declared in the *Bangkok Post*:

> I for one sincerely hope that if any of the arrogant and unpleasant
> Immigration officials we encountered during our short stay should

visit Thailand, they are singled out for grossly offensive treatment for no other reason than the single fact that they live in Hong Kong.

The Thais also resent the xenophobic attitude of the Singapore government, which announced in 1989 that illegal workers from foreign countries would henceforth be liable to imprisonment and three strokes of the cane. In an interview with a Bangkok journalist, Prime Minister Lee Kuan Yew said that corporal punishment was a legacy of the British tradition and that it 'worked' for Singapore. Reports like this in the *Bangkok Post* suggest that the punishment only applies to people of non-Chinese race:

> On Boxing Day it [the Singapore government] caned three Indians. They were not the first; more than 20 men – Indians, Malaysians, Filipinos, Thais, Burmese – have had their buttocks bruised with a rattan cane, soaked overnight in brine, at the Kaki Bukit prison here since the canings began in December.

The same report in the *Bangkok Post* (23 January 1990) said that Singapore's ban on foreign workers had led to a labour shortage, hurting industries such as ship repair:

> Singapore hopes however that this would be a passing phase, and that the thousands of Hong Kong workers it hopes to attract would take up the slack. About 6,000 of these are now in already, the advance guard of the exodus it hopes to attract with special privileges, incentives and legal guarantees as the 1997 deadline for the change of flags in Hong Kong nears.

The Hong Kong Chinese arriving in Singapore will not be subject to the levy imposed on the employment of workers of another race. This is part of Lee Kuan Yew's frequently stated plan to change Singapore's multi-racial society into one based on Chinese culture, 'the core values', as he expresses it. The pressure for 'core values' has led already to an exodus of the island's Indian and Malay minorities, many of whom have gone to Canada, Australia and even Britain which is at the same time offering shelter to those Hong Kong Chinese who have not been lured to Singapore. In the House of Lords debate on the British Nationality (Hong Kong) Bill, which grants British citizenship to up to 50,000 Hong Kong residents, their spouses and minor children, the Archbishop of York, Dr John Habgood, denounced this number as an 'indictment' of Britain. He said 'racist pressures were responsible for the government's unwillingness to be more generous' (*Daily Telegraph*, 30 June 1990). It is instructive to compare what the Archbishop of York calls Britain's 'racism', with Lee Kuan Yew's belief in the 'core values'.

Having looked at the surrounding countries, I marvel still more at the great success of the Thais at integrating the Chinese. Many things contributed to this happy outcome: the absence of colonialism which sets race against race to divide and rule; a land tenure system which does not drive farmers into the hands of money-lenders; the readiness of the Chinese and Thais to intermarry. As always in Thailand, the two great forces for good are the monarchy and the Buddhist religion. Monarchy unites all races in one common allegiance, just as republicanism divides people in squabbling over their 'rights'. Buddhism teaches tolerance and the Middle Way.

Although the Thais have permitted and even encouraged Chinese immigrants, they never felt under an obligation. They have never given state subsidies towards Chinese housing or education. There is no law to stop the Thais calling the Chinese jek. The Thais cannot begin to understand our European, especially English, feelings of guilt about 'racism'. Perhaps this explains the ease, grace and courtesy of the Thais in their dealings with foreigners.

CHAPTER EIGHT

Brothel Culture

Arriving in Bangkok during the rainy season, which lasts from June to the end of October, you have to be prepared for the vagaries of the ever more frequent flooding. I first encountered this in 1979, when the world had not yet started to worry about the ozone layer and the rise in the ocean level. It was June, one of the hottest months, when I landed at Bangkok Airport; and of the taxi-drivers who touted for custom, I chose the one who boasted about the air-conditioning in his Japanese car. When we got on the highway, Peter, for so he had introduced himself, asked me the name of my hotel and, as usual, gave me the card of one that was 'very much better, number one massage, number one girls'. I smiled, knowing the ways of Bangkok taxi-drivers and answered that, thank you, I still wanted to go to my hotel near the river.

Peter was most persistent. There had been heavy rain that morning ... there were very bad floods by the river ... the hotel he suggested was on our way into town. I smiled and said, OK, I would take a look, but I still wanted to go into town. The hotel he recommended was one I had visited ten years earlier, when I was writing an article on American 'R & R' in Bangkok. There had been something unspeakably sad about those hotels, where the apprehension and fear of the GIs seemed to grow with every day snatched from Pleiku or Camp Eagle. I returned to the taxi and told Peter to head into town. He pointed to overflowing gutters and patches of flood-water and said it would get worse. I did not believe him.

Peter asked me again what hotel I wanted, then shook his head and said it had changed since I stayed there last. 'It is cheap but very much crime. Two Americans murdered there last week. Thieves took all their money and jewellery. Security is very bad.' I mentioned another hotel in the district but this one he said was full of hippies and heroin dealers. I smiled again at these warnings, although I later discovered that they were true.

Peter complained of the world fuel shortage which started in 1973–4, and still gravely affected Thailand:

> In Thailand today gasoline is very expensive and often we can't buy it. Thailand's a poor country and all our gasoline used to come from Iran. Often now you see cars lying in the street where people have left them because they have no gasoline. Now everything is expensive. Taxis are expensive because of the gasoline. Hotels are expensive because of the electricity and the air-con.

And modern Bangkok is built of those box, cement houses which make life unbearable without air-conditioning.

A few minutes later the traffic grew very dense, which did not accord with what Peter had told me of petrol shortage. We reached the Victory Monument and soon afterwards came to a halt in a four-lane traffic jam. The cars in the opposite lanes were making some progress but we made none. After about fifteen minutes the engine began to steam from the heat and Peter grew anxious. He muttered something about the air-conditioning, too embarrassed to say right out that if it was not switched off the car would break down. I got the point and we switched off the cool draught. He apologized for the heat and said that the air-conditioning only worked when the car was in motion. But of course if the car is in motion you open the windows and catch the breeze and do not need any air-conditioning. About every few minutes we moved a few yards until we came to a small hotel where Peter suggested I check in, as I was glad to do.

The hotel reception staff, a lady and a girl, confirmed what Peter had said about the flooding. It would take from two to three hours to drive the two or three kilometres to the river, 'but maybe an hour on foot if you try hard'. I paid off Peter who said there was good security at this hotel. The security was rigid. 'May I see your passport, air ticket and travellers cheques,' said the lady at the reception desk. 'These must all be put in the safe. If you bring a woman into your room you must pay 100 bahts extra.' There was a desk clerk on every floor to enforce this rule, and provide the girls. Security was so strict that the bedroom windows were barred and the fire escape door was padlocked. When I mentioned this to the girl at the reception desk, she giggled. 'If there's a fire, we fry like eggs,' I said, at which she giggled even louder and passed on the joke to her colleague.

From next day's *Bangkok Post* I learned that the flooding had been the result of the heaviest downfall the city had known in twenty-five years. More than six inches of rain had fallen during the small hours of the morning and many streets had been waist-high in water. My inconvenience could not compare with that of the woman who stepped into an open drain and disappeared from sight before she was rescued. General Lek Neaomali, the Minister of the Interior, took three hours to get to work and afterwards sneered at the city council: 'Nobody can solve the flood problem in Bangkok unless we build a roof over the whole city.'

Even ten years ago, people had warned that the vast weight of building in Bangkok would sink it, literally into the water. The covering over of the canals had wrecked the ancient drainage system. Ten years ago, in 1979, we had not yet heard of the 'Greenhouse Effect' which raises the temperature of the sea and also its level. The low-lying country of Bangladesh is sinking at an astonishing rate, losing arable land and living space. Thailand faces a worse problem, since Bangkok, the capital and greatest supplier of wealth, is only just above sea level.

Coming back this time from the south I decided to change my habits and stay this time in the east of town, in a stretch of Sukhumvit Road, which is close to some of the places I needed to visit, like Reuters and the British and Vietnamese Embassies. The small hotel where I stayed has a first-class swimming pool and is right next door to the vast Ambassador Hotel, whose services include the Ambassador City Food Complex. Here, for one or two pounds, you can pick a delicious meal from some thirty stalls offering food from as many cuisines including Thai, Chinese, Japanese, Korean, Vietnamese, Italian and Muslim. The Thais are such marvellous cooks because they also delight in eating and, still more, in buying their food each day in the market. Even in Bangkok, with all the latest aids to refrigeration, the Thais insist on fresh food. Rich women continue to go to the market rather than sending the maid to shop. Unlike the French, for example, they do not fret over their cooking, nor wax pompous. They do it for fun.

The sois on either side of Sukhumvit Road begin at Soi 1, near the British Embassy, continuing into the hundreds through what is practically countryside. Around Soi 21/23, there is a cluster of German beer-houses and pubs, like Lord Mike O'Henry, a Dutch establishment, as well as Soi Cowboy, a less brash and aggressive version of Patpong Road. In the lower numbered sois there is an 'entertainment' district, catering mostly for Arabs who are unpopular in this country. Here is found the Grace Hotel, a legend in Bangkok's entertainment industry, and which used to feature in sex tour advertisements in the British Press. It was also a favourite hunting ground for the mass murderer, Charles Sobhraj.

I was there in September, which is an anxious month in Bangkok. It is then that the army announces the annual promotions, which are republished in full on the front of the newspapers. Promotion goes logically but not always automatically by the year that the officers left the academy. This was the year of Class 5, who finished in 1953. The years on the way up are always at odds with the years on the way out, who want to cling on to power. Any class year that is disappointed may stage a *coup d'état*. Students of politics here have to keep a map of the country, showing which class year governs in which military region.

September is also the month of flood, when the brimming Chae Phraya River meets a freak tide. The army commanders vie with the Bangkok municipality to get control of the pumping equipment which can be used to divert the water away from one suburb into another. Angry politicians and generals always blame the floods on someone else, which could also lead to a *coup d'état*, except that the tanks and infantry cannot move through the water-logged, traffic-jammed streets.

During September, both the government and the army try to create a diversion. As the public was getting bored with the AIDS scare, they had to be offered a crackdown on crime, especially on firearms. The Chief of Police announced the creation of 'Weapons Free Zones' at boxing stadiums, football grounds and some of the sleazier entertainment districts. A picture appeared in the Press of the manager of the Far West bar standing in front of his swing doors under the notice 'Weapons Free Zone'. A day or two after the crackdown on crime, someone exploded a bomb by the Grace Hotel, killing a Saudi Arabian tourist. Those who come from the West on sex tours now have more to contend with than AIDS and the old-fashioned poxes.

The sleazy part of Bangkok during a flood in September forms the setting for a novel I have been reading, *Paradise Eater*, by John Ralston Saul, a Canadian who had been living here as a businessman. Inevitably, for a thriller set in Thailand, there is much about heroin, murder, corrupt politicians and generals, Patpong Road and girls popping ping-pong balls from their genitals. Unlike most writers on Bangkok, Saul dwells on the squalor instead of the glamour. He tells us more than we want to know of the sexual diseases that still are a much greater menace than AIDS. He is well-informed on the links between Chinese bankers, Thai generals and US intelligence agencies, as well as the protocol of the *coup d'état*.

This novel afforded me many new insights to life in Bangkok, for instance, on subsidence. When the hero is walking beside a skyscraper, 'his left foot was lower than the right because these new buildings with deep foundations were not sinking while the road was, so that the pavement hung around the skyscrapers like a billowing skirt.' He also says that when floods hit the suburbs, the cobras come out from under the houses to sun themselves on the porch. I think I had heard before that the statue of Queen Victoria in the British Embassy courtyard, was looked upon by the Thais as a fertility goddess but did not know that the sceptre and orb were symbols of the male and female generation. I certainly did not know that the slaughterhouse for pigs, which Saul describes in repulsive detail, was manned by Catholic Vietnamese, since Thais will not perform this work. Nor did I know and still do not quite believe, that drinking beer while eating the durian fruit can make the stomach explode.

Several identifiable people appear under false names, or even under their real names. There is a Thai-British doctor called Meechai, also nicknamed the 'Condom King' who leads the campaign for birth control. Nor does it take much guesswork to find out who at the *Bangkok Post* writes columns entitled 'Crappe at the Flicks', 'Crappe Reads for You', and 'Crappe's Bangkok'. There is a reference to a Bangkok con man, Vichit, who specializes in faking exposure stories for foreign writers: 'He got some London pinko front page hot shot last year'. There is a sharp portrait of 'George Espoir', a world-famous writer of espionage fiction, who comes to Bangkok to do research for a new book. Field, the hero, 'could even, with a little effort, have dredged up the man's real name; the one he didn't sign his novels with. The expression of serious self-contentment on Espoir's face stopped Field from betraying any sign of recognition.' Later, Espoir explains the tricks of his trade:

Mind you, I'm no worse than a Balzac or a Dickens. Each one has his touch you see. Mine is to dress it all up in a kind of convoluted upper class verbiage that sounds like an Oxbridge crossword puzzle, if you see what I mean. That makes them all feel good; well, either good or impressed. Either way it sells. Then you shove in some seedy spies for the *bas monde* and the moral aspect for the intellectuals.

For all the horror that Field endures in Bangkok, 'the seamless web of filth and of noise filled him as always, with a wonderful, meaningless sense of pleasure.' The very viciousness of Bangkok produces a kind of innocence. Because Field and his prostitute girl friend are both riddled with sexual diseases, they have not made love to each other before the end of the book and their marriage.

This book presents such a dismal picture of modern Thai woman-hood that it was pleasant to turn to a story that Thai women themselves love, first in its original form as a newspaper serial, then as a two-volume novel and later a play, several films and a TV epic. This is *Si Phaendin*, or *Four Reigns* by Kukrit Pramoj, the scholar and wit who played the part of a Southeast Asian premier in the film *The Ugly American*, before going on to become the real life Premier of Thailand. The translation of *Four Reigns* by Tulach-andra, published by D. K. Bookhouse, is one of three Thai novels in English that I have read with delight as well as illumination. The story about an aristocratic lady who lived through four reigns, from 1882 to 1946, provides a foreigner with an understanding of the life style in what is now a remote epoch. To Thais and above all Thai women, the story of Ploi expresses not only what they would like to be, but what, in a way, they still are. It is by the most popular novelist in Thai.

The story opens almost a hundred years ago in the reign of King Chulalongkorn (1868–1910), when Ploi as a girl of ten is taken to serve a Royal Princess in the Inner Court of the Grand Palace. Ploi's mother, who also served the same Princess, a distant relation, has walked out of her role as junior wife to a kind-hearted but ineffectual nobleman. The relationship between senior and junior wives, and half-brothers and half-sisters, adds complication but also richness to what is a family saga. Although the four kings are seen from the edge of a crowd at their public appearances, the whole book centres on the Grand Palace, since most of the Thai aristocracy were em-ployed as royal courtiers, civil servants or army officers. The govern-ment and the Court were until 1932, virtually indistinguishable.

Although Ploi has suffered at home from the spite of a stepsister, she is at first lonely and shy in the all-female world of the Inner Court. She has to study the etiquette and the arts of a Thai lady, including the preparation of food and betel nuts, the making of scented water, the care of clothes and the rules on what colours go with each day of the week: 'Both bean colour and iron colour are correct for your Wednesday *palai*. And this is for Thursday: green *palai* with bird's blood red . . .' Many Thai women still follow such rules on colour, and also on matters like which day of the week to visit the hairdresser.

Ploi's mother stays for a time at the Inner Court, where she had been as a child, before leaving to start a new life with the money she made out of money-lending. This again struck me as true to life. A Thai woman I knew in the 1960s would chatter away about her two businesses of money-lending and lorry rentals. When Ploi's mother returns to the Palace to say she is getting married again, she brings Ploi the charming gift of a basket of miniature foods, like brown crispy fish the size of a little finger, and salted eggs, not of the chicken or duck but of the tiny rice bird. The gift is typical of the Thais in their fondness both for food and children.

Ploi's mother dies in childbirth. When Ploi reaches puberty, she goes home for the ceremony of removing the topknot. Her father, a sad and put-upon Chekhov aristocrat, says it is hard to get servants these days:

> Not like when your grandfather was alive. Those days there were hundreds and hundreds of people living in the house under his care. There were his clerks, his oarsmen, his labour corps, his musicians and women dancers – a whole troupe of them, and relatives and hangers-on, drifting in and out all over the place . . . you should have seen the cauldrons we had for cooking rice, rows of them, like in a regular barracks . . .

Ploi gets engaged to a young army officer, who is sent to the provinces, feels lonely and marries the daughter of a rice-and-curry seller instead. After a few weeks of grief, Ploi is coaxed back into the current amusements, like bicycle riding. She goes on the new train to Bang Pa In, on the river between Bangkok and Ayutthaya, and it seems that even in those days the Thais suffered from railway sickness, as they frequently do today. At Bang Pa In, she is wooed by her new admirer, a rich, handsome Thai-Chinese in the civil service called Prem. After a suitable courtship, Ploi marries and takes up charge of a big household. Her maid, Pit, a ribald woman like Juliet's nurse, makes friends with the cook: 'they loved to eat, and like many serious eaters, they enjoyed drinking . . . Pit also loved to sing, especially after a certain amount of imbibing.'

Soon after the marriage, Ploi discovers that Prem has a son by a mistress, but gladly accepts the boy and eventually comes to love him as much as her own three children. Her attitude to her husband is very Thai: 'We live together and it's natural that we love each other. But over and above this, I feel infinitely grateful to you. I'm in your debt. I owe you everything.'

When King Chulalongkorn had gone on a visit to Europe, his Queen acted as Regent. A cheeky friend of Ploi's in the Palace had boasted, '"I'm not afraid of men any more. I'm a woman, and a woman reigns over all in this land of ours."' For her impudence she was given the usual warning, '"If you don't shut up, you'll get a coconut in your mouth to shut it for you."' When King Chulalongkorn dies in 1910, he is succeeded not by a woman but by a new kind of king, an English-educated dandy, a lover of theatre and country sports, a man always happier with his own sex. Ploi's husband Prem is keen to adapt to the latest court fashions like collecting ivory boxes or walking sticks, dressing in foppish pink and having his jackets sent to be laundered in Singapore. Ploi herself is made to abandon the betel chewing which blackens teeth: '"There's something else you must do now that you're so fashionably coiffed . . . scale your teeth, make them white again, you know."' White teeth came into fashion throughout Indo-China. In Vietnam, the advertisements for the toothpaste Hynos, showed a grinning African. The popular Thai toothpaste Darkie, also shows a black in a top hat and tuxedo.

The day comes when Prem urges Ploi to abandon the *Pamung* dress for the *Pasin* costume worn in the north: '"What's got into you, I'm not a Lao",' Ploi complains, only to be reproved with the pious sentiment: '"Don't call them Lao . . . We are all Thai. The people of the north are citizens of Siam just as much as we are."'

At Prem's insistence, Ploi sadly agrees that her two sons should go to an English school from which Awd goes to Oxford and Un to Paris. He consorts with communists and revolutionary Vietnamese, at last bringing home a French wife. When King Prajadhipok comes to the throne, Prem loses his job at Court and becomes despondent. Ploi meekly suggests that he take a minor wife, but

instead he consoles himself with riding. He is killed in a fall and
buried, after the Chinese fashion, with the burning of paper models
of his more loved possessions.

Ploi is horrified by the *coup d'état* of 1932 and puzzled by all the
new words like 'democracy' and 'revolution'. Her son Un is one of
the revolutionaries, a Pridi figure, and soon is at odds with her
stepson, Oan, who is an army officer and loyalist. She goes by
river to visit Oan when he is under sentence of death, past palaces
that are now closed and forlorn:

> On such a morning on the Chao Phraya ... your thoughts could
> keep going back to the days long past, the days of giggling boatfuls
> of Inner Court girls on their way to Bang Pa In, of candle-lit flower
> boats under a bright moon, of processions of the Royal barges with
> their fabulous prows moving to the accompaniment of the boat
> chant ...

King Prajadhipok abdicates and all Ploi's hopes now rest on the
boy King Ananda, who comes on a brief visit from Europe. A new
war breaks out and Thailand grabs back from defeated France the
lost regions of Laos and Cambodia. That skirmish is now recalled
in the Victory Monument.

The Pibun government apes the Japanese in banning betel nuts,
and enforcing the use of hats and gloves. Wives are encouraged to
kiss their husbands in public, or at least blow kisses. The air raids
start and Ploi is bombed out of the family home and goes back to
live in her father's house. The British replace the Japanese and the
youngsters along the canal banks shout 'OK! Thank you!', instead
of *'Bansai!'* and *'Arigato!'*

At last King Ananda returns to Bangkok, where Ploi is in the
ecstatic crowd: 'We've been bereft for so long, now we'll have him
back with us, with his Gracious Power to reign over us'. Ploi's life
and the story of *Four Reigns* end with the catastrophic death of
Ananda on 9 June 1946, the most woeful day in Thailand's
history.

After reading of the gentle, virtuous, dutiful Ploi, who is nevertheless a creature of flesh and blood, it is sad to reflect that much of
the world now thinks of Thai women as prostitutes. Why is this
country such a brothel? It is the first question that foreigners ask,
one that puzzles and also disturbs me. Even now, before I offer my
thoughts, for what they are worth, on prostitution, I should say
something of Pattaya on the coast near here. When I first came to

Thailand, Pattaya did not exist except as a fishing village; it grew during the 1960s as a resort for US troops on R & R from Vietnam; in the 1970s, Pattaya looked instead to single male tourists, especially from Western Europe; it may now be in decline because of the AIDS scare. In all my visits to Thailand, I never had been to Pattaya, and came to regard it with dread and horror. Perhaps because of this, when I finally went there, I found it charming.

The crescent beach is so long that, even at the height of its popularity, Pattaya did not go in for high-rise building. The sea is infested with motor boats but there are beaches further along the coast and swimming pools in most hotels. Although this was during the off-season, when business is slack, I did not encounter much touting or hassle. When an elephant came down the street, promoting a show, it was not the tourists but some of the bar girls who came out to feed it bananas. The tone of Pattaya is overwhelmingly vulgar, proletarian, Anglo-Saxon and old-fashioned. There are signs like: 'Aussie Ken. We speak English, right bloody good, Mate', 'The Leaning Tower of Pizza', and 'Mince and tatties, just like back home'. The typical Pattaya visitor is a Western oil man on holiday from the Gulf, which may partly explain the signs in Arabic, Thai and English: 'No Arabs to sit down here. We don't want Arab people consuming alcohol and annoying women'. There are middle-aged Americans who came here on R & R twenty years ago and took to the marijuana and girls. Some are on pensions. Others keep talking of getting away to earn some money: 'I'm going back to Alaska to pan me some f. . .ing gold.'

Most of the bar or brothel keepers are Westerners, including a high proportion from northern England, born into working-class homes, but now disgusted by the trade unions, immigration and football hooligans. These northern English sit round the bar watching spaghetti westerns on video, while in the back the bar girls play snooker. 'I came out here', said one man from a famous northern mining town, 'because I didn't want to pay tax and rates and see some lazy bugger pissing it against the wall . . . My girls look after the business for me. They fix the police. And I look after them like daughters. If they get sick or need to go back to their family, I'll see they're all right.'

These north country bar keepers wax furious over the AIDS scare. 'Don't mention it to me,' one said, 'I couldn't trust myself to keep my temper. We've had reporters down from the local press to

write about it, pissed out of their skulls from morning to night.'
The bar keepers blame AIDS on the 'gay bars' which still advertise
blatantly in Pattaya. One English bar keeper has put up a poster
depicting crudely and rudely, two men, over the caption: 'Stop
AIDS. Don't bend for a friend.' Another English bar has a map of
the world with Britain and the Falkland Islands very large, and
other regions described as 'Union of Soviet Commie Bastards;
Slanty-eyed, Chinky takeaway land; greasy, goucho spic land; Fede-
ral Republic of Bullet Head Krauts; Coon Coast; Pakis; and Much
Maligned South Africa.'

Thailand's best-known feminist comes to Pattaya when the US
fleet is in town; so too, I am told, do sociologists wanting to study
the bar girls and their customers. One evening, at one of the
English bars that also has rooms, a good-looking European woman
took a place beside me. She said that she stayed there, was a
sociologist and yes, she was interested in the bar girls. I started to
feel uneasy, and yet she was not your average sociologist. She was
funny. She liked John Wayne films. I got the impression that she
was laughing at me. She also got on extremely well with the bar
girls, whispering and giggling a good deal. When she went up to
her room, the owner told me confidentially: 'She's AC/DC. There's
quite a lot of them here in Pattaya. She normally takes two of my
girls to bed with her every night. I don't mind, and nor do the
girls. Some of them are a bit AC/DC too.' Pattaya really was quite
different from what I expected.

Before asking why Thai women are ready to go into prostitution,
one first has to answer a different question: why do the sex tourists
come here? A silly question, you think at first. The US soldiers on
R & R were young, randy and frightened of dying. They wanted a
woman, but few, I imagine, specifically wanted a Thai woman,
any more than they wanted the Vietnamese scrubbers who hung
round the camps. Most GIs would almost certainly have preferred
one of the tall, long-legged and big-bosomed American girls they
saw in the *Playboy* centrefolds and had known back home. This
knowledge of Western taste explains why the bar girls of Pattaya
and Bangkok have tried, unsuccessfully, to imitate Western
women, by a display of nudity and the bump and grind of the go-
go dance, which do not become their slender gracefulness. Why
should a man want to see an Eastern girl pretending to be a
Western girl?

I advance the idea that the great majority of the sex tourists in

Thailand are not looking primarily for the act of sex. Most human beings breed with and are attracted by their own kind, nation or race. Of course, there are exceptions but as a general rule it applies all over the world. So why should Western men come to Thailand to have sex with women so unlike those in the West. Perhaps timid men like Thai girls just because they are small and docile.

But there is more to it than that. We come nearer the truth when we start to look at one particular nation, the Swedes, whose men have been pioneers in the Thai sexual tourist industry. There have always been Swedish bars, Swedish VD clinics and Thai girls who speak some Swedish. The fondness of Swedish men for South-east Asian women is matched by the fondness of Swedish women for men in other exotic countries. Swedish women tourists used to flock to the beach hotels of the Gambia, West Africa, most of them with the avowed intent of enjoying a 'black experience'. Gambian peanut pickers left for the coast to be beach boys and gigolos. The sexual traffic there is as open and unashamed as at Pattaya. A Zimbabwean friend says that the Swedish women who go to his country will not look at their own fellow-countrymen but are easy game for the locals. At Larnaca, in Cyprus, where the Swedes formed part of a United Nations force, I have seen two Swedish soldiers standing at one end of a bar, while two Swedish women tourists, equally tall and blonde, stood at the other. They had no eyes for each other. It seems that the Swedes, like the geese of their frozen tundra, head south to mate and breed, but not with each other. In view of the sexual diseases spread this way, the World Health Organization ought to set up a project to teach the Swedes to find each other attractive.

It seems to me that the Swedish men and the sexual tourists from Europe are looking for something other than sex in Thai girls, perhaps for sympathy, laughter, romance, even love. The feminist movement in countries like Sweden has killed off most of the virtues that men used to regard as feminine. Swedish women who once might have dreamed of a midsummer idyll beside the Baltic now are content with the services of a Gambian beach boy. Many sex tourists to Pattaya look not only for love but marriage. West Germans in particular often take their bar girls home with them. Some may also want children, either their own or by adoption. The demand for babies from all Third World countries, and in particular Thailand, has risen enormously now that abortion makes them scarce in Europe.

All this does not anser the question of why Thai women are so ready to meet the needs of the sexual tourists. It has little to do with poverty, since even the people of north-east Thailand are rich by comparison with the rest of Asia. It can have nothing to do with Buddhism, whose teachings condemn the practice. It may have something to do with Thailand's freedom from colonization and conquest. Western visitors to Bangkok in the early nineteenth century were shocked by the forwardness of the women who flirted with them even inside the temples. The Thais have no experience of living under a foreign tyranny and having to guard their daughters' honour. From as far back as the records go, it seems that Thai women enjoyed an unusual independence, so that in the fifteenth century they were ready and eager to marry Chinese. They have always been businesswomen. Those Chakri kings who took scores of wives are not known to have punished them for infidelity. From *Four Reigns* we know that women like Ploi's mother left husbands and remarried.

A few Thai feminists have addressed themselves to the age-old question of why Thai women are so submissive to men. For example, Sanitsudo Enachai complained in one of a series of newspaper articles:

> Not one single university in Thailand has a systematic women's studies programme to examine the root causes of the widespread exploitation of women. This gap in academic inquiries should come as no surprise. The academic world is not cut off from social reality. And after all, this is the country where there are more than one million prostitutes to supply the demands of institutionalized polygamy, where there are more women than men who cannot read or write, where women receive low pay for the same job, cut off from promotion because women are 'irrational and indecisive', and where wife-beating is considered a private and isolated matter rather than a social disease as a result of the male quest for domination. Of some twenty universities in Thailand, only four offer some scattered courses to correct misconceptions about women, to question double standards. At Chiang Mai, a group of feminist lectures had an unexpected boost when the faculty received foreign grants to set up such a programme.

Certainly, Chiang Mai is a feminist centre and source of much of the agitation against the sexual tourist industry. The main Chiang Mai bookshop has a display of feminist works. But the books, like the lectures, refer largely to the experiences and the grievances of women in the United States and Britain, rather than Thailand. Only a few Thais have tried to explain the peculiar status of women in Thailand. One of these, Assistant Professor Pranee Wongtet, believes that the subjugation of women began with the arrival of patriarchal Indian and Chinese culture which introduced the idea of the 'good woman', selflessly looking after her menfolk. The indigenous culture, she says, was matriarchal, with women owning the land and houses and acting as medium with the *Pii Fah* or sky spirit. Husbands in those days were treated like guests.

A Buddhist feminist, Dr Chartsumarn Kabilsingh of Thammasat University in Bangkok, says that the status of Thai women is culturally determined. However, she says that the culprit is Brahminism, not Buddhism: 'The core teachings of the Buddhist faith preach that enlightenment can be attained regardless of sex, race or age.' Although admitting that animism, Buddhism and Brahminism are intertwined, Dr Chartsumarn blames the third of these for the growth of 'male chauvinist' attitudes. This was especially so during the period of Ayutthaya and its constant wars. 'Masculinity, courage, military expertise and virility' were seen as the male virtues, Dr Chartsumarn argues.

The arguments of these feminists are convincing up to a point, but do not explain, to me at least, the matter of prostitution. Neighbouring countries like Vietnam, Cambodia, Burma and India have all to a greater or lesser extent, come under the influence of Brahminism. They have all been engaged in war for much of their history, and therefore come to admire military virtues. But Saigon, Phnom Penh, Rangoon and Calcutta have never attracted millions of sexual tourists.

My own explanation of this phenomenon lies in the royal polygamy practised during the nineteenth and early twentieth centuries. Not only the Chakri kings and the royal nobility but Thai men of the middle classes thought it proper to take a number of minor wives and this practice was often condoned by the legal first wife, as we have seen in the novel *Four Reigns*. This institutionalized polygamy, often compounded with incest, has given the Thais their peculiar freedom from sexual guilt. Any man who has a sexual relationship with a Thai woman, whether a prostitute, a girl friend or wife, is bound to be struck by her lack of bashfulness. The Thai Eve bites cheerfully on the proffered apple and afterwards feels no shame at her nakedness. The prostitute may regret not having a proper home with husband and children but does not regard herself as a fallen woman. Women of all stations tend to regard sex as something between a pleasure, a game and a joke.

Thai prostitutes may often have been abused by pimps and sent into something approaching white slavery. After a fire at a Phuket brothel, several women were burned to death because they were chained to a bed. But the great majority of the girls go voluntarily into prostitution because of the good money they earn from not too arduous labour. If Thai men misbehave, this is not because Thai women are drilled into submissiveness. European women who marry Thais have often found it impossible to control their husbands, hence the club in Bangkok where these unfortunate wives gather to swap advice and commiseration. Thai wives who do not expect their husbands to be monogamous, feel less inclined to jealousy and a sense of rejection. Even those Thai men who mistreat their wives are more inclined than men in Europe to honour their parents and love and care for their children. The feminist cause has failed in Thailand, not because it defends the status of women but rather because it is seen to attack the family.

Most Thai women feel secure in the three all important institutions of family, Buddhism and monarchy. This explains why Thai women love Kukrit Pramoj's great novel, *Four Reigns*, which celebrates all three institutions. It also helps to explain why so many Thai women and men as well, are hoping that when the King's long reign eventually ends, he will be succeeded, not by the Crown Prince, but by one of his two very popular and respected daughters.

PART THREE

The North-east

CHAPTER NINE

Three Towns

KHORAT

You cannot stay long in Thailand without starting to hear about the troubles of the north-east. Most of the Thais you meet in Bangkok, as distinct from the ethnic Chinese, are likely to be some of the millions of immigrants from that region, bulging out on the map between Cambodia and Laos. The labouring class, like navvies and porters, probably started work in the paddy fields, under the even more punishing north-east sun. The menial staff in tourist hotels and restaurants usually come from the north-east, as do most of the bar girls, go-go dancers, masseuses and prostitutes. These girls often say they are from Chiang Mai, which sounds more glamorous. They are sadly ashamed of the north-east, or Isaan as they call it.

If you have come to Thailand, meaning to take a serious interest in her problems, all the old-timers will lecture you on the north-east: 'Forget Bangkok, that's strictly a Chinese city. Forget Chiang Mai, that's tourist country. Go to the north-east, that's the real Thailand, the one that foreigners never see.' The same kind of person tells you, in Rio de Janeiro, that you should see the real Brazil, in the starving north-east. In London, he tells you to witness the real England of unemployment and squalor in Newcastle or Middlesbrough.

However, the north-east is not the real Thailand. For one thing, the people of the Isaan are not real Thais but Laotians, the same as the people across the Mekong. I am told that their language is just as different from Thai, as French is from Spanish. The north-east is not the real Thailand because, in a country richly endowed by nature, it suffers from poor soil and a harsh climate. The flat, low-lying plain is sparsely covered by what geographers call a 'dry monsoon forest', which means that for most of the year it is parched by the sun and then, for a short while, drenched. The cycle of drought and flood appears to have grown more severe during this century, causing an exodus of the young to Bangkok and, more recently, to the Middle East oil states.

Ecologists blame the poverty of the north-east on the cutting down of the forests by Danish timber companies at the start of the twentieth century. The Royal forests department gave the Danes a licence to fell, without the obligation to replant teak and other trees, as the British did in northern Thailand and Burma. This does not imply any particular wisdom and virtue for British forest-ers, as opposed to the Danes, but more that, as colonists, they looked on the timber as property to be preserved. The Danes, having no long term interest in the timber, were eager to get as quick a profit as possible, without regard to the future. Nor is it true that people a hundred years ago were unaware of the dangers of deforestation. As long ago as a thousand years BC, the Indus valley was shorn of its trees to fire the furnaces used in making bricks, and now is the desert of Sind. The kings of England during the Middle Ages struggled to keep the forests for deer and the timber for shipbuilding. Their failure is seen in Sherwood Forest, where Robin Hood and his descendants claimed the right to cut down trees as avidly as they poached the game. It is now a treeless plain.

The north-east suffered more than the rest of Thailand, more than the rest of this part of Asia, from the Depression in the 1930s. At the same time, Isaan was opposed to the military politi-cians who took power after the King's abdication. During the Japanese occupation, the north-east supported a number of 'Free Thai' groups of guerrillas, many of whom were allied to Laotians over the river. After the war and the re-emergence of some of the military politicians, the north-east came under the influence of the Viet Minh, who were fighting the French in Laos as well as Viet-nam. By the 1960s, communist groups were active around Sakon Nakhon, whose Member of Parliament, Nai Krong Chandawong, also took to the forest. An article in the *Bangkok Post* uttered a scream of warning:

> On a sturdy pony, this stocky agitator rides the bullock-cart trails and the thirsty-ground routes, raising dust behind him – and raising

hell before him. He swiftly covers the distances isolating the various villages of north-east Thailand ... This is a dedicated man on a deadly mission, the devil's mission, the Red Devil's mission ... He rides like Paul Revere of old; he sounds the alarm like Paul Revere. However, while Paul Revere sounded the alarm to wake the people to fight an incoming enemy, he is sounding the alarm to rouse the people to join an enemy. Specifically he is trying to separate the north-east region from the rest of the kingdom and bring it under the communists in a territorial amalgamation with Laos.

That was in 1963, when I was first in Thailand, and the United States was fearful that the disease of communism would spread from Vietnam. Economic advisers and Peace Corps volunteers were poured into north-east Thailand. Gawky and earnest young men, who had studied *The Ugly American* and had voted for John F. Kennedy, preached to the peasants on miracle rice, fish farming and hog cholera vaccine. Here in north-east Thailand, almost as much as in Vietnam, the battle was on for the 'hearts and minds' of the people.

At the same time, in the early 1960s, the US set up a number of air force bases in north-east Thailand, first for intelligence-gathering, then for bombing attacks on Vietnam, the 'Ho Chi Minh Trail' of supplies through Laos and ultimately on Cambodia. As many as 30,000 American Air Force personnel at any one time were stationed in north-east Thailand, as well as the hundreds of thousands who spent their 'rest and recreation' in Bangkok. By the late 1960s, when Thailand had two combat divisions in South Vietnam, north-east Thailand was very much part of the war. Then in 1976, Prime Minister Kukrit Pramoj annulled the lease of the bases, thereby depriving the north-east of its largest source of revenue, after rice. Tens of thousands who had lived off the US Air Force, went to find jobs in Bangkok or the Persian Gulf. The girls who had learned how to please American servicemen, now had to get used to West European tourists.

The communist take-over, first of Cambodia, then South Vietnam and, more quietly, Laos, soon created an influx of refugees, most of them coming to north-east Thailand. Scores of thousands of Laotians crossed the Mekong. The new Cambodian rulers, the Khmer Rouge, planted minefields along the border to keep their own people captive. Many got through. After the Vietnamese invasion of 1978–9, hundreds of thousands of Khmer Rouge victims, as well as the Khmer Rouge Army, crossed into Thailand, most of them settling near to Aranyaprathet, east of Bangkok and not strictly part of Isaan. Once more Thailand was caught up in the seemingly endless troubles of Vietnam, Laos and Cambodia. Inspired by fear and dislike of Vietnam, Thailand became the ally of China. With China, Thailand armed and supplied the Khmer Rouge forces fighting the Vietnamese from bases inside her frontier. Sometimes the Vietnamese shelled over the border into Thailand, often hitting the refugee camps.

Those foreign observers who took the side of the Vietnamese now looked on the Thais as their enemy. Newspaper and television reporters focused upon the squalid aspects of Thailand, especially the poverty of the north-east and above all the prostitution. The region, which once used to be famous as a breeding-ground for rebellion, is now best known for its white slave traffic.

It is true that foreigners seldom visit the north-east. One cannot blame them. The landscape is flat and monotonous. The few old temples near the Cambodian border cannot compare with the splendours of Angkor Wat on the other side of it; they serve to remind us that this region has in the past belonged to the Khmers, as well as the Laotian kings at Luang Prabang before it came under Thailand. The towns of the north-east are modern, charmless and quite indistinguishable from one another. The villages are still more drab now that the roofs of the houses are made of tin rather than of thatch.

Before Laos fell to the communists, many foreigners passed through north-east Thailand, making their way to Vientiane, but few would have thought of stopping even a night at Khorat, or Udon. Those who did, talked of their stay as 'interesting' rather than 'fun'. But for those wanting to learn about Thailand and her relationship with the neighbouring communist states, a trip to the north-east is necessary and often surprising.

On this occasion, I went to Khorat almost by chance. Coming from London in the tourist season in early December, the only flight I could book had arrived on Saturday morning, the start of a three-day weekend, for Monday was also the King's birthday. Not wanting to spend a long weekend, or indeed any weekend, in Bangkok, I took my bag from the International to the Domestic building and asked if there were any flights north or south. All the flights were fully booked, except to Khorat, the nearest town in the north-east. The ticket cost little more than a taxi fare to down-town Bangkok.

Just before Khorat, our plane went over the one range of high hills in the north-east. I have seen them also from buses and trains, a pleasant relief from the tedious landscape. Arriving at Khorat, the principal town in a region notorious for its poverty, I was struck by the cleanliness, neatness and fresh air. Municipal buildings, shops and houses are smart and well kept, the citizens well dressed and fed.

The north-east may be poor compared to the rest of Thailand, but not by other standards. Even the north-east of Thailand belongs to the affluent world of Asia, along with Japan, South Korea, Taiwan, Malaysia and Singapore. The 'poor' of north-east Thailand simply cannot be compared with the poor of India or Bangladesh. The peasants may have bad years but there is not the starvation and misery, leading to armed revolt, that you meet in some of the Philippine islands.

Whereas, twenty years ago, people in north-east Thailand anguished about their plight the mood is now optimistic. In Khorat, as later in other north-east towns, people told me that there was more money around and offered as proof of this the great number of cars and scooters. Whereas in Europe people attribute economic change to the politicians, here in Thailand the politicians do not even pretend to direct affairs. There is little or no social engineering. Thai politics largely consists of Bangkok versus the rest of the country.

The north-east people tend to attribute any benefits to the King, who is tireless in visiting backward parts of the country, to promote irrigation projects, crop improvements, fish-farming and re-afforestation, the kind of work that was once undertaken by US aid organizations. On the King's birthday, the young people of Khorat marched through the street in his honour, with pipe bands dressed in a scarlet uniform. Like the Trooping of the Colour, the marching is done in the easy English fashion, with none of the goose-stepping so popular in the modern world.

The oddest thing about Khorat is something you do not see: the American influence. During the Vietnam War this was a major air base and home to thousands of US servicemen. There is now no sign that they were ever here. There are no American films in the cinemas, few in the video shops, little American music on the cassettes and the radio. Most of the cars and motor scooters, as well as the electronic and plastic gadgets come from Japan, Hong Kong or other parts of the East. The menu in my hotel is written also in French, not from any pretence at a French cuisine – it is Thai and Chinese – but because a French tour company sends a coach through Khorat each week; heaven knows why. The bars and massage parlours are few and cater for Thai men only.

NONG KHAI

Taking the train north from Khorat, you come to the end of the line at Nong Khai, on the stretch of the Mekong River that flows due east before turning south to Cambodia and Vietnam. In the old days, visiting Laos, you crossed the Mekong from here in a long boat, powered by an outboard motor. Just a few hundred yards over that scented, sun-dazzled, chocolate stream, you would find yourself in the Land of the Million Elephants, with its opium parlours, outdoor French restaurants, Bohemians, spies, gun-runners, psychedelic nightclubs, soldiers and airmen of fortune, and Lao girls, even more beautiful than the Thais. The passage over the Mekong had the enchantment for me of the Lethe River, with often the same result that I could not remember anything that occurred to me on the other side. My last visit, in April 1975, is only too clear in my memory. Having been in Saigon, when Phnom Penh fell to the communists, I was in Vientiane when the end arrived for Saigon. Laos itself was in the last throes of its independence. Already the communist Pathet Lao troops, in apple-green uniforms and curious pastry-cook caps, were on patrol in the capital. The foreigners, from the crooks to the crackpots, were leaving across the Mekong. A few months later, the Pathet Lao evicted the rest, sometimes treating them to additional gaol and torture. The King was sent to a labour camp where he and most of his family died. Some two years earlier, in the old royal capital of Luang Prabang, I had met a Cambodian who had escaped from his own country. *'Laos, c'est le dernier paradis'* he had told me sadly. By the end of 1975, Laos as well was gone.

On that same day, 30 April 1975, when I was over the river in Vientiane, the hero of John le Carré's thriller, *The Honourable School-boy*, woke up in a brothel here in Nong Khai and watched the fishermen casting their nets on the river. I think he was quarrelling with an American agent and planning to murder someone else, but I never could follow the plot of a John le Carré novel.

When John le Carré, or David Cornwell to give him his real-life name, had come to Saigon in 1973 to do research for his book, he took out to lunch three of the English free-lance journalists who were living there at the time, including myself. He took us for Sunday bouillabaisse at the best Corsican restaurant in the city, treating us lavishly to the French wine and pear brandy. At about six o'clock, he asked us what he imagined to be an all-important question: how did we fiddle our expenses? We gaped at him, for none of us had an expense account. We paid our accommodation and meals from the money we earned writing articles, or in my case a book. John le Carré then said he had come without his travellers cheques, filling us all with alarm; but he paid before catching the plane the next morning. It was a very good lunch and I did enjoy what I understood of *The Honourable Schoolboy*.

Four years after Laos fell to the communists, much of the population had crossed the Mekong as refugees to Thailand. Near Nong Khai was a camp with a population of 47,000, or nearly as many as those still left in Vientiane. The camp was really a town of wooden or reed houses. There was a fleet of hundreds of tricycle taxis. There were meat and vegetable markets, photo shops, barbers, chemists and even a dental surgery. It struck me as far more friendly and hopeful than other refugee camps I had seen in Asia, or anywhere in the world for that matter. The inmates were free to go into Nong Khai where many had taken jobs. This part of Thailand is lacking in population, so no one resented the newcomers. The main restriction was that they must not fish in the Mekong. Although the camp included a number of tribespeople from up in the mountains, most were ethnic Laotian and therefore kin to the people of Nong Khai.

Most of the refugees I met had found it easy to get out of Laos. I heard tales of privation and ill-treatment rather than death and atrocity. They all complained of the forced labour and poor conditions. One young man said he was made to join in a 'seminar', which is the latest euphemism for Marxist indoctrination or 're-education'. Another was taken from school to join in building a dam. They said that Laos was bossed by the Vietnamese, who in turn were under the orders of the Russians. An American diplomat here told me: 'Laos is about as much a part of Vietnam as Lithuania is of the Soviet Union'.

Returning to Nong Khai ten years later, I found that most of the refugees had either gone back to Laos or been absorbed in the local community. Although foreigners still have to get a visa in

Bangkok to visit Laos, the locals constantly cross the river in small boats flying the colours of one of the two countries. Australia is providing most of the money to build a bridge here over the Mekong, a waste of money it seems to me, since most of the traffic between the countries is done in contraband. The Laotians float across teak, for like the Burmese they are rapidly cutting down forests. They have also started to process heroin out of their rich opium crop. The Thais in return send all kinds of electronic devices, cigarettes and, above all, cars and lorries, floated across the Mekong on rafts. Since Thai cars all have right-hand drive, they must be conspicuous in a country that drives on the right, but the Laos authorities seem to connive at the illegal imports.

Nong Khai has grown into one of the most delightful towns in Thailand, reminiscent of Vientiane during the old days. There are several very good wooden restaurants perched on stilts over the river bank. It is best to arrive for a drink in the early evening, in order to watch the sunset, upstream and slightly over the Laos side of the river. The fierce Isaan curries of deer, rabbit, frog, snake or catfish need to be tempered with plenty of rice and beer, but I have never had in Thailand the stomach complaints so common in India, Latin America and the Middle East. The Thais are scrupulously clean; they cook meat and fish on the day they bought it; there are almost no flies to spread disease.

The main problem in Nong Khai is finding a place to sleep. The staff at the one Chinese commercial hotel are rude beyond sufferance. The guest house down by the river is loud with American pop music. I eventually found a derelict three-storey hotel in a derelict garden. The elderly maid spoke French and indicated that most of the staff had come from Laos. They certainly have a Laotian work ethic. The reception clerks or porters were almost always asleep behind the desk, except when eating. When I wanted to pick up my room key, I had to step over snoring, prostrate bodies. Three large dogs slept in the foyer, a room furnished with empty and broken cupboards and bookcases. There was no room service, or any service. However the fan in my bedroom worked; I did not get bitten by bugs or mosquitoes; and who could complain about £2 a night?

The King comes to Nong Khai at least twice a year to see the statue of Buddha in Wat Po Chai. This solid gold figure was brought from Vientiane by General Chakri, the future Rama I, whose boat overturned and sank in the Mekong. A miracle raised the figure to the surface, so I was told by a monk, and it is now one of the most prized statues of Buddha in Thailand. The temple is bright, clean and cheerful, like Nong Khai itself.

Two or three miles from town there is one of the most bewildering sights in Thailand, a park full of statues built to express the philosophy of a Brahmin holy man, Luang Pu, who came from Vietnam and Laos after the communist take-over. Most of the figures at Wat Khaek are towering thirty-foot Buddhas, built of brick with a concrete surface. The compound also has a profusion of representations of eight-armed Kali, humans crossed with deer, dogs or tigers, a group showing an elephant chased by dogs, a warrior holding a sub-machine gun, and one man holding a severed head, an image that comes I think from a photograph of the war in Cambodia. The local people and Thais from all over the country love Wat Khaek, which is always full and always turning out fresh grotesques. To the foreigner, it is a useful reminder of how strongly the Thais believe in animal spirits, wizards and demons.

Around Nong Khai and Udon, where I was heading next, there are several important archaeological sites from Thailand's prehistory. As is usual with archaeologists, they cannot agree on what the artefacts mean, or who were the people that made them, so I shall not venture my own interpretation. It does, however, seem there was some sort of civilization here thousands of years before the arrival from China of those we would now call Thais or Laotians.

UDON

After a very delightful stay in Laos, in 1968, I had felt the need to do penance by visiting one of the US Air Force bases in Thailand – at Udon, forty miles south of the Mekong River. This was all part of observing the Vietnam War. Udon impressed itself on my memory as more unpleasant even than South Vietnam. There was no actual danger from enemy action, but the atmosphere of the town was more rowdy and hostile than anything I had experienced. The American servicemen that I met in the bars were drunker and more eager to quarrel than those in the great Vietnamese base of Danang, which was sometimes subjected to rocket attacks. I stayed at what used to be called a Chinese hotel (a

misleading term, for virtually all hotels are Chinese-owned), where
the wall partitions stop short of the ceiling, so that you hear all the
fighting and fornication that goes on next door. At one point
during the night, it sounded as though the drunk American airman
wanted to use a broken bottle against the hotel porters. Udon was
a vile and alarming town after Laos, although that country was at
war.

Udon was a base for the B-52 bombers, which later became one
of the most familiar images of the Vietnam War, like the soldier
using his zippo lighter to burn down a hut, or General Loan
shooting a Viet Cong prisoner, or the naked small girl splashed by
napalm. The B-52s were immense eight-engined propeller planes
which, from a great height, dropped a cascade of bombs, or sometimes anti-personnel weapons, like the flechettes, inch-long steel
darts I had seen stuck in the trees of Hue.

Neither at Udon nor anywhere else have I actually seen a B-52.
At Vientiane, sitting beside the river at nightfall, I saw the crimson,
blinking lights of the B-52s heading north; so close to Udon, they
had not reached top altitude. Later they flew so high that their
victims could not hear or see them. Destruction fell from a quiet
sky. I was never close to a B-52 strike, but even ten or twenty
miles away, they made the earth shudder.

Opinions vary still on whether the B-52 raids helped the United
States in the war. They caused great havoc in the North Vietnamese countryside, but because they were seldom employed
against cities like Hanoi and Haiphong (what military jargon called
the 'population centroids'), they probably took less life than did
the air-raids on Germany in the Second World War. The B-52
raids failed to stop the supply of weapons and ammunition along
the Ho Chi Minh Trail from North Vietnam, through Laos into
South Vietnam. The effect of the raids on Cambodia is a still more
controversial matter, which I discuss elsewhere. The B-52 raids
were, in one respect, most counter-productive. Later historians of
the war conclude that almost all the communist mines and booby
traps were produced from unexploded American shells and bombs,
causing at least 20 per cent of total American casualties. They
constituted a still greater cause of terror because they struck, by
surprise, at the legs and genitals. I can remember staying with US
Marines who were so obsessed they could hardly sleep for fear of
these hidden mines, especially the 'Bouncing Betty', which sprang
from the ground to explode at groin level. It was a terror I shared.

Back in 1968, I was one of those who argued against the B-52 raids and other attempts to win victory through technology. I still think that the B-52 raids were not only savage but ineffectual. So, I believe, was the bombing of cities like Dresden during the Second World War. But we who opposed this bombing should not impugn the courage of those who carried it out. The B-52s were never safe from ground-to-air missiles. Many were shot down over North Vietnam. Pilots and crew who parachuted to safety were made to endure both physical and psychological torture in the prison camps, collectively nicknamed the Hanoi Hilton. Many prisoners never came back.

In Udon, during that brief visit in 1968, I did not meet any bomber crew, but a few years later, beside the pool in the Oriental Hotel, I got into conversation with an American on holiday. On learning that I and the woman with me were British, his face lit up and he asked if we happened to know his favourite restaurant in the world, the Gay Hussar in Greek Street, London. We said that we both had quite recently eaten the cold pike with beetroot, the cauliflower soup, the goose and red cabbage, the paprika chicken and other Hungarian delicacies of the famous proprietor, Victor Sassie. Then he told us he was a B-52 pilot. The Labour party regulars at the Gay Hussar, like Lord Longford, Michael Foot, Roy Hattersley and Tom Driberg, might well have choked on their boar's head pâté if they had known their fellow diner's profession.

When I next came to Udon in 1979, the B-52s had gone, and most Americans with them. The exceptions I met were two of the Air Force men who had chosen to stay on here in retirement; apparently they could get their full pension at an absurdly young age, like forty. Housing and food were cheap, and of course they had married their Isaan girl friends. One of these men was with his wife in the hotel bar where I met them. Without wanting to sound ungallant, I have to report that the sweet, lissom girl that she may have been ten or fifteen years ago, was now a plump and ferocious matron. 'We go home now!' she kept insisting, and when he demurred, marched angrily out to a taxi. After a few more beers, the two Americans told me of the complaints they get, 'Why you drink so much? Why you no get job? Why we no get new automobile?' The boredom of Udon, quite apart from a nagging wife, must have made their retirement miserable.

Today, twenty years or so after my first visit to Udon, I found no relics of the American presence. The new, big hotel where I stayed the first night was crammed with officers of the Thai Army, here on exercise. Some of them were escorted by what I should guess were 'travelling wives', but there were only two bar girls around. Neither spoke English. The next day I moved to a cheap hotel in the Chinese shopping quarter, grandly described as the City Centre. In the street outside, some twenty or thirty young men were doing a dragon dance, with their heads encased in a long, gaudily-painted monster. There was much banging of fireworks. Unfortunately, I have seen these dragon dances so often in movie thrillers about Hong Kong, or San Francisco, that seeing the real thing is a disappointment. Far from adding local colour to Udon, it actually emphasized the prevailing drabness.

After a long and vain search for a second-hand book stall, with English books (such stalls used to be plentiful round US bases), I went to eat at a restaurant near the hotel. The food that sizzled away in the pots and pans had smelled good from the street and I liked the look of the manageress who ushered me to a table. Since few people in this part of Thailand now speak English, I had to order in basic Thai, or by pointing. When I had chosen, the manageress and some of her family gathered to watch me eat. She herself chose with her chopsticks the right combination of rice, fish, duck, duck's liver, greens and chilli or fish sauce. With every mouthful I took, she nodded encouragement and approval. A party of Thais at another table sent me over a bottle of Singha beer. It is odd and heartening to find in a town once teeming with noisy and unloved strangers, that a lone farang like myself is now an object of amiable curiosity.

Also from my visit to Udon in 1968, one conversation sticks in my memory, perhaps because I wrote of it at the time. I was passing a cinema in the evening when one of a group of young men shouted to me in English. Thinking he was a pimp of some kind, I started to move on. Then he asked me where I was from. From England? Not from America? His attitude was more friendly. Then looking at him and his friends, I asked, 'You're not Thais?' No they said, they were Vietnamese. They were not only Vietnamese but communists. 'Ho Chi Minh, Number One!' said the man who had spoken first. He was sitting astride his scooter, and as he became more excited, his leg started to twitch, as so often happens with Vietnamese. 'America, Number Ten Thousand!' he went on, for he had learned the enemy's language. He raged at the B-52 bombers that went from here to attack his homeland. It was like meeting a group of Germans beside one of our bomber bases in Suffolk during the Second World War.

Later I learned that there were 70,000 Vietnamese in the Udon district. They had left their homes after the French defeat in 1954; because of this, they were sometimes known as the Dien Bien Phu refugees after that famous battle. However, this new generation in Thailand contained many communists.

When I came back to Udon in 1979, I found that the Vietnamese were once more in trouble. Communist Vietnam had just conquered communist Cambodia and briefly fought against communist China. Vietnam had also driven out thousands of Chinese, the Boat People, and others who crossed the northern frontier. Thailand was now an ally of China and hostile to Vietnam. Many Vietnamese in the Udon area, the Dien Bien Phu refugees, were anxious or willing at least, to go home. The governments in Bangkok and Hanoi arranged for the repatriation of 30,000 people from round Udon.

Perhaps in order to speed this exodus, the Udon authorities posted an order in June 1979: 'Vietnamese refugees in Udon are permitted to carry out twenty-seven occupations . . .' These included bicycle repairs, vehicle body assembly, laundry, pens and glasses repair work but not the two occupations, of engine and radio repair, in which the Vietnamese had almost a local monopoly.

CHAPTER TEN

Missing in Action

From Udon, I took the bus east to Nakhon Phanom, where the Mekong River now heads south on the slow journey to Vietnam and the sea.

The Vietnamese had a leading role in the international drama that took place in and around the north-east of Thailand after the Second World War. The Vietnamese, the Chinese, the Laotians, the French, the British, the Americans and, of course, the Thais themselves were all engaged in a struggle for power that was no less bloody because it was little publicized at the time. It was here on the banks of the Mekong River that Thailand first got involved in the still continuing struggle for Vietnam and the rest of Indo-China . . . the war that never ended.

The Japanese had moved into French Indo-China after the fall of France in June 1940; it was from Vietnam that they launched the invasion of Malaya, eighteen months later. From the end of 1941 till August 1945, Japan was the occupier of Thailand, from which she launched the assault on Burma. Thailand was also compelled to declare war on Britain and the United States. The Thais, like the French in Indo-China, did not actually fight for Japan but carried on the civil administration. Towards the end of the war, however, resistance movements appeared throughout the region. Chinese communists joined with Britain in fighting the Japanese in Malaya. The Karens and other hill-people started an insurrection in Burma. Thai politicians in exile called for the setting up of a 'Free Thai' resistance which found a response in several regions, especially the north-east.

The majority of the French in Indo-China supported the Vichy government after the fall of their country in June 1940. Those who sympathized with De Gaulle's Free French either kept their silence or made an escape to one of the British or Dutch colonies. After the liberation of France in 1944, virtually all the French who were not actually Fascist, now wanted to share in freedom. The Japanese knew this. In March 1945, they arrested most Frenchmen of military age, leaving their families vulnerable to attack from the indigenous people. The Japanese now tried, rather late in the day, to play on racial, anti-colonial feelings. This policy had met with success in Burma but failed in Malaya and still more the Philippines whose people stayed loyal to the United States. In Indo-China, the Communist party led the largest anti-colonial movement, which came to be known as the Viet Minh, and many years later the Viet Cong. Many of its supporters were nationalists rather than communists, and many afterwards served in the army of South Vietnam but the Viet Minh were led by veteran communists such as Ho Chi Minh and his brilliant army commander, General Giap. In the official histories, published now from Hanoi, it is claimed that the Viet Minh fought all foreign oppressors, the Japanese as well as the French. This is arguable. After the purge of the French in March 1945, the Japanese permitted if not encouraged the Viet Minh to murder French nationals.

Although the Viet Minh were, by definition, a Vietnamese movement, they also were active among the Vietnamese in Laos, Cambodia and Thailand. The Vietnamese have for centuries settled the lands to the west, sometimes as military conquerors, sometimes as farmers, fishermen, artisans and traders, where they compete with the Chinese. They occupied much of northern Cambodia, near to the Thai border, until 1970, when they were massacred and their bodies thrown in the Mekong, to float back to Vietnam.

The Vietnamese were just as prominent in Laos, where their industry and ability gave them the edge on the dreamy Laotians. The French loathed the Vietnamese as much as they liked the Laotians, but came to depend on their talent. In most of the riverside towns of Laos, the Vietnamese were the middle class and sometimes formed a majority. The Vietnamese had for centuries crossed the Mekong to trade and settle in Thailand.

As the Japanese went on the retreat in Burma, New Guinea, the Philippines and the smaller Pacific islands, they paid little attention to Thailand and French Indo-China, far from the battle lines. This gave freedom of action to local guerrilla groups like the Free Thai, the Free Lao and the Viet Minh. There was also a Chinese army moving south, in theory loyal to Chiang Kai-shek, but actually run by private war lords. The American OSS officers wanted to use this army not only against the Japanese but also against the French, who were sending agents in to try and reclaim their former colonies. The British sent officers into Thailand, and after Japan's surrender, they sent a force into South Vietnam. Although Britain now had a Labour government, she was helping the French and the Dutch to regain their former colonies. There were thus two rival coalitions here by the Mekong River. On the one side were the British, French and Thais; on the other, the Chinese, Viet Minh and Americans. In view of what followed, it was an odd alignment.

In mid September 1945, the Allies 'at top level' divided the spheres of influence in French Indo-China. Everything south of the sixteenth parallel came under the Southeast Asia Command of Lord Louis Mountbatten, who handed over to French troops the job of disarming the Japanese and restoring law and order. North of the sixteenth parallel, including the north and centre of Laos and Vietnam, the same duty fell to the Chinese Army. The decision alarmed the French, who feared that the Chinese would help the Americans throw them out of their colonies. The Thais feared that China wanted to regain her ancient sovereignty, helped by the large Chinese minority in Bangkok. Thailand's declaration of war against Britain and the United States had placed her, nominally, in the same class as Germany, Italy and Japan.

When the Chinese Army reached Vientiane, their first action only increased such anxieties. They invited all the French officers to a party where they were held at gunpoint, robbed of their weapons, equipment, money and even watches, then thrown out of the country. The Chinese had the delighted support of the American OSS and the Viet Minh, who started to ambush French and British officers. Outside Vientiane, the Viet Minh murdered dozens of French civilians, including women and children.

The struggle along the Mekong River, which went on till March 1946, was seen at its most bizarre round Nakhon Phanom which faces Thakhek in Laos. Here, a tiny detachment of Britain's Special Operations Executive (SOE) supported the French against the Viet Minh in a war that involved the betrayal of allies, murder, kidnap and naval engagements on the river. The British commanding officer, Peter Kemp, has not only written a book on his adventures but he has come back over the years, on many visits to Thailand, Laos and Vietnam, where I first met him in 1973. Few men have had longer experience of the Indo-China War, or seen such changes of fortune and friendship.

Another British officer, David Smiley, had dropped into north-east Thailand in May 1945, making contact with some of the Free Thai guerrillas. After three weeks, he became the victim of one of the SOE's James Bond-like devices, a self-igniting briefcase which plastered him with five pounds of blazing thermite. After a week in agony, with a hole in one arm full of maggots, Smiley was flown to Calcutta where he met Kemp, who had served with him for a year in the mountains of Albania. In August, Smiley returned to Thailand, followed by Kemp who landed at Sakon Nakhon, where he met 'Pluto', the code name given to Tiang Sirikand, the Free Thai leader and north-east politician. He was a close friend of the regent Pridi Panomyong and, like Pridi, was later called a communist. However, Kemp considers the accusation false, and having already fought three years in Spain on the Franco side, he was not a man to be taken in by communists disguising themselves as nationalists. Although Pluto was allied with Laotians over the river, he loathed the Viet Minh. According to Smiley, Pluto's guerrillas shot any Vietnamese they caught, suspecting them, often with good reason, of spying for the Japanese. At Nakhon Phanom, where Kemp made his headquarters, there was and still is a separate Vietnamese quarter. The Vietnamese outnumbered the Laotians in Thakhek, over the river.

Nakhon Phanom in 1945 consisted of one muddy high street and one hotel and it has now expanded into a town of four paved main streets and about as many hotels. The one where I stayed had prospered during the Vietnam War, when American airmen flew from the Royal Thai Air Force base, which they called NKP. The words 'NKP 1969' are visible in the deep end of the hotel swimming pool. The Americans used this base not for B-52 bombers but for rescue and reconnaissance operations, also as a listening post for radio and electronic sensor devices. Visitors to Nakhon Phanom claim that the foodstalls sold fried bananas wrapped in discarded computer print-outs of traffic along the Ho Chi Minh Trail. The Americans have vanished, though I did meet a local man who now lives in the state of Virginia, running a restaurant with his family. He called me over to join him where he was entertaining his friends with beer and Mekong whisky. He talked of the States but I noticed he did not boast of his wealth and success. He earned a living but there was too much competition from the Koreans. He seldom went into Washington DC: 'Too many blacks.'

The main attraction, if not the only attraction of Nakhon Phanom, is walking down to the bank of the Mekong River, which here runs north to south. At dawn, you can watch the first pale yellow or rose on the skyline clearing the mist from the forest and from the knobbly, mis-shapen foothills of the Annamite Chain. The boom of temple gongs and the metal twangling of loudspeaker music sounds from over the river, which at this hour has a milk chocolate colour. Behind me, a party of monks in saffron robes proceed in a line with their tin bowls, begging for rice and vegetables. Their shaven heads and sullen expressions give them the look of convicts rather than of holy men; the smile of the Buddha is not always seen among his disciples. These monks probably come from the ramshackle wat through which I passed on my way to the river.

When the sun comes up, boats start to cross from either side of the river, heading upstream to allow for the pull of the current. They are really wooden canoes with an outboard motor. At the stern they fly the national flag, either the marzipan red, white and blue of Thailand, or that of Communist Laos which still seems to show a pagoda as well as a star. Customs and immigration are both at the top of the bank, which must be at river level during the summer spate. Now the passengers have to climb up the steps from the jetty. There are no formalities, no inspection of papers; little sign of a frontier, let alone of a frontier between two rival ideologies.

As the sun climbs to midday, the colours are drained from the river and from the far shore, until, in the late afternoon, the darkness begins to edge forward from the horizon, on to the forests and the stumps of hills, as the sky changes from green and lilac to indigo and purple. Reason may tell you that Thakhek, over in Laos, is even more sleepy and dull than Nakhon Phanom; but at dusk or at dawn, it becomes a place of mystery and danger.

It was Peter Kemp's job, when he got to Nakhon Phanom, to find out what was happening on the other shore. He heard there were French people interned by the Japanese in Thakhek; that French and Laotian guerrillas were out in the jungle, seriously short of food, medicine and money; that armed Viet Minh controlled much of the interior. Japan had now surrendered, so Kemp was impatient to cross the river and take over authority for Thakhek. The Thai governor of Nakhon Phanom implored him not to do so, his eyes filling with tears. The reason for this was explained to Kemp by a US missionary who had lived in this region:

> These people are terribly afraid for their independence. They feel they're in bad with the Allies – even though it wasn't their fault they were sold out to the Nips. They are responsible for your safety and they think that if at this critical time something should happen to you, or to any British officer in Thailand, they would lose their independence.

Two days after getting to Nakhon Phanom, Kemp saw a Dakota flying low over the other side of the river. Later he heard that the plane had dropped two French officers, Lieutenant François Klotz, an Alsatian ex-Maquis fighter, and Lieutenant Edith Fournier, his wireless operator. The new arrivals got in touch and came to stay in Nakhon Phanom before returning to Laos to rescue their own civilians there. The Viet Minh were murdering French people all over Indo-China and now the defeated Japanese were proving as dangerous as they had been in victory. One of the drunk and mutinous Japanese at Ubon, down river, actually bit his colonel during a brawl in a whorehouse.

When Kemp, Smiley, the Thai province governor and Lieutenant Klotz arrived at Thakhek on 7 September, they found the French community close to despair. Eighteen women and fourteen children were crowded into a convent under the leadership of a woman whose husband, the Resident, had had his head cut off in March. The other women begged for news of their husbands, most of whom were probably dead. They were terrified of the Viet Minh guards who wanted to keep them as hostages.

Only three Frenchmen had come through the massacre. One, the electrician attached to the power station, had rashly waved to the plane that brought Klotz and Fournier. A Vietnamese had reported him to the Japanese who killed his wife and child as he fled to the jungle. After two days, he begged for help from a Vietnamese charcoal burner who hacked him about the arms with a machete, then turned him in to the Japanese who would have killed him but for a warning from Kemp. The French Resident's widow told the visitors: 'I think, Gentlemen, you have only just arrived in time. The Annamite [Vietnamese] guards who have replaced the Japanese have become extremely menacing. They show us their knives and make gestures of cutting our throats.'

Both the Viet Minh and the Japanese refused to hand over their captives, so Kemp and Klotz remained in Laos to show the Allied presence.

Driving north, they met convoys of trucks carrying Viet Minh to Thakhek. They rescued a French girl who had been shot in the gut by a drunken Japanese guard. Approaching Boneng, about thirty miles north of Thakhek, they found a battle in progress between a party of French and Laotian troops besieged in the village school and 150 Viet Minh, with four machine guns. A British uniform still had the power to stop the fighting. A few days later, the British succeeded in getting the French civilians over the river to Nakhon Phanom.

Here, on the border of Thailand and Laos, as in Saigon and all South Vietnam, the British supported the re-instatement of French rule. Here, as in North Vietnam, the Americans backed the communist Viet Minh. Already the OSS had virtually handed power in Hanoi to Ho Chi Minh. In mid-September, a party of ten OSS agents, under a Major Banks, arrived without warning at Nong Khai, in spite of the fact that Thailand belonged to the British sphere of influence. Banks went over to Vientiane, the Laos capital, and told the French in no uncertain fashion to 'cease their aggression' against the Viet Minh and the Pathet Lao. The British officer in Nong Khai thought it a good joke to get rid of the OSS by sicking them on to Kemp at Nakhon Phanom. The joke was to turn very sour.

After a trip to Laos, Kemp got back to Nakhon Phanom to find Banks already installed: 'He had taken it upon himself to scare my French refugees out of their lives by telling them that they were going to be returned to Thakhek.' Over in Thakhek, Banks promised the Viet Minh that he would put an end to 'French aggression'; also that Chinese troops would arrive to disarm the French and take over administration until the establishment of a 'national and democratic government' in Indo-China. The French commander in Thakhek, Lieutenant François Tavernier, later complained to Kemp: 'He spoke to me as I would not dream of speaking to a servant – in front of my own soldiers and the Annamites, all of whom understand French. He called me a pirate . . .'

The attitude of the OSS astonished the French as much as the British. As Kemp now recalls:

Like ourselves, the French had been accustomed to thinking of the

Americans not only as allies but friends; it never occurred to any of us simple officers that the most powerful country in the free world would deliberately embark upon a policy of weakening her allies to the sole advantage of her most dangerous enemy. We have learned a lot since, but in those days it all seemed very strange.

That is British understatement. The attitude of the Americans to their French and British allies was soon to result in murder. One day in September, Kemp and Klotz decided to cross the Mekong to take medicine to the French. Major Banks had instructed Klotz not to go but the Frenchman, a veteran of the Maquis, answered: 'I can certainly go to Thakhek if I wish. I am a French officer and Thakhek belongs to France.' He boarded the yacht with Kemp and one of the OSS men, Lieutenant Reese. At Thakhek they jumped ashore and climbed the bank to the road where they heard a high-pitched command and saw a platoon of Viet Minh, led by a certain Lieutenant Tu, holding a drawn revolver. Tu ordered his men to train their guns on the visitors, then uttered his ultimatum: 'The British and American officers may go free. They are our allies. The Frenchman is under arrest and will come with us. The French declared war on us yesterday in Saigon.' Kemp protested, but the American officer, Reese, had already passed through the ranks of the Vietnamese and was leaning against a house across the road. 'I guess we're neutral,' he said, refusing to become involved.

With or without the support of Reese, Kemp determined to get Klotz back to safety. 'Monsieur Tu,' he said, addressing the Viet Minh commander, 'since our presence here is unwelcome to you, my friend and I are returning to Siam.' He put an arm around Klotz and together they turned to go to the ramp leading down to the boat.

'No!' screamed Tu, 'you may go but he stays here.' Kemp heard the rattle of rifle bolts, and orders shouted in Vietnamese. Only a few yards lay between them and the launch under its dirty canvas awning. The Vietnamese fired a burst of shots, apparently in the air. Kemp was now walking almost behind Klotz to give him maximum protection. He heard another burst of shots, then 'a figure ran up on my left, thrust his rifle under my arm into Klotz's back, fired once and disappeared.' Klotz staggered and let out a terrible, despairing gasp, '"Oh Peter!" he whispered, "Oh, Peter!"' He was dead by the time he was in the boat.

Kemp returned to Nakhon Phanom tortured by grief and

remorse: 'All the way across I sat watching the poor dead face of this gallant, warm-hearted young man who in such a short time had become so close a friend.' It was monstrous that Klotz should have fought through the war to be shot in the back when it was over. Kemp brooded on whether he should not have trusted Klotz's instinct to draw pistols and shoot at the first Vietnamese raising a rifle. Even today, forty-five years later, Kemp cannot forget the murder of Klotz.

Back in Nakhon Phanom, Kemp had to break the news to Edith Fournier the wireless operator. As the tears rolled down her cheeks, she muttered '*C'est la deuxième fois, mon Dieu, c'est la deuxième fois!*' On her last mission in occupied France, her chief had been grabbed by the Gestapo. Later, Kemp asked Edith to help break the news to the French refugees and nuns at the hospital. The crowd stared anxiously at Kemp's grim face and blood-stained shirt, then broke into sobs when he told them what had occurred. Sorrow gave way to anger on hearing about the 'neutrality' of Lieutenant Reese.

All that night, Kemp, Edith and some of the French kept vigil over the corpse that lay on a camp bed, dressed in a clean uniform. He was buried the next day in the Roman Catholic cemetery on the north side of Nakhon Phanom. To the surprise and indignation of most of the mourners, the OSS officer, Lieutenant Reese, came to salute the grave. He was not wanting in manners and courage; perhaps he disliked the orders he had obeyed.

The cemetery was in the suburb occupied by the Vietnamese, who hated Klotz even in death. Time and again in the next few months they desecrated the grave by stealing the cross. This dishonour, coming after the murder, expressed the malignant hatred felt by the Vietnamese for the French in Indo-China, a feeling not shared by the Laotians and Cambodians. They, in fact, tended to side with the French against the Vietnamese.

The savagery of the Viet Minh in 1945 helps to explain if not excuse the later cruelty of the French towards the Vietnamese. Even Peter Kemp, who later came to admire the South Vietnamese in their hour of adversity, detested the Viet Minh he had met in 1945. After Klotz's funeral, Kemp walked back by the Mekong: 'Gazing at those hateful hills above Thakhek, which only yesterday I had thought so beautiful, I felt Edith's tight grip on my arm. "*Nous le vengerons,*" she whispered fiercely, "*nous le vengerons.*"'

Defeating the Viet Minh was now a priority for the British in Thailand. The SEAC command was pressing for the removal of

Banks and his OSS team who had no right to be acting in Thailand. Paradoxically, it was the Viet Minh who brought about a change in the OSS when they shot up their Saigon headquarters, killing the man in charge, Colonel Dewey. In October, Banks and his party left Nakhon Phanom and Kemp was free to get on with supplying arms to the French in Laos who were now operating virtually as guerrillas.

For tactical and political reasons, all supplies had to be dropped in Thailand, then ferried over the Mekong by canoe, at night. On his first effort at gun-running, Kemp and his little flotilla were ambushed by the Viet Minh on one of the islands, losing three men. He later acquired a motor *pirogue*, a sturdy and swift craft with a Bren gun mounted in the bows. For the rest of 1945, Kemp was largely engaged in gun-running, with frequent naval engagements along the river.

The Viet Minh put a price on Kemp's head, a sum that many attempted to win in Thailand as well as Laos. He was several times ambushed on this side of the river. He was shot at one evening at dinner, causing him to spill Indo-China rum on his newly washed, khaki drill slacks. The rather left-wing government in Bangkok was sabotaging his efforts to help the French. Laotian soldiers loyal to France, who came to Nakhon Phanom to visit friends or relations, frequently vanished, to turn up later without a head.

On a visit to Ubon, Kemp was himself coshed and kidnapped by people hoping to get the head money or ransom; but he escaped. Ever since the death of Klotz, he had dreamed of getting revenge on the Viet Minh Lieutenant Tu and his superior Le Hoq Minh. Both made frequent visits to Nakhon Phanom. If he could catch them, Kemp intended to hand them over to the French or, if necessary, kill them and throw the bodies into the Mekong. He got tentative approval from the British in Bangkok. At last Kemp got good information that Le Hoq Minh was to pass through Nakhon Phanom next evening. He sent a 'most urgent' signal to Bangkok asking permission to go ahead with the operation but got the disappointing reply in one word of cable language: UNOFFBUMP.

By the end of 1945, Kemp was in charge of 500 miles of the Thai frontier with French Indo-China. Much of his time was spent in supplying the French, who got almost no help from their own command in Saigon. On 19 October, the French got their first reinforcements; sixty-four parachutists dropped at Nakhon Phanom, making their way to Laos by canoe. By the time the

British missions left Thailand, late in January 1946, the French were on the offensive in Laos and two months later took possession of Thakhek.

Thanks to the British troops in Saigon and the efforts of men such as Kemp in Thailand, the French got back most of their Indo-China possessions except northern Vietnam. Here the communists fought the return of the French and kept up resistance until their decisive victory at Dien Bien Phu in 1954. Then, for the next twenty or thirty years, the communist Vietnamese struggled to win back and hold the south of their country, Laos and still perhaps, Cambodia. For this is the war that never ended.

From Nakhon Phanom, Kemp was despatched to Bali to keep the peace in that most enchanting island. This was his last assignment in ten years of fighting in Spain, France, Albania and Poland, where he had spent a month in a KGB prison.

In a second career as a journalist, Kemp continued to visit countries at war, such as Hungary in 1956, the Congo, Rhodesia and Nicaragua, where he and I spent a hilarious week observing the Sandinistas and their gullible foreign admirers. Peter has also been back on long visits to Thailand, Laos and Vietnam, where I first met him.

Sitting on one of the park benches, overlooking the Mekong River, I brooded on the events that occurred here and in Thakhek, forty-five years ago; they were some of the first shots fired in the Indo-China tragedy. Laos, as far as we know, is once more run by the Vietnamese communists. Many Laotians from there have fled to this side of the river. The Vietnamese on this side of the river are no longer loud for the communists; they no longer wear their distinctive conical hats or *ao dai* dress and pantaloons. The Vietnamese are still as disliked by the Thais as they are by the Laotians and the Cambodians.

That the French were enabled to get back their Indo-China colonies by a British Labour government is explained by Peter Kemp: 'British policy was made by Ernie Bevin, who was quite simply the best Foreign Secretary that this country has had in my lifetime.' It is less easy for Kemp or anyone else to understand why in 1945 the United States, through the OSS, the forerunner of the CIA, was helping to power the very people who two decades later would prove her deadliest enemies. Had communists infiltrated the intelligence services of the United States, as Senator Joe McCarthy was later to claim? Or were the Americans still naïve concerning the postwar ambitions of Joseph Stalin?

*

Brooding about the Americans here in 1945, I came back to the still odder Americans who continue to come to Nakhon Phanom, forty-five years later. These are the searchers for MIA, the Missing in Action in Vietnam.

The searchers believe, with countless millions in the United States, that Communist Vietnam is still holding as prisoners more than two thousand Americans listed as missing two decades ago. They also believe that the MIA can be found and rescued from where they are slaving, somewhere just over the borders of Communist Indo-China.

The searchers have therefore made their base in Thailand and concentrated attention on places like Nakhon Phanom, where you can actually see over the border. Why the Vietnamese would want to hold American prisoners not only in Laos but in a frontier town, is not a question that worries the searchers. They have released into the Mekong plastic bags full of dollars, to float over to Thakhek with printed offers of up to a million dollars for news of any Americans living in Laos. Some searchers have actually crossed into Laos, where they were caught and gaoled, but none heard news of the MIA.

The obsession with MIAs, which started during the war, grew still more powerful after the first film about Rambo, the muscle-bound hero who leads an expedition from Thailand to rescue Americans held in Communist Indo-China. Belief in the MIA increased when Iran took American hostages. It fostered the notion that Vietnam too was holding the MIA as hostages. The belief has survived, though Vietnam still has not demanded a ransom. There is now a plaque to the MIA on the Vietnam War memorial in Washington DC. President Reagan gave his implied assent to belief in the MIA, suggesting them as a reason for the United States's refusal to make peace with Hanoi. It is almost as though the Americans need a belief in the MIA to ease their guilt and bewilderment over what happened during the Vietnam War.

Belief in the MIA goes with hatred of Vietnam, which adds to its popularity here in Thailand. The first Rambo film broke all box office records here. It was even more popular than *The Deer Hunter*, another film showing the Vietnamese as sadistic monsters.

CHAPTER ELEVEN

The Refugees

Some people in Bangkok believe that the north-east is a trackless wasteland where people live hundreds of miles from public transport. In fact, you can now get around on luxury buses equipped with air-conditioning, a toilet, a hostess and all too often a video. The roads are narrow by national standards and seem narrower still because of the habit of bus drivers in north-east Thailand of greeting each other as they pass by swerving inwards and practically brushing sides. Water buffaloes also present a hazard; they are too lazy or proud to look both ways before crossing the road.

Heading south into Ubon province, I found it harder than usual to take much interest in the drab, monotonous countryside of the north-east. It is tempting to reason that the lives of the north-east peasants must be depressing, just as you do when you look from a train passing through bleak industrial northern England. To a foreigner, as to a Bangkok sophisticate, north-east Thailand is strange and forbidding. Some of those who grew up there, however, look on it as a region of beauty and wonder.

The proof of this is a quite enchanting novel by Kampoon Boontawee, *A Child of the North-east*, now translated by Susan Fulop Kepner. The story covers a year in the life of a boy of about eight, named Koon, during the economic depression of the 1930s, when north-east Thailand suffered outstandingly. It is a genre of fictionalized autobiography that often, in England, leads to self-pity and facile political rant. But *A Child of the North-east* is overwhelmingly joyful, tender and funny, without ever straying to sentimentality. I have seldom read such a cheerful and convincing account of childhood.

This book and the introduction by Mrs Kepner also taught me much about life in Isaan, including the fact that this name can be translated as Siva, the Hindu regent of the north-eastern quadrant of the world. We learn, as Koon learns, the knack of survival in an unfriendly countryside. We learn about hunting the local exotic game. We learn how to set the dogs on a mongoose; how to snare a chameleon with a noose, or bring it down with a blow-pipe; how to pluck the cicada on the wing, and where to net quails. Frog hunting sounds easy. You first catch one of the giant bull-frogs, whereupon all the females hop to the sound of its croaking.

At the end of a year of drought, all the village goes off in a caravan to a distant river, there to catch fish to barter for rice and meat. Koon learns how to grope in the mud for catfish without getting spiked by the fins. He learns to net for the more valuable white fish. He and his friend are entertained to a feast by a village near the fishing ground, for the book makes clear that the Isaan people try to live in harmony with each other, as with nature. On the way home, their wagons laden with fish, the villagers greet the long-awaited rain, the arrival of which brings the book to its joyful conclusion.

The translator says in her introduction:

> An altruistic view of life permeates *A Child of the North-east* . . . Isaan villagers believe that the poor man, the poor family, and even the poor village are the responsibility of the relatively comfortable man, family and village . . . To North-easterners, virtue is synonymous with honesty, kindness, hospitality, cheerfulness, industry, generosity and courage.

Does this all sound a bit too good to be true? Peasants in other parts of the East, or Europe for that matter, have not always shown such care for their fellows but the Isaan people have certain advantages. The climate is hostile but no more so than it is to the peasants of Bengal, northern Vietnam, or those who drowned by hundreds of thousands in China. Moreover, north-east Thailand has not suffered the twin scourges of Asia: the money-lender and rack-renting landlord. Because Thailand escaped colonization it also escaped the high taxation imposed by the French, British and Dutch to force the people into a wage economy. The Isaan land may be poor but it does belong to the farmers.

Nature sometimes appears harsh but should not be blamed for misfortune. When Koon, during the drought at the start of the book, says that he hates the sky, his schoolmaster, an old monk, canes him and makes him repeat: 'From this day on I will never

blame the sky because the sky never punished anybody.' The
monk reminds him of this at the end of the book, at a feast in the
wat after the rains have come. Now all are happy. A singer has
come, so exquisite that the men shout: 'Girl you are so beautiful
... You can shit in my field any time!' Koon asks why they say
this. Because if a girl that beautiful shits in a field, just think what
the rice will be like.

This was the knowledge that Koon had won:

> He knew that there would be other years when the sun would blaze
> in a cloudless sky, and when the rain would not fall, other years
> when the earth would crack, and rice grow low in the silos. He
> knew, too, that he would meet those years, and he would survive,
> because he was a child of the north-east. He had descended from a
> thousand ancestors who had met such years, and survived, and
> who had never blamed the sky.

These days there are many who blame, if not the sky, what man
has done to the sky by wrecking the ozone layer and causing the
'Greenhouse Effect' which threatens to raise still further the heat
in north-east Thailand. The sky never punished anyone; but have
we not punished the sky?

The province town of Ubon is yet another former US air base
that prospers in the American absence. Like all the towns I have
seen in the north-east, Ubon is clean, smart, progressive and dull.
It could be anywhere in an opulent, capitalistic Asian country,
such as Japan, South Korea, Taiwan or Malaysia. Fifty years ago,
travellers used to say of a new city, built for the age of the automobile, that 'it could be anywhere in the Midwest'. The United
States no longer has a monopoly on the motor-car civilization.
American cities now have a decrepit appearance, racked by the
problems of crime, drugs and racial hatred. It is here in East Asia
that capitalism is still on the up-and-up, confident in itself and the
future.

As in America, fifty years ago, the smart hotels are the meeting
places for businessmen and politicians, to which should be added
here in Thailand the military and police. My hotel on the outskirts
of town was typical of its genre, with a vast, glittering lobby, a
reception desk the size of the Shanghai Long Bar, a shopping mall,
a massage parlour with coloured lights, an almost Olympic swimming pool and a restaurant-cum-nightclub, plunged in darkness,
so that I could not see to avoid eating chilli and other violent

spices. It was horribly loud and garish, but since the cost of a room was £10 a night, I certainly did not complain.

During this two-day visit, I saw only one other farang, an Australian army officer, who had been visiting local units. Since Ubon is right in the forward line of defence against Communist Indo-China, I said that it must be a favoured posting for officers wanting to make a career. Apparently not. He said that ambitious young officers wanted to stay in Bangkok. That too, makes sense. Power rests in Bangkok, as many soldiers have proved with successful *coups d'état*. However, the army is influential all over Thailand, as I had witnessed when I was last in Ubon in July 1979.

The occasion for this was a visit by HRH Princess Anne, the President of Save the Children Fund, to a nearby refugee camp. It was just at the height of world concern over the plight of refugees from Indo-China. The Boat People were still fleeing from Vietnam and often finding no haven. The Vietnamese invasion and conquest of Cambodia had shown to the TV cameras of the world the horror done by the Khmer Rouge. Children were starving to death inside Cambodia. The hundreds of thousands of Khmers who had now escaped into Thailand were scarcely in better condition. The Thai government, fearful that Vietnam was trying to swamp the country with refugees, was now forcing some of these wretched people back into Cambodia, often over the minefields. Although most of the Cambodian refugees were living in camps near Aranyaprathet, due east of Bangkok, the Thai authorities had been loading them into lorries and shoving them over the border just south of Ubon. The visit by Princess Anne was therefore a major news event. I was in Bangkok at the time, and caught the overnight train to Ubon.

The Princess Royal's visit was like a military exercise. The road to the airport was blocked more than an hour before her arrival and when I had talked my way past the guards, I saw dozens of heavily armed, steel-helmeted soldiers crouched in menacing postures around the runway. This was the old American bomber base, and its café still had a number of paperbacks from that epoch, including Arthur M. Schlesinger Junior's *The Bitter Heritage: Vietnam and American Democracy 1941–1968*. I started to read a chapter contesting President Johnson's theory that North Vietnam was simply the puppet of Communist China. Full marks to Schlesinger as a prophet: Communist China and Communist Vietnam had gone to war that year, 1979. Halfway through the chapter, I heard somebody say that the Princess's plane was about to land, so I went out to the runway through the departure room, which was decorated with photographs of planes that had crashed on this airport.

No misadventure attended the Royal Andover bringing the Princess, who soon appeared on the steps wearing a khaki trouser suit of austere military cut. She was accompanied by her husband Mark Phillips, the British ambassador, some of his staff, the military, naval and air attachés, and also the Bangkok head of Save the Children Fund. This gentleman too was an ex-Major who cut an impressive figure in blue shirt, pink face and lime-green hair. The Princess, the diplomats, the attachés and the Major were introduced to the various Thai generals and colonels on the tarmac, then got into some of the leading cars of a heavily armed procession of fifteen vehicles. I have never seen such a cavalcade even for the Queen herself, nor one so well protected. The roads wherever we went had been cleared of traffic, and armed sentries guarded the crossings with all side roads.

Since Indo-China was much in the news, the Princess came with a dozen or so reporters, two top Fleet Street photographers and TV crews from the two main companies. The Princess met the two doctors and three nurses from Save the Children Fund; she saw some of the children and asked some pertinent questions about the camp. It was left to the Press to ask some impertinent questions, like how many refugees were murdered each month by the guards. The answer was two or three. One of the Save the Children Fund doctors, who had shown the Princess round the camp in the morning, was privileged to have drinks with her but not invited to sit at her luncheon table, his seat having been taken by one of the service attachés, who probably got on better with the hosts, the Thai Army.

What was Save the Children Fund actually doing in Thailand? This question was put by the *Guardian*'s reporter to the Major who had spent ten minutes challenging her to provide some proof that she had been a correspondent here for twelve months. When she finally convinced him, the Major said: 'If you have been that long in Thailand, you should know what Save the Children Fund does here.' End of interview. When we got to the refugee camp, we found we had not known many things concerning Save the Children Fund. We found out, for instance, that all the food, housing and medicine they gave the children was actually paid for by the

United Nations. They did offer the children tinned baby food paid for by an English manufacturer but these concoctions caused the children tummy upsets; the doctors badly needed the soya bean milk which these children relish.

Save the Children Fund paid the salaries of the five Europeans employed at the camp. Excellent though this work may have been, it hardly seemed to justify the expense of Princess Anne and her entourage coming to north-east Thailand, or putting the province into a state of armed alert. The seventy refugees who helped the five Europeans had done so free in the hope of getting resettlement in the West. But when they found there was no such reward, most of them drifted away to paid jobs in the camp or in town.

The British public, seeing the TV film of the Princess and these children, naturally thought that these refugees were in the same plight as the Boat People from Vietnam, or the starving Cambodians. This was not so. Almost all the refugees at this camp were from Laos. The Thais were most unlikely to send them back. They had suffered no danger in escaping. The only sacrifice they had made was paying some £40 to bribe the Thai army to 'intercept' them on reaching this side of the Mekong. All the Laotians here, like those I had seen in Nong Khai, would soon assimilate in Isaan society.

While the Thai Army accepted Laotians, at a price, it was busy sending back the Cambodian refugees at gunpoint. This was happening sixty miles south of the camp which Princess Anne visited.

The new Vietnamese rulers of Cambodia accused the Thais of having beaten and stoned the refugees in order to drive them back over the border. Correspondents and those working for refugee organizations had no doubt the Cambodians went back unwillingly and in terror of all the dangers they faced: the murderous Khmer Rouge troops, starvation, disease and worst of all landmines. It appears that most of the refugees who were pushed through what the Press called 'safe exits', were in fact despatched into a minefield. Two of these unfortunates who survived and then managed to reach Thailand a second time, reported that people were dying at a rate of two hundred a day, not sixty miles from the place where Princess Anne was entertained by the Thai Army. The visit by Princess Anne was used by Thailand to demonstrate that the British supported its policy to the refugees and that was the object of the exercise at Ubon.

When Princess Anne, Captain Mark Phillips, the ambassador

and his attachés and the Major had gone, I went to see the Roman Catholic Bishop of Ubon, a Thai who expressed real concern for the refugees sent back to Cambodia. He asked me not to publish what he and his priests had been doing, which was sending food and medicine through the minefields. The Catholic Church was not as keen as the British charities to win publicity from the Press and TV. Listening to the Bishop was like rinsing the mouth of a bad taste.

CHAPTER TWELVE

On the Edge of the Killing Fields

Few of the millions of foreign tourists in Thailand come to Aranya-prathet on the Cambodian border, known to the world for its refugees from the 'Killing Fields'. Considering all the horrors that have gone on here, it was odd to find that the border post is now a tourist attraction for Thais. For the ten-minute trip from the town out to the frontier, I hired one of the elongated motor tricycle taxis. It is a local model, a stretch tuk-tuk. The road went past neat wooden farmhouses, a Buddhist temple, a football field and the bungalows of one of the town hotels. The guests sometimes complain of the noise of artillery fire at night, which is hardly surprising, given the fact that the region is home to three Cam-bodian exile armies, including the Communist party, or Khmer Rouge.

We pulled up in front of the sentry box beside a barrier over the road. On one side, the thoughtful Thai Army has built a roofed wooden gazebo, with benches for tourists who wanted to sit in the shade. On the other side of the road, a lady keeps a stall from which you can buy such Cambodian curios as a chess set or a walking-stick with a handle shaped like a sea horse. Some of the Thai women tourists started to chat and flirt with the soldiers manning the sentry box who, to my surprise, lifted the bar and let us approach the thirty yards to the frontier. This is a row of sandbagged bunkers, each equipped with a heavy or light machine gun pointing towards the Cambodian lines, which are fifty yards away across no-man's-land. Some of the troops were manning the guns but most were talking to tourists, especially the women, while one man strolled into no-man's-land to chat with his Khmer opposite number.

Behind the bunkers, the soldiers have planted rows of ornamental trees, and several cacti, each of them ringed with a circle of white-painted stones. There was yet another gazebo here in this forward position which reminded me of the seats and viewing platforms sometimes provided on hilltops, waterfalls and other proven beauty spots. Beside one of the bunkers I noticed part of the railway line which once connected Bangkok with Phnom Penh.

The sound of a few shots brought to mind that we were, after all, on the edge of the Killing Fields. There are still hundreds of thousands of refugees living beside this border. And still the horrors continue. All warring parties during the last twenty years have sown Cambodia with as many as three million landmines, most of them plastic and almost impossible to detect. A few miles south of here at the time of my visit, the Khmer Rouge were clearing a site for a camp on the other side of the border and losing dozens of killed or maimed. A British nurse in Aranyaprathet told me that some of the amputees had gone for a week without treatment before reaching the hospital where she works. The smiling Thai troops who had invited us up to the line, are not so hospitable to the refuges from communism. Only that month, the authorities sent back to Vietnam a party of eight, including a woman and a monk, who had tramped most of the way here from Saigon.

The international refugee organizations continue to do good work; but it cannot be said that Aranyaprathet is a hardship posting. A clean, friendly and prosperous town, with many old wooden buildings, it offers some of the best food in Thailand. The foreign relief workers congregate in the Kim-Kim café, which offers a range of twenty-seven brands of coffee, and almost as many of ice cream. At the restaurant Lao Gim Nguen, I started my meal with a bottle of export Guinness and three large oysters at the equivalent of 30 p each. The manager, Mr Nguen, has imported for sale a large number of old Cambodian vases and jugs, as well as stags' antlers. These he grafts on to the cast metal stags' heads which he makes at home and hangs on the restaurant walls. The row of vases, the metal animal heads and the sexy pictures make for a pleasantly weird atmosphere.

Because there are no foreign tourists, the nightclubs are free of bar girls and amplified rock music. Instead there are plaintive love songs similar to the ones I heard in Cambodia in the 1960s, under the happy rule of Prince Norodom Sihanouk.

Some of the foreign aid workers disapprove of the good life here, which affronts their puritan conscience. They accuse the Thais of exploiting the refugees and of hoping to make a profit from trade with Cambodia. They cling to the ancient fallacy that the rich only prosper at the expense of the poor. But the industry and prosperity of the Aranyaprathet merchants helps the Cambodians, here and in their own country. When I went down to Trat province, in the extreme south-east, I found that the Thais were openly shipping goods to the southern ports of Cambodia: cars, videos, brandy. Even the Khmer Rouge have moved into the trade in precious stones which are found in Trat and still more at Chanthaburi, a violent and nasty town.

This wheeler-dealing and trade may offend socialist principles but it certainly does no harm to the refugees. Because the Thais are themselves well off, they do not steal the food and medicines which arrive for the refugees, as happens in the Sudan or Ethiopia. The refugees benefit most from competition and therefore low prices. And for all its commercialism, Aranyaprathet is a town that respects the Thai belief in the family, the Buddhist religion and the King. It is the only place I have been in Thailand, except for Bangkok railway station, where every day at eight in the morning and six in the evening, everything stops for the national anthem. The traffic comes to a halt; men, women and children stand to attention, as this dignified but inspiring hymn blares from the town's loudspeakers.

Aranyaprathet is much more cheerful than when I was here in 1979, the year that hundreds of thousands of people fled Cambodia to escape the Killing Fields and the Vietnamese invasion. The world had seen for the first time the full enormity of the Khmer Rouge terror; the starving, ghost-like children, the piles of human skulls and the empty streets of Phnom Penh, the capital. The main refugee camp here in Thailand, Khao-i-Dang, was now Cambodia's largest city. Almost a quarter of a million people were fitted into this great collection of huts and tents and cared for by the United Nations.

The day I spent here was one of the glummest in my life. I had got a lift from Bangkok in the chauffeur-driven car of a Scandinavian doctor, employed by the UN. She was a cool, efficient crusader for all those social welfare ideals for which Scandinavia is famous. She believed in women's rights, birth control and free abortion on demand. She did not belong in Indo-China. She was perfectly decent in her way, but I do not admire her way. For instance, some of the women refugees were terrified and appalled by the obligatory contraceptive injections, especially harsh for a people who had endured the loss of hundreds of thousands of children under the Khmer Rouge. They wanted to breed and re-build their nation. They also suspected, with reason I think, that some of the Western charities at the time were looking for children to sell for adoption in Western Europe.

However, the UN officials I met at Khao-i-Dang were friendly and sensible. They had done well in coping with such an enormous influx, many of whom were near to death from disease and starva-tion. It was a dreadful place, quite different in every way from the camps I had seen for Laotians. I saw children in shock, who had never been taught to read or write and could scarcely speak their own language. One little girl of about ten, when given paper and crayons, would draw only corpses and skulls. There was not even the anger and indignation you generally find among refugees: just listlessness and despair.

The despair at Khao-i-Dang changed into something more sinister at the Khmer Rouge camp that I visited. The faces there showed nothing but hatred. Even the children were scowling zombies. The Khmer Rouge ran these places as military training camps, drilling the men to fight and the women to carry supplies through the minefields. Even here in Thailand, the Khmer Rouge exercised powers of life and death over everyone in their camps, often placing minor offenders in metal punishment boxes, to bake in the sun.

While Cambodian refugees were reaching Thailand across this border near to Aranyaprathet, thousands of Vietnamese were leav-ing as Boat People, some of whom came to the south coast of Thailand, as I describe in a later chapter. The plight of the Boat People, harassed and often murdered by pirates, was both more telegenic and shocking than that of the people who crossed over-land. However, in its effect on Thailand, the war in Cambodia has been by far the most important event of the last fifteen years, overshadowing other foreign and even domestic affairs.

For one thing the war has encroached on to Thai soil. Until the Vietnamese troops withdrew from Cambodia in 1989, their artil-lery often shelled over the border, aiming perhaps at the rebel armies but frequently hitting civilian camps and Thai villages. The Bangkok newspapers still show pictures of Thai children who lost an arm or a leg in the shelling. At various times in the last twenty years, Thai military leaders have talked of invading Cambodia, or claimed that Vietnam was poised to invade Thailand. This genuine fear and hatred of Communist Vietnam explains why Thailand now has a close alliance with Communist China.

For twenty years, the Cambodian War has threatened Thailand's international reputation. Those in the West who took the side of the Vietnamese communists, have always regarded Thailand as an enemy. The newspaper and TV journalists who exposed the atrocities of the Killing Fields were quick to point out that Thailand supported the perpetrators, the Khmer Rouge loyal to Pol Pot.

The most prominent friend of Vietnam, the Australian journalist and TV reporter John Pilger, supplemented his condemnation of Thailand's foreign policy with vilification of Thailand's capitalistic social system. He led an angry and rather erratic campaign against what he called child slave labour in Thailand. The opponents of Thailand cling to the very anachronistic view of the country as tied to the United States. For instance, one of the many films on prostitution at Pattaya, concentrated on the arrival there of the US Navy on shore leave. For most of the year, there are few Americans at Pattaya. Television producers tend to support Vietnam and denigrate Thailand, in just the same way that they back the African National Congress and Central American Marxist guerrillas. Thailand has fallen foul of the Western liberal or left-wing establishment.

The story of Thailand over the last twenty years has been so densely entangled with that of its eastern neighbour, that here I must sketch in a summary of the tragic events of Cambodia. As I have mentioned, I first went to Phnom Penh from Bangkok in 1963, when the eccentric Prime Minister, Prince Norodom Sihanouk, was raging against the United States. Apart from his shrill harangues on the public address system, Phnom Penh was a tranquil, prosperous and enchanting city. I wrote of that first visit:

> I remember Phnom Penh as a city of broad streets, trees, flowers and flamboyants; of dusk at a café beside the river, and after dark the floating dance halls where Vietnamese girls, insubstantial as shadows, swayed in the moonlight to music that I had never before heard or imagined. In the mornings, I sat under the green awning at La Paillotte in the market place, drinking orange juice and bitter tea, watching the slow crowds by the foodstalls, crammed with the abundance of a fertile land. There were Vietnamese lunches and

French dinners and late at night a soft tap on the door from a
barefoot girl who smiled as you unwound her from her sarong.

Returning to Phnom Penh in 1968, I found the country still at
peace and still more prosperous, although it had so far resisted the
garish, steel-and-concrete civilization of Bangkok. 'I have seen the
past, and it works', I wrote, a remark that at first annoyed Prince
Sihanouk, until he saw it was meant as a compliment. Although
Prince Sihanouk insisted upon his neutral status, he permitted
North Vietnam to use Cambodia as a sanctuary for its troops.
Arms and supplies for the communist army were brought overland
from North Vietnam, or shipped to the port of Kampot, then called
Sihanoukville.

Nobody knows if the United States or any other country took
part in the *coup d'état* against Sihanouk in March 1970. The
Soviet Union and the United States both seemed to welcome the
man who supplanted him, Lon Nol. Fighting broke out all over
Cambodia, as local communists, dubbed 'Khmer Rouge' by Prince
Sihanouk, joined with the Vietnamese against government troops.
Lon Nol responded by an incitement to massacre the civilian Vietnamese. The United States Air Force, which had been bombing the
sanctuaries near Vietnam, extended its raids to anywhere in Cambodia where there were anti-government troops. More than a
million people fled the bombing and fighting to go to Phnom Penh,
which itself came under rocket attack from the Khmer Rouge.

The Khmer Rouge took Phnom Penh in April 1975, forcing its
huge population back to the countryside and work in the killing
fields. The Cambodian communists soon fell out with the Vietnamese communists, who had taken Saigon at the end of April.
They massacred or expelled those Vietnamese civilians who had
survived the previous right-wing persecution. They made savage
attacks into Vietnam itself. At last, in December 1978, the Vietnamese Army invaded Cambodia, captured Phnom Penh and drove
the Khmer Rouge Army into the sanctuary inside Thailand. Some
of the Khmer Rouge sided with the Vietnamese and set up a
puppet regime in Phnom Penh. Communist China, which had
been backing the Khmer Rouge, invaded Communist Vietnam in
January 1979.

This war between communist states produced confusion both
on the Right and Left in politics. To the Right it meant the end of
the cherished Domino Theory, as once advanced by Eisenhower,

Kennedy and the Quiet American of the Graham Greene novel. According to this, the 'red tide of communism' threatened to pour from China through Vietnam into Laos, Cambodia, Thailand, Burma, India, Japan and the Philippines. Now, five years after the fall of Saigon, the tide seemed to be flooding in reverse. The Right had always warned of the danger of 'international communism', frequently with the adjective 'Godless' tagged on the front. They had claimed that the quarrels between the Soviet Union and Yugoslavia and later with China, were ruses to fool the West. Now in 1979, the various communist countries were not merely swapping insults but fighting each other.

Events in Indo-China were still more baffling to the Left. They had dashed for good the hopes expressed by singing the Internationale. The slogan 'Workers of the World, Unite!' was now proved meaningless.

The overthrow of the Khmer Rouge dealt a blow to the international Left, from which it has never recovered. The journalists and the camera crews who went to Cambodia, saw the full enormity of the horror that communism inflicts on human beings. The evils of Nazism came to be known because Germany lost the war, and the Allies sent camera crews into Auschwitz and Belsen. No foreign camera crews or journalists ever went to Vorkuta, Kolyma or other camps of the Gulag Archipelago. Only one foreign journalist, Malcolm Muggeridge, witnessed and tried to report the mass starvation and murder that wiped out millions in the Ukraine in the 1930s. The Left refused to believe Malcolm Muggeridge, just as they later refused to believe Alexander Solzhenitsyn and other survivors of the Gulag. In Cambodia, in 1979, the world for the first time saw incontrovertible evidence of the evil of communism, before it has had time to reform and mellow, as it has recently done in Eastern Europe.

The Left attempted to argue first, that the Khmer Rouge were not really communists, and second, that the brutality of the Khmer Rouge should not be blamed on the Khmer Rouge themselves but on the United States bombing. Neither argument really stands up. The Khmer Rouge leaders like Pol Pot and Ieng Sary joined the Communist Party as students in France in the 1950s, worshipping at the feet of French and Russian terrorists, from Robespierre to Stalin. After Stalin's death, the Cambodian communists found a new hero in Mao Tse Tung, who had just embarked on the murder of forty or fifty million Chinese. The Khmer Rouge, in 1979, were not alone in their veneration of Stalin. The Vietnamese Communist party still showed his portrait in the politburo in Hanoi. The difference between them was merely that while the Cambodians still believed in communism, the Vietnamese had started to have their doubts. When the communists took power in North Vietnam, in 1954, they were truly Stalinist in their liquidation of landlords, kulaks and bourgeois. Later they saw that this was an 'error', but it was not till 1986 that the Vietnamese communists moved towards the abandonment of Marxist-Leninist theory.

Prince Sihanouk, who had coined the term 'Khmer Rouge' was quite aware of their fiendish nature when he suppressed and jailed them during the 1960s. When the Prince was deposed and fighting erupted in 1970, the Khmer Rouge soon revealed themselves as far more pitiless than the Vietnamese communists. Several journalists who strayed into no-man's-land were captured and murdered. For the next five years, the Press regarded Cambodia as far more risky than Vietnam. In short, the Khmer Rouge had won their bloodthirsty reputation even before the US bombing which later was used to explain it.

By 1974, there were frequent reports of Khmer Rouge atrocities, such as tearing babies limb from limb and crucifying women. A few years later, nobody doubted the truth of these stories but some people heeded them at the time. The poet James Fenton, who wrote from Phnom Penh for the *New Statesman*, warned of the evil character of the Khmer Rouge, somewhat to the annoyance of *New Statesman* readers – who also did not like what I was writing from Saigon. When Phnom Penh and Saigon were both under siege in April 1975, those of us in the Vietnamese capital felt almost safe by comparison. When Jon Swain of the *Sunday Times* said he was off to Phnom Penh, I warned him that he might be killed, as he very nearly was. The Press in Saigon fully expected a bloodbath to follow the Khmer Rouge victory in Cambodia, though no one imagined the full enormity of the horror.

The stories written by Swain and others shocked the world. But soon, he and all other foreigners had to leave the country. Silence and darkness fell on Cambodia. Attention was turned to the still more dramatic fall of Saigon and what people vainly believed was the end of the war in Indo-China. It still goes on, fifteen years later.

The Left turned a blind eye to the misery of Cambodia. The *Guardian*'s Foreign Editor, Richard Gott, praised the example set by the Khmer Rouge in moving people out of the cities into the countryside. The British sociologist, Malcolm Caldwell wrote a number of articles in *The Times* and other journals, praising Pol Pot and his achievements. I met him once and found him a strangely pleasant and harmless man to hold such monstrous opinions. 'If only', we used to say, 'Malcolm Caldwell would go to Phnom Penh and see for himself.' He did go, in December 1978, and was murdered on Christmas Eve by his hosts, the Khmer Rouge, in their government guest house.

The Left also rejected the evidence of the first book exposing the Khmer horror, *Cambodia Year Zero*, by Father François Ponchaud, a Jesuit priest who had lived in the country and spoke the language. After his expulsion by the Khmer Rouge, Father Ponchaud started to interview refugees in Thailand, forming a picture of what had happened in Cambodia. He revealed that all over the country the Khmer Rouge had rounded up army officers, civil servants, shopkeepers, teachers and students and driven them to the forest where, in the words of one survivor, 'the servants of the Prince of Death, hiding all along the road, and in the forest, all armed, began to send a rain of fire upon us'. Whole companies of the former army were massacred with their wives. Their children were made to watch and, if they cried, were also murdered.

The Khmer Rouge set out to smash even the memory of the old Cambodia. Families were deliberately split, and the members given new names. The ancient music and songs were abolished, temples destroyed and the bonzes murdered. The Khmer Rouge smashed statues of Buddha, used them as clothes racks or wheel blocks, and urinated on them; all this in a country even more Buddhist than Thailand. The Khmer Rouge banned from the language the subtle and intricate forms of address to show respect for age, social position, family ties and religion. All adults had to be called 'mum' and 'dad' by the young 'cadres', itself a bastard word from the French for 'framework'. All other foreign words were abolished except for 'fascist' and 'meeting'. Those to be shot were sent to the 'higher organization'. The party, the government and the agents of death were called the Angka.

After the overthrow of the Khmer Rouge in 1979, everything Father Ponchaud had described was proved to be only too accurate. Those on the Left who had lauded the Khmer Rouge, or stayed silent about their behaviour, were looking around for a way of excusing their error. They latched on to the recently published book by William Shawcross, *Sideshow: Kissinger, Nixon and the Destruction of Cambodia*. This was not, of course, an apology for the Khmer Rouge, or any kind of communism. Unlike most of the people who used his book for their own purposes, Shawcross had known Cambodia during the war and had studied with horror the book on the Khmer Rouge by Father Ponchaud.

The theme of his book was the US policy that Shawcross blamed for involving Cambodia in the Vietnam War. Shawcross put the blame for the crime, and he used that word, on Richard Nixon and Henry Kissinger. The conclusion was fully endorsed by Prince Norodom Sihanouk, the Cambodian leader deposed in 1970 who, as Shawcross so rightly says, was the only man who could have saved his country from five years of atrocious war and four subsequent years of still worse suffering under the Khmer Rouge. The book is essential for those wanting to understand the still continuing troubles of Cambodia, in which both Vietnam and Thailand are deeply involved.

According to William Shawcross, the crimes of Kissinger and Nixon began in 1969 when they ordered the secret bombing of communist Vietnamese bases in eastern Cambodia, afterwards falsifying the flight reports in order to hide the aggression from Congress, the Press and even from senior government colleagues. Later efforts to guard secrecy and to suppress investigation involved further government illegalities in the United States including the Watergate burglary. After the *coup d'état* against Sihanouk in March 1970, the United States and South Vietnam sent troops into Cambodia, first to smash the North Vietnamese bases and then to support the Cambodians in what had become a new anti-communist war.

Meanwhile, the United States stepped up and extended its bombing of Cambodia, employing fighter-bombers by day and giant B-52s by night. According to Shawcross, the South Vietnamese pilots were so eager to kill Cambodians that they bribed their superiors for the privilege of working seven days a week. I find the story hard to believe. Perhaps some pilots felt like that but not all of them. In Hue, in 1971, in the Cercle Sportif, I met a Vietnamese who had been flying helicopter combat missions into Cambodia. He adored Cambodia, where he had been in time of peace. This love of the old Cambodia was not confined to romantic Westerners like myself.

The bombing of Cambodia created an exodus to the larger towns, especially Phnom Penh, whose population quadrupled to two million. It should be pointed out that those who fled the bombing had not become Khmer Rouge. Many had fled the Khmer Rouge as much as the bombing. The bombing was cruel and counter-productive but cannot be held accountable for the subsequent crimes of the Khmer Rouge.

Lon Nol, the politician who led the *coup* against Sihanouk, had proved both bullying and incompetent in his dual role as head of state and commander-in-chief. He refused all urgings to sack some of his generals however cowardly, venal or dotty: one, in his youth, had placed a cat on his own head and told a soldier to shoot it off. The subordinate aimed low, sparing the cat but scalping the future general.

Until the very end, Nixon and Kissinger blocked all attempts to bring back the one man popular enough to save his country, Prince Norodom Sihanouk. He lived for a time in exile in Peking enjoying a heated swimming pool and French, Chinese and Cambodian food cooked for him by nine chefs. He loathed and feared his supposed allies, the Khmer Rouge, to whose morose and puritanical leader, Ieng Sary, he used to show blue movies, just to annoy him. Not till shortly before the fall of Phnom Penh did Kissinger try to lure back Sihanouk, who refused. After the fall of Phnom Penh, the very courageous Prince went back to his country although he knew that the Khmer Rouge might kill him. Instead they kept him under house arrest until 1978 when they too tried to cash in on his reputation to save Cambodia from a military defeat, this time at the hands of Communist Vietnam.

Although William Shawcross deftly recounts the process of the Cambodian tragedy, I think he overstates the case against Nixon and Kissinger. Certainly they were cynical, brutal and power-mad, but so are most politicians. It just happens that only in the United States, the supremely open society, do we get to know what politicians are doing. Top secret presidential documents are reproduced in the Press; we can read despatches written by diplomats only a few years earlier; politicians and civil servants chatter happily and maliciously to reporters. It goes without saying that such information is unavailable in Peking, Moscow, Hanoi, or even London.

There were other, specific reasons why I thought it was wrong to blame Nixon and Kissinger for the horrors of Cambodia. It is easy, now, to say that Sihanouk was the best man for Cambodia, but Nixon and Kissinger were not the only outsiders who failed to

see this during the 1960s and 1970s. At the American Embassy in
Phnom Penh in 1963, a senior diplomat told me that Sihanouk
was a madman who planned to deliver his country to the Chinese.
That was shortly after the *coup d'état* in Saigon, almost certainly
fixed by the CIA, which led to the death of President Diem and the
escalation of war.

The memory of that fatal attempt to play God in a foreign
country – it is the theme of Graham Greene's *The Quiet American* –
haunted American governments. It explains why the CIA apparently took no part in the *coup d'état* against Sihanouk. It helps to
explain why two years later they did not dare to get rid of Lon Nol
for fear of seeming to interfere. Anyway, Sihanouk's credibility as
a patriotic leader would not have survived returning to Phnom
Penh under American protection.

Again, with hindsight, it is easy to say that the 1970 *coup d'état*
was disastrous, that Lon Nol was a nincompoop, and the invasion
of Cambodia a crime. Such views were not popular in Phnom
Penh when I was there in June 1970, even among the most
liberal diplomats and reporters with whom I argued. Those, like
myself who regretted the old regime, were written off as reactionaries and romantics. Was not Sihanouk a tyrant who tried to
make the university graduates go off and teach in the countryside?
Had not the country suffered from widespread amoebic dysentery?

We have Sihanouk's word, as told to Mr Shawcross, that he did
not authorize or know of the B-52 raids in 1969. I wonder. In
1968 I saw on display in one of the Phnom Penh squares the
wreck of an American aircraft which, so it was claimed, had been
shot down crossing the frontier. Surely Sihanouk must have
known of the B-52 raids, if only from the reports of his eastern
provincial governors? Then why did he not protest? Perhaps Nixon
and Kissinger were telling the truth for once and Sihanouk
welcomed the attacks on the North Vietnamese intruders.

In trying to show that the 1969 bombing raids into Cambodia
were illegal and wicked, Shawcross suggested that they were also
unnecessary. He scorns the idea that the Vietnamese communists
depended on having a haven across the border: ' "No guerrilla war
in history was ever won without sanctuaries" was a favourite
phrase.' It may have been a favourite phrase but it was largely
true. In other Southeast Asian countries, like the Philippines and
Malaysia, the communists never succeeded because there was no
neighbouring country in which to hide and obtain supplies.

Ironically, by the time of the publication of Shawcross's book, the Vietnamese Army was faced with the problem of Khmer Rouge guerrillas using Thailand as a sanctuary. The Bangkok newspapers reported a massive build-up of Vietnamese troops just over the border from here in Aranyaprathet. Were they preparing to cross the border in 'hot pursuit', to use the Americans' phrase?

The bombing of Cambodia took an appalling toll of life. But was it also responsible for the cruelty of the Khmer Rouge, the interpretation eagerly seized upon by the Left? If the Khmer Rouge tore babies limb from limb and crucified old women, this was because they were maddened by years of continuous bomb attack. It was pointed out that some B-52s had missed their mark, striking villages or even towns.

There are several flaws in this argument. In the first place, most of the Khmer Rouge had spent the war in the countryside, often in jungle or hilly terrain, where they offered a difficult target. The sort of people who lived in towns came from the class that the Khmer Rouge wanted to murder. If they were bombed, they were much more likely to go to Phnom Penh than to join the guerrillas.

The theory that bombing caused the savagery of the Khmer Rouge does not explain why still worse bombing did not have the same effect on the Vietnamese, who suffered for many more years from B-52 and low-level bombing raids, from napalm strikes and artillery fire. In Operation Canyon, in sixteen days of 1969, at least 750,000 pounds of bombs were dropped on the river island of Go No, which is five miles long by two miles wide. The Vietnamese troops and civilians were tough to survive these attacks but they came out of the war as normal human beings, not monsters.

Shawcross's anti-American thesis reappeared in what was to be the most forceful commentary on Cambodia, the film called *The Killing Fields*. It was shot here in Thailand, and simply in visual terms it was stunning. Chris Menges, the director of photography, had learned that war can sometimes heighten the beauty of nature and people. He is not only an artist in his profession but he has worked for years in Asia as a documentary cameraman. He told me that he was once with guerrillas in Burma when they were bombed by government planes dropping large stones, because they had no explosives. I worked with him for a few weeks making a film about a village in the Mekong Delta in South Vietnam. I was both amazed and exhausted by his energy and enthusiasm which drove him and us to work from, literally, dawn till dusk. When our crew eventually got permission to stay the night in the village, instead of the local town of My Tho, Chris Menges was furious that an armed CIA man insisted on joining us. After a sumptuous meal at the Catholic priest's house, Menges berated the CIA man over his country's role in Vietnam. I seem to remember the argument started again at the pre-dawn breakfast which, I see from my diary, consisted of bacon, a whole roast chicken, salami, lettuce, tomato, radishes, oranges, bananas, toast, butter, coffee, rum, whisky and banana liqueur.

The film begins in 1973, when Phnom Penh is already besieged by the Khmer Rouge soldiers, who fire the occasional rocket into the city. The protagonists are the *New York Times* correspondent Sydney Schanberg, and Dith Pran, his Cambodian legman and interpreter, on whose experiences the film is based. The action begins when Dith Pran gets wind of the scoop that US planes have accidentally bombed one of the few towns still held by the government. Schanberg runs the story large. In March 1975, when Phnom Penh is about to fall to the communists, Dith Pran agrees to send his family to America but decides to stay on himself. When the Khmer Rouge arrive and turn out to be bloodthirsty maniacs, Dith Pran successfully pleads for the lives of Schanberg and two other foreign journalists, Jon Swain and the US photographer Al Rockoff. They all seek refuge in the French Embassy where it is found that Dith Pran's papers are not in order. He is taken away by the Khmer Rouge and sent to slave in one of the rural concentration camps to be known as the Killing Fields. He gets a job as a houseboy with a sympathetic Khmer Rouge official, then makes his escape through the minefield to Thailand, freedom, reunion with his family and Schanberg.

The Killing Fields blames the Yanks for the war in Cambodia, and even for the murderous character of the Khmer Rouge. The film is frequently interrupted by breaks for political messages (crudely lifted from *Sideshow*) denouncing Kissinger, Nixon and the B-52 raids. When Schanberg is taxed with not having predicted the Khmer Rouge atrocities, he pleads in defence that he could not have known the effect of the US bombing.

If *The Killing Fields* encouraged the view that America was to blame for the tragedy of Cambodia, it incidentally produced the most telling rebuttal. This came in a book written not by a journalist, like Sydney Schanberg or his interpreter Dith Pran, but by the highly intelligent man who played the part of Dith Pran in the film. This was Haing S. Ngor, a doctor of half-Cambodian, half-Chinese ancestry, who had gone through horrors worse than those in the film before he escaped to Thailand. He had also toiled in the Killing Fields, been hideously tortured, and forced to witness the torture and murder of others, including the disembowelment of a pregnant woman. He saw the pillage, rape and banditry at the Thai border and was himself nearly forced back by the Thai Army. Yet he is wholly opposed to the Left's ideas on Cambodia. The book, *Surviving the Killing Fields*, impressed and moved me far more than the film in which Haing Ngor acted the leading role. Whereas the film projected on to Cambodia all sorts of Western obsessions and neuroses, the book tells the story through Eastern eyes. Ngor thinks that US bombing did little to boost the popularity of the Khmer Rouge, which he blames largely on Sihanouk. He claims that the Vietnamese are in his country mainly in their own interest, and stay in power through violence and torture. He blames the madness and cruelty of the Khmer Rouge almost entirely upon the Cambodian character, with its obsession for revenge. He admires and is grateful to both Thailand and the United States, where he now lives.

At the end of his book, in a summing up of Cambodia's recent history, Mr Ngor says that America helped to unbalance the country in 1970: 'Once Lon Nol was in power, the United States could have forced him to cut down on corruption, and it could have stopped its own bombing, but it didn't until too late.' He notes that in 1973 the United States ended its bombing missions over Cambodia, but it was not till 1974 that the Khmer Rouge almost completely took over the communist side of the fighting from North Vietnam. The Americans gave a number of war planes to the Cambodian government, one of which bombed and destroyed the Ngor family home, but he says they were ineffective against the Khmer Rouge who shelled Phnom Penh with artillery and their fearsome rockets. Perhaps because I had been in Phnom Penh during the siege, I cannot resist the impression that these attacks on a crowded city probably did at least as much damage as random American B-52 raids.

Like most Cambodians, Haing S. Ngor greatly respected Sihanouk when in power: 'Domestically, he kept the support of the dark-skinned, ethnic Khmers . . . by appealing to their racial pride and by telling everyone over and over again how lucky they were to be Cambodians.' He also protected the rights of the light-skinned

Chinese and Vietnamese. 'When he spoke to us in his loud, high-pitched voice, shouting and gesturing wildly, eyes bulging with excitement, we listened with respect.'

After the *coup d'état* in 1970, Sihanouk could have chosen to live in his villa in France. It would have been better for Cambodia if he had done so, Mr Ngor thinks. But the new regime's campaign against him, especially the burial of his statues in pig manure, hurt Sihanouk's pride. He had lost face. He went on Radio Peking to say he was setting up a government in exile. He called on the people to take up arms to 'liberate' their country from the 'reactionaries'. To Mr Ngor, this sounded like Sihanouk joining the Left, and not just Russia and China but the Cambodian communists, whom he had once detested. 'For years he had persecuted them relentlessly, throwing them in jail, having them tortured, driving them out into the forests.'

Then, in 1973, Sihanouk came from North Vietnam along the Ho Chi Minh Trail to visit the 'liberated zones' in Cambodia. As Mr Ngor writes: 'compared to Lon Nol, who was despised even by those who worked for him, Sihanouk was highly respected. Even if Sihanouk was only a figurehead for the Khmer Rouge, it was hard to believe that the cause he represented was cruel or bad.' This is a telling point against Sihanouk, though I do not cease to admire him.

Western writers do not believe that dark Asian people are capable of destroying themselves by their own efforts. It must have been we in the West, with our B-52 bombers, who made the Cambodians kill each other. I tend to believe with Haing S. Ngor that much of Cambodia's trouble comes from 'an old, old grudge against the Vietnamese'. All Cambodians know the legend of the cooking stones. According to this, some Vietnamese soldiers took three Cambodians and buried them up to their necks in the ground. They then built a fire between them, using the heads as cooking stones.

The *coup d'état* against Sihanouk in 1970 started off as an anti-Vietnamese riot. A mob sacked the embassy, then murdered dozens of Vietnamese, throwing their bodies into the river. The new Lon Nol government organized rallies at which the crowd burned colossal effigies of a Vietnamese conical hat. When I went to Phnom Penh a few weeks later, the walls were covered with crude posters inciting hatred against the Vietnamese. Lon Nol himself was very dark-skinned and liked to be called 'Black Papa'. The hatred of

Vietnamese was founded on colour as well as on cultural difference.

The Vietnamese return this dislike but with less passion. They too have a strong colour prejudice but in favour of whiteness. In the American war, I saw a Vietnamese point to a black soldier, sneering, 'same, same, Cambodian'. The Vietnamese look down on Cambodians with disdain. They behave to them as to a backward, almost colonial people. Although they no longer use Cambodian heads as cooking stones, they have often been harsh in the last ten years. According to Haing Ngor, who cites reports from Amnesty International:

> They arrest people for making remarks against the regime, for listening to unauthorized radio broadcasts and for marrying without permission. They do not give their prisoners hearings or trials. The prisons are filthy and excrement-filled. Torture is common. The interrogators beat their victims, whip them with chains and rubber hoses, attach electrodes to their skin and suffocate them with plastic bags.

These things sound mild compared to the devilry of the Khmer Rouge. But they are still intolerable.

The hatred of all things Vietnamese is part of the darkness that seems to lie in the heart of Cambodians, masked by their charm, smiles and apparent gentleness. Father Ponchaud says that they cling to the old Hindu regard for authority as a divine incarnation. '*Khmer men chaol* – the Cambodian sticks to the rule; the Khmer people respect authority with a respect which to us is tinged with fatalism, even passivity . . .'

This respect for power, this fatalism, even passivity took physical form in the temples of Angkor, which are frightening in their lack of humanity, humour or individual artistry. The whole place is totalitarian in its profusion of almost identical stone gods, dancing girls and elephants, so that I wrote when I saw it first in 1963 that Angkor must have been built 'by some mad Cambodian Stalin'. I little realized that a mad Cambodian Stalin was waiting to make not monuments but the Killing Fields. The Khmer Rouge leader, Ieng Sary, is quoted as saying: 'How many human lives it must have cost to build Angkor Wat!' I suspect he said this in admiration or even envy.

Towards the end of his harrowing but magnificent book, Haing Ngor examines the harm done to Cambodia by France, the former colonial power, by China, the United States and by Vietnam: 'But sad to say, the country that is most at fault for destroying Cambodia is Cambodia itself'. He attributes this to *kum*:

> *Kum* is a Cambodian word for a particularly Cambodian mentality of revenge – to be precise a long-standing grudge leading to revenge much more damaging than the original injury. If I hit you with my fist and you wait five years and then shoot me in the back on a dark night, that is *kum* ... It is the infection that gnaws at our national soul.

Under the Khmer Rouge, *kum* was directed against the whole existing order of society, against family, religion, teachers, engineers and doctors. 'If someone needs to have his intestines removed,' said the lecturer at one of the re-education classes, 'I will do it.' The Khmer Rouge talked of the millions who worked on the forced labour farms, as 'the war slaves', a phrase that suggests the age of the building of Angkor Wat. *Kum* had become *kum munuss*, or *kum* of the people, which was a play on the word for 'communist'.

In April 1979, Haing Ngor was at Battambang when attacking troops drove out the last of the Khmer Rouge Army. He saw to his astonishment that his liberators were not fellow Cambodians but Vietnamese. The conquerors tied up Ngor and other civilians then punched them, demanding information about the Khmer Rouge. He noticed that the Vietnamese beat only those who were light-skinned and therefore of part-Chinese ancestry. He did not know whether they did this because they hated the Chinese, or because they thought them better sources of information.

Later, Haing Ngor got to know three Vietnamese soldiers and asked them why he had been mistreated. They said they could not distinguish the Khmer Rouge from other Cambodians. Haing Ngor was sceptical. The answer did not explain the hostility of the soldiers who had interrogated him, though at least the Vietnamese, unlike the Khmer Rouge, would hold a rational conversation. He did not want to stay in Cambodia under a foreign or any kind of communist occupation and therefore resolved to leave for Thailand.

Thailand and Vietnam are Cambodia's two traditional enemies. A Siamese invading army overthrew the Cambodian Empire at Angkor. Like the Vietnamese, the Thais have pale yellow skins and tend to look down on the dark Cambodians. But of their two neighbours, Cambodians greatly prefer the Thais. They and the

Thais follow the same kind of Buddhism, called the 'Lower Vehicle'; their religious sculpture, temples and services are similar. The Vietnamese follow the 'Greater Vehicle'. The Khmer and Thai languages have many words in common, but few in common with Vietnamese. The Thai and Cambodian country people built houses on stilts; the Vietnamese tend to build on the ground, except in the Mekong Delta region which many Cambodians claim as theirs. So although the Thais and Cambodians are ancient enemies, they also have much in common and, as Haing Ngor says, have mixed feelings about each other; sometimes of friendship, sometimes hostility, often of both.

Ngor's book reminds us that other countries, especially China and Vietnam, contributed to the tragedy of Cambodia, just as much as the United States. It shows that national pride is more disruptive than ideology. Above all, it says that what the Vietnamese and the Cambodians do to themselves, and each other, is basically their fault, not ours. The author refuses to shift the responsibility for the plight of Cambodians on to the country, Thailand, which for ten years now has offered them sanctuary. For in the aftermath of 1979, the Western partisans of the Vietnamese cause, who had always regarded America as the leading villain in Indo-China, began a campaign of vilification against Thailand, which they regard, erroneously, as a puppet of the United States.

When the Vietnamese invaded Cambodia, exposing the infamy of the Khmer Rouge, they at first had the support of most Cambodians as well as the outside world. The other countries in Southeast Asia and most of the United Nations gave support to a government in exile, including Prince Sihanouk, followers of Lon Nol and the Khmer Rouge, all of whom loathe one another. All three factions had their armies, using Thailand as a base for raids into Cambodia to fight the Vietnamese. In ten years of war in Cambodia, 1979–89, the Vietnamese lost more than 55,000 dead, about the same number that the United States lost in Vietnam.

Rightly or wrongly, Thailand believed herself threatened by Vietnam, which had not only swept through Cambodia but had defeated a communist Chinese army. Thailand claimed that the Vietnamese were driving Cambodians over the border to swamp and disrupt the country. It should be remembered that in 1979, when hundreds of thousands of Cambodians came to Thailand, even more were fleeing Vietnam itself, the Boat People. The plight of the Boat People lost for the Vietnamese most of the sympathy they had won by defeating the Khmer Rouge. Moreover, it soon became clear that those Cambodians who had at first welcomed the Vietnamese for getting rid of the Khmer Rouge did not want them to stay. Vietnam itself, when I went back there in 1980, struck me as grim and hellishly poor.

As the war of words over Indo-China entered the 1980s, the Left set out to defame Thailand. Annoyed by Thailand's prosperity and free economy that showed up the failure of socialism, more and more TV films and newspaper articles told of the prostitution, the drugs, the corruption, the poverty of the north-east and the spoliation of sea and forest. Bangkok was reviled for the very things that made it attractive to Southeast Asians: the cars, TV sets, electrical goods, skyscrapers, shopping centres and girlie bars. These things were often described as 'American', although they were more Japanese.

Hatred of Thailand is part and parcel of love of Vietnam. Some people on the Left hate the Thais because they are smiling and prosperous and have not gone communist. They have disproved the Domino Theory. The forty-year sacrifice by the Vietnamese communists did not bring revolution to Southeast Asia but death, despotism and poverty to Laos, Cambodia and Vietnam itself. The dog it was that died.

PART FOUR

The South

CHAPTER THIRTEEN

Spoiling the View

After a night in the train travelling south from Bangkok, most of the foreigners get off at a town called Surat Thani, near to the Gulf of Thailand coast. Some, like myself, are catching a bus to Phuket Island, an old-established seaside resort on the other side of the Kra Isthmus but the great majority of the young are heading for Samui Island, the latest and fastest-growing tourist attraction. Like all such places, Samui was at first proclaimed as an unspoilt island paradise, where crystal waters lapped against pure white sand, where no sound was heard but the cool breeze whispering in the palm trees, or the laughter of village girls at play. Like all such places, Samui is becoming a hellhole but at an even faster pace than usual.

With almost half-a-million tourists each year, and 221 hotels and bungalows lining its shore, the little island seems to be close to disaster. The Director of Samui Hospital, Dr Suvit Nantapanich, who is a native islander, said in an interview with the *Bangkok Post* that the worst problem was sewage: 'One person produces an average of two litres of waste a day. Samui has a population of roughly 30,000. That makes 60,000 litres a day. Last year we had about 480,000 tourists, staying an average of three days each. Add all that up, and you can now see how heavily overloaded Samui is with waste.' Since the local rubbish collectors can handle only 20 per cent of the total waste, the hotel and bungalow owners usually dump and burn the refuse on the coconut plantations. However, the rapidly rising land price has pushed the rubbish dumps further inland and made it ever more hard to find a suitable dumping ground.

Water is also a major problem. In 1989, for the first time ever, the reservoir on Samui ran dry. The Imperial Hotel, the largest on the island, now has three water delivery trucks, each of them making three runs a day, as no doubt will the three even larger hotels which are soon to be built. More clean water will soon be an urgent need and the people who suffer will be those ordinary Samui islanders who cannot afford to pay for extra supplies.

Sewage and water were now the most serious problems facing Samui, said Suvit, who mentioned almost in passing the tourist-related dangers of AIDS and motoring deaths. In this paradise isle, there are now twenty-nine AIDS victims, twenty-four of whom are local villagers, all of them drug addicts, aged between twenty and thirty-five. In an attempt to stop the spread of the virus, Dr Suvit said that his hospital now did a blood test on every foreign patient. When asked why Thai patients were not given the same he said, 'It's too costly, each blood test costs about thirty baht.' Almost as an afterthought, Dr Suvit mentioned the problem of road accidents which kill, on average, two people a month on Samui Island. Road conditions are dangerous, the speed limit is too high and there are not enough traffic signs. Most of the deaths happen to tourists who hire a motor cycle without a licence and often learn to ride it as they go along.

On the way south from Samui, I overheard some young English people discussing the times they had had on the island. 'It was fabulous,' said an elated, shrill young woman, 'I'd never ridden a motor bike before. I spent seven or eight hours a day just whizzing around the island. I got these . . .', she indicated some cuts and bruises, 'falling off the back of a bike when Bob took a corner too fast. But he stayed on. Typical! I got the cuts from the gravel and the burn from the exhaust. It was really wonderful!'

Who are these young people, the backpackers, who come all the way to Thailand to fall off a motor bike? I had met some of their kind in the north and was to meet more in the south, though I stayed away from their favourite haunts such as Samui Island and Krabi, another up-and-coming beach resort. The backpackers are mostly from Britain, Australia and northern Europe, with just a few these days from the United States. Apart from youth, they have little in common with their predecessors, the hippies. Their hair is short and their clothes are drab. They take no interest in Eastern religions, or indeed in anything about the East. Some of them smoke marijuana and, from their sickly appearance, I would guess that others take harder drugs. This may also account for their singular dullness and listlessness. They show no sign of excitement or *joie de vivre*, except for the girl who had thought it thrilling to fall off the back of a motor bike.

It is easier to describe what backpackers are not, rather than what they are. They are not the same as the young tourists I met at Sukhothai who were interested in Thailand and its history and were generally undergraduates at good universities, taking a long vacation out East. Nor do the backpackers resemble the sexual tourists in Bangkok and Pattaya. The sexual tourists are virtually all single men, in their thirties or over. The backpackers are almost all moving around in pairs, in a relationship as they call it. Although the backpackers like to stay on a beach, very few of them have the physique or suntan that marks out the surfer. Even the many Australians have a weedy appearance. Nor, mercifully, do the backpackers have anything in common with the English yobboes who now infest the Mediterranean seaside resorts. Few people will travel six thousand miles just to get drunk, in any case alcohol is expensive in Thailand. Nor, finally, are the backpackers like the middle-class tourists at Phuket, whom I would later meet.

One further thing puzzled me about backpackers. The size and weight of the burden they carry are comparable with the Full Service Marching Order that used to be carried by British soldiers. What do they put in these packs? A spare pair of shorts, T-shirts and trousers take little space. A sleeping bag is not a necessity in a land where it is always warm at night and you can get a bed for a pound or less. When I come to Thailand, I bring a suit in case of an invitation to formal parties. I also come with some books and notebooks for work. Yet all I need goes easily into an airline bag. The only problem is books to read in the evening or on train journeys. The kind of books that I like are long nineteenth-century novels, for instance Dickens, Trollope and Tolstoy, which are hard to find in a local bookshop and are also very expensive, so it means lugging around an extra parcel during the first few weeks of the journey and then selling them off in Chiang Mai at the second-hand bookshop.

In the minibus from Surat Thani to Phuket, we went through the jagged limestone mountains that run down the length of the Kra Isthmus. Precipitous cliffs, white but streaked with the green of the vegetation that somehow clings to the rock face, loom over the road. Twice we took side roads, avoiding the work in progress on bridges and culverts wrecked by the previous winter's flood. On one of these side roads, the driver slowed to a walking pace as we passed two elephants, ridden by mahouts. These slow and imperious animals do not adjust to motor traffic, and therefore command a respect greater even than that of the water buffalo.

There is now a causeway crossing to Phuket Island, whose fine beaches have made it one of the major seaside resorts of Asia. As you can see from the road, Phuket is also a centre of rubber plantations. The pale, slender trees, slashed by the knife of the tapper, look out of place in these rain forests because the surrounding undergrowth has to be cleared and weeded. Rubber plantations are also dangerous places for troops engaged in a counter-insurgency war, as the British found in Malaya and the French and then the Americans found in Vietnam. The guerrillas in the surrounding jungle are given an excellent field of fire.

There are still some communist bands around the rubber plantations of southern Thailand. Tin and rubber are the two great sources of wealth both here and in Malaysia. The British, who were installed in Malaya, also ran most of the tin mines here in Thailand, acting on behalf of the State. Phuket was the tin capital back in the nineteenth century. Out on the point in Phuket Town, I saw what looked like an abstract sculpture, a Q-shaped disc, which in fact is a testament to a British tin-dredging device.

There are tin tips, or tailings, in front of one of the beach hotels and there is a mine still in use just west of the town. All this I learned from a Phuket man who had studied in England and took the concerns of the island much to heart. Had there not been a row, I asked him, vaguely recalling something I read, when the Phuket people objected to having a factory? Yes indeed, he told me, it was a smelter and factory for tantalum which is a very fine metal used in aeroplanes: 'It's something like tin. It was an international consortium of West Germany, Singapore and some Bangkok people who thought they could do what they like down here. But the Phuket people like their air clean. They know what a smelter can do. And the hotel trade thought that the fumes would be bad for tourism. So people were very strong against the smelter and factory.'

'Did they manage to stop it?' I asked.

'Stop it? They burned it down, and they smashed all the windows of the bank that was behind it.'

The people of Phuket fill me with admiration. Some twenty years ago, I was writing a book on an international company, *River of Tears: Rio Tinto Zinc and the Politics of Mining*. At that time

RTZ were seeking permission to build a foul-smelling and poisonous aluminium smelter on Anglesey, the Welsh island about the size of Phuket. Thanks partly to good public relations work, RTZ succeeded in winning over the local politicians. Protest was largely confined to a few elderly nature-lovers, most of whom were dismissed as cranks or, worse still, Englishmen. On another part of Anglesey, the Shell oil company managed to get the same politicians to let them establish a ship-to-shore depot, in spite of the fact that these installations often cause spillage.

Here again, Phuket puts Anglesey to shame. A few years ago, another international company wanted to mine for tin off Patong Beach, one of the loveliest in Phuket. The fishermen said it would poison the water. The hoteliers said it would spoil their trade. So the offshore mine was abandoned. But Patong now faces a worse threat from the tourist bodies that tried to preserve it. Already it has a noisy 'village' of German restaurants and girlie bars, where touts offer you fake precious stones and genuine massage. The *Nation* newspaper warned that an advertisement 'boasts about the construction of a shopping area and multi-storey tower on Patong Beach'. The man who told me about the smelter enlarged on the peril to Patong Beach:

> There has always been planning here in Phuket, unlike Bangkok, where people will get permission for three storeys, then add three more on top. The only exception here is Patong Beach, where there's no planning, no water supply and no proper fire guard training. If there's a fire there, the old fire engine here in town will hardly be able to get up the hill to reach it. If I had the money, I wouldn't buy a condominium in Patong.

The recently formed Phuket Environmental Protection Club (PEP) is also campaigning against a plan by the international capitalist Bruce Rappaport, to build a resort at Ta Chatrchai. As usual, those who are making money out of this project claim that the protesters are in the pay of a rival company, or are not Phuket islanders. In fact most of the members of PEP are local students who have the protection of monks at a Buddhist temple. Some of the young protesters live at the temple, sleeping at night wrapped up in their protest placards, in order to keep out the cold.

A retired Frenchman who rented a house in Patong two years ago told me:

They're mad. They're putting up all these tall buildings because
they think that's what Europeans want. But the Europeans want
quiet. They should bring in the same law they have in Indonesia:
no building higher than the palm trees. I love Thailand but I'm not
going to stay here. I'm going to wait till things have calmed down,
then go to live in Cambodia or Vietnam. There are good beaches.
They speak French. And because they have socialism and therefore
don't produce anything or have any money, they haven't ruined
the country, as the Thais have done.

I fear he is wrong on the last score. The Chinese and Rumanians
have shown that socialists can ruin the cities and countryside
even more thoroughly than the capitalists.

My guidebook speaks well of Karon Beach, 'the more peaceful
option – a good place to go if you're not into crowds'. I spent a
depressing afternoon there, mostly in one of the three- or four-
storey cement hotels which utterly spoil the look of the shore.
Between the hotels and the sea was a road with taxis touting for
custom and several boutiques. Red flags announced that swimming
was dangerous. In the immense, grandiose and musty hotel, piped
music tinkled out songs from the 1950s. The few guests lay round
the flower-shaped pool, rubbing sun cream on to their bodies. An
Australian woman exposed her leathery breasts. A small elephant
walked round the children's pool. Most of these tourists come on a
charter flight from Europe to the kind of hotel that is indistinguishable from those I have seen in places like Acapulco, Sri Lanka and
Kenya. It is a long way to go for a suntan, especially since it was
not much warmer than London during the summer of 1990. But
then I have an aversion to sweltering seaside resorts, preferring
the coasts of Scotland and the north of England.

The actual town of Phuket is charming, and the hotel was fun,
with a lively band in the evening, Thai clientele and a rectangular
swimming pool, conducive to exercise rather than lazing. Phuket
has a few houses dating back to the days of the Chinese and
Portuguese traders, as well as a modern Shopping Centre in what
is described as the Chinese-Portuguese style. The tall arcade, with
double row of ornamental balconies, suggested to me at different
times a set for Chu Chin Chow, a Stalinist art nouveau, Hollywood
Regency, with hints of Venetian, Gothic and Jugendstil. Among
the boutiques I noticed 'Le Café', which also serves as an antique
shop and patisserie. Because of some whim of the architect, the

ground floor rooms are immensely tall and the kitchen is also upstairs, so that when the cook has prepared his order of hamburger, say, or spaghetti, he lowers it through a hole in the ceiling, gently down thirty or forty feet to the tune of 'Jingle Bells'. This bizarre but pleasant and restful place is also a centre of gossip, like a café in Belgrade or Barcelona. People go there to read the papers and then discuss their content.

The south leans to the civilian side in Thailand's politics and is more opposed than other parts of the country to Bangkok's present government. Although not wanting to dwell on passing political squabbles, I think I begin to see how the system here works. From the Revolution of 1932 till after the Second World War, power alternated between the civilian and military factions under Pridi and Pibun respectively. Since 1947, when Pibun drove Pridi into his permanent exile, the army has been in charge with brief interruptions such as the Premiership of Kukrit Pramoj and his brother Seni. The military rulers had most to fear from other ambitious generals. As I have mentioned, Pibun himself was overthrown by Field Marshal Sarit Thanarat. He was followed by General Kittikachorn and then by General Kriangsak Chomanand who came into power by a kind of *coup* in 1977. His successor, General Prem Tinsulanonda, brought in the present system of much less autocratic rule, with the government answerable to the politicians, the Press and public opinion. In Prem's long term of office, he faced a mild but persistent opposition from various heads of the High Command who hoped to go into politics. These military rulers start to make their challenge every year, around August and September, when it looks possible that they might be kicked upstairs in the next round of promotions which follow the system of Buggins's turn.

The present Prime Minister, General Chatichai Choonhavan, was constantly under pressure in 1989 from the head of the Armed Forces, General Chavalit Yongchaiyudh, who clearly wanted to move from active service into the Premiership. The Bangkok papers, as usual, talked of a *coup d'état*. The army denied this. 'Military coups are a thing of the past,' said Armed Forces Information Officer Director, Lieutenant-General Naruedol Detoradiyuth, answering journalists' questions. Some of the journalists did not believe him. Noting the recent statement by Chavalit that he did not aspire to be Prime Minister, the journal *Matichan* pointed out that this was just what Sarit told Pibun in 1957, before he got rid of him.

Prime Minister Chatichai, in his military days, was often involved in intrigue, and helped to bring down the government of Seni Pramoj, Kukrit's elder brother. For this he was sent into a kind of exile as an ambassador abroad. Since becoming Prime Minister in 1988, Chatichai has been eager to show himself as a respecter of constitutional freedoms. His rival, General Chavalit, takes a populist, even left-wing stance. He took up the fashionable cause of the 'Green North-East'. He called for an agricultural revolution against the Bangkok politicians and businessmen, whom he calls corrupt. This language may have contained a coded appeal to the Thais of the countryside against the Chinese. It may have been an appeal to the radical left. When Kukrit Pramoj suggested that Chavalit was a communist, some 500 officers picketed Kukrit's house. The following year, in 1989, Chavalit tried to exploit the anger against the logging firms. Then he took up the AIDS scare, ordering mass blood tests of the entire army, quite a few of whom turned out to be HIV positive. He brought in the birth-control-turned-AIDS-campaigner, Dr Meechai, and with him promised to set up army centres for AIDS victims, called 'Villages of Light'.

After a few months in Thailand, you start to grasp what the generals mean in their sometimes curious statements. For instance, Chavalit announced, apparently apropos of nothing, that the corruption in Thailand had risen to 90 per cent, in contrast to Singapore where apparently people are honest. A few days later, Prime Minister Chatichai told the *Bangkok Post* that Thailand has the best anti-corruption record of anywhere in the region after Singapore, 'which is only a small country'. He then went on to muse that the social aspect of Thai life should not be confused with real corruption: 'Accepting invitations to attend dinner parties is common practice here'.

Then a few days later, General Chavalit suddenly said it was time to scrap the anti-communist law from the 1950s. This sounded reasonable enough, for the liberal reforms of the Prem regime, and the lenient treatment given to Communists who defected, had brought their numbers down to a mere two hundred. But then Chavalit called instead for a comprehensive internal security law, like those in Malaysia and Singapore. He did not mention those countries but Thais know well enough what he had in mind. The *Nation*'s leading article, which attacked General Chavalit's proposals, also refrained from naming Singapore and Malaysia. But again Thais knew what was meant, especially the southern

Thais like those who frequent 'Le Café'. They understood the *Nation*'s references:

> In neighbouring countries where an internal security act is in effect, civil rights and liberties are severely restricted by the authorities, wielding the power given them by the law. Dissent is stifled in the name of preserving the security of the country – which in practice usually means continuing the control of an autocratic group over the government and society. Those who can, emigrate, those who cannot have to put up in silence or rebel through anti-social behaviour, such as urinating in lifts and refusing to flush public toilets.

A Thai in 'Le Café' was telling me about the repression of freedom in Singapore and Malaysia. 'It's not true by the way, that Singapore politicians are less corrupt than ours,' he said. 'When a Minister is going to announce bad news, he sells off his shares and when the market collapses, buys them back again. Insider dealing.'

Going still further south to the border town of Hat Yai, I found the Thais still more preoccupied with their neighbours in Singapore and Malaysia.

CHAPTER FOURTEEN

Shades of Green

The town of Hat Yai has grown in the last few decades from little more than a railway halt to a teeming city, the third in the country, with half-a-million tourists a year and shops and girls to amuse them. The fish from the nearby Indian Ocean and South China Sea is some of the best in Asia, and you can eat it cooked in Thai, Chinese or Malay style, for all three races are found here. They seem to live together in harmony. A European who lived here several years and speaks good Thai said that only three times did he hear a Thai disparage the Chinese. He also remarked that the Chinese here took pains not to offend the Muslim Malays by cooking or eating pork in their presence.

The two local industries of tin mining and rubber have been eclipsed by the tourist trade, which is quite distinct from that of the rest of Thailand. Whereas most of the visitors to Bangkok, Chiang Mai and Phuket are Westerners, 90 per cent of those who come to Hat Yai are from Singapore and Malaysia. Whereas most Western tourists are young, or at any rate randy men on their own, the Malaysians and Singaporeans tend to come in a family group, or even in groups of women. They come principally for the shopping at what is really a vast black market of goods smuggled in from Japan, Hong Kong and Singapore. The electronic, video, stereo gadgets are a bargain, so I am told, as are the jewels, precious stones and objects of gold which so entrance all Asian shoppers. The fashion goods greatly appeal to women from Malaysia, a puritanical country that frowns on such things.

A Thai restaurant owner told me complacently that people from Singapore and Malaysia 'don't go to Bangkok and Phuket and Samui Island because they are too expensive and there's nothing to do. They don't like sunbathing'. Above all, Hat Yai is close, only a mile or two from the border, and very much nearer even to Singapore than it is to Bangkok. And most important of all, Hat Yai has the naughty glamour for which Thailand is famous, or infamous, all round the world. As Americans during the Prohibition era trooped off to Cuba and Mexico; as gloomy Swedes and Norwegians troop to Denmark or West Germany, so Singaporeans and Malaysians come to Hat Yai to make whoopee. In spite of the high proportion of family tourists, Hat Yai offers the sexual frolics of Bangkok and Pattaya, with only the mask of respectability. The girlie bars are disguised as nightclubs. The massage parlours call themselves Ancient Massage parlours. The brothels are 'entertainment' complexes.

Although prostitution is not so big a part of the tourist trade in Hat Yai as it is in Bangkok, the town has suffered more from the AIDS scare that broke out in 1989. The scare began in Bangkok, where the health authorities, taking a lead from Europe and the United States and backed for their different reasons by feminists and the homosexual lobby, claimed that the virus was spread as much by heterosexual intercourse as through intravenous drugs and sodomy. Although the Thai government has to admit that 85 per cent of the victims are heroin addicts and has not produced a man who caught the disease from a woman, the AIDS alarm took off. General Chavalit, the army commander, Dr Meechai the 'Condom King' and even a royal princess became concerned with the AIDS scare. The ever-increasing demand for condoms no doubt brings benefit to the south Thailand rubber plantations but the AIDS scare has badly damaged its sexual tourism.

Sexual tourists continue to go to Bangkok and Pattaya. These people know about AIDS from warnings in Europe and the United States and, if they have any sense, would anyway use a condom against the far more likely risk of syphilis or gonorrhoea. Western tourists probably have not heard of the AIDS scare in Thailand, since most of the newspapers they read accept advertisements from the sex tour operators. But in Malaysia and Singapore, the newspapers, TV and radio played up the AIDS epidemic.

In vain, the local province head of tourism, Sawaj Na Phattalung, tried to play down the scare. He blamed the Bangkok government for 'exaggerating the AIDS danger, just as previously they had exaggerated the danger of communist guerrillas'. He said that the seven known victims of the disease in the province had all caught it from tainted needles. He said that the scare had already, in August 1989, produced a 30–40 per cent drop in tourists, and threatened to cancel a new 1,000-bed 'entertainment complex'. Of course, one can see Mr Sawaj's point that fear of AIDS can lead to hysteria. The newspaper in which I read his remarks carried an article on the AIDS risk from getting a haircut, or even having your nails clipped.

A few weeks later, Mr Sawaj was in print again, this time accusing Malaysia of 'playing the AIDS card', in order to stop her citizens going as tourists to Thailand. The Malaysian government brought out pamphlets concerning the danger of going to Thai border towns; it clamped down on the issue of permits for civil servants wanting to visit Thailand; it introduced random blood tests on the returning tourists. Small wonder that Mr Sawaj could accuse the Malaysian government of undermining the Hat Yai tourist trade. It may have been a sign of the times that at one posh hotel, I saw a notice on the lift: 'Dear Guests. Durian Cannot Be Allowed To Take To Your Room.' Durian is a fruit that most East Asians love, while others cannot abide its overpowering, corrupt smell. But unlike some of the Hat Yai girls, it is safe to take to bed with you.

Apart from the shops, the restaurants and the Ancient Massage parlours, Hat Yai has little to offer the tourists. There is a temple nearby of quite breathtaking garishness, with a reclining Buddha, 100 feet long by 48 wide, housed in what looks like an aircraft hangar and wearing a wide, ruby smile, like the late entertainer Liberace. The temple has plenty of monks who greet you, like taxi-drivers, with cries of 'hey, you!' and, strangest of all, a merry-go-round, on which there are not the traditional horses but plaster monks, with plaster begging bowls.

In the lobby of the King's Hotel, there is a pleasant coffee shop, but the waiters and waitresses spend most of their time playing computer games, whose electronic pings and poings compete with the noise from the television. One day in the coffee shop, I got into chat with a European who owns a number of bars in the South of Thailand. Since he knew Hat Yai well, I asked if the town had suffered during the floods in November 1988. It was like asking an ancient cockney if London had had any bombs during the Second World War. 'I was trapped in this very hotel for three days, with nothing to eat but a packet of crisps and a bottle of water,' he told me, then took me next door to a Chinese printer, who kept an album of photographs of the tragedy. These showed a car submerged to its roof, a bus overturned, and a Buddhist monk with nothing visible but a grinning face and a suitcase balanced above it. The two men were sorry they had no photograph of the crocodiles that escaped from a local breeder and roamed the streets of Hat Yai.

Everywhere in the south I saw signs and heard reports of that great disaster. Everywhere there were gangs repairing roads and bridges. Thousands were still homeless. At Nakhon Si Thammarat, hundreds of farmers were keeping vigil in front of the Province headquarters, demanding government help to provide seed for their rice fields. At Krabi, the homeless had even invaded the tourist beaches. And everywhere I saw signs of what had caused the disaster, the deforestation by loggers, tin miners and to a lesser extent by farming, rubber plantations, market gardening and tourist development.

In January 1989, the Minister of Agriculture and Cooperatives, Major-General Sanan Kachornprasat, ordered a total ban on logging in Thailand, which pleased the mass of the population but made him unpopular with some of his fellow generals and politicians who had an interest in the business. General Sanan, who has a collection of pets, including a talking crow ('I love crows because of their loyalty') is eloquent on the need to respect nature. He says that over the past few decades, Thailand's jungle has been reduced from 50 to 28 per cent of the land, while satellite pictures show it at only 18 per cent. Yet he has high hopes that this will be up to 40 per cent by 1999 when Thailand will celebrate the seventy-second birthday of the King. 'This will be the best gift for our beloved King ... As I understand it, the King has been paying a lot of attention to this deforestation problem.'

People in Hat Yai say there is still surreptitious logging. 'Power comes before justice', one man told me darkly. But because there is now in Thailand great freedom of speech and publication, actual breaches of this logging ban have soon become known and are punished. This is in contrast to neighbouring countries like Laos, Burma and Malaysia where wholesale logging continues under the secrecy imposed by authoritarian governments. The outcry against logging and other affronts to nature comes principally from the country people whose lives are affected and not, as in the West, from urban intellectuals. As I found in the north, the Buddhist monks are especially strong for conservation, as is the King. And these are the two most powerful institutions in Thailand.

In writing of deforestation, I know that most people find the subject depressing. I used to believe that what I wrote on 'environment issues' – itself a depressing and tedious phrase – was anyway futile. Now I am not so sure. The fine example shown by the Phuket people in burning down an unwanted smelter shows what can be done. And I recently learned that something I myself had written appears to have taken effect, almost twenty years later. In the book, *River of Tears*, which I mentioned when writing of Phuket in comparison with Anglesey, I also examined the doings of RTZ in southern Africa and in Australasia, including the huge opencast copper mine on the island of Bougainville in Papua New Guinea. This was 1971, before we were all so well aware of the dread effect of deforestation. In that year, although the mine had only just come into operation, an RTZ official told me: 'Before, it used to rain regularly at one each afternoon. Now we can go for a week without rain and then it will rain at night. Or we'll get two days' rain on end.' This change in the climate was only one of the dire effects of the mine on the natural and human life of the island. I wrote in 1972:

> The excavation, refining and shipping of this ore to the smelters of Japan could bring great profit over the twenty years to the shareholders of RTZ at the cost of damage to the physical, social and spiritual well-being of Bougainville, which until the mine came, was a peaceful and prosperous island. Moreover, there is a danger that arguments over the mine could cause political strife, even civil war, in this part of the South Pacific.

The publishers of the book went bankrupt shortly afterwards, and I heard no more about Bougainville until 1989 when I read reports of revolt on the island by something described as the Bougainville Liberation Army, which had attacked the mine installations. Three thousand troops of the Papua New Guinea Army were now engaged in fighting the BLA which wanted secession for Bougainville, as I had forecast all those years ago. Then somebody sent me a cutting from the *Times of Papua New Guinea* in which I learned with amazement that the leader of the revolt was in part inspired by my book. The armed guerrillas wore yellow T-shirts inscribed with the words 'Valley of Tears'. Although not by nature friendly to revolution, I could not resist some slight feelings of gratification. It also encouraged me to go on nagging about the conservation of nature here in Thailand, even although it may bore some readers.

These things need to be said more strongly because there is now an intellectual fashion in Britain for playing down or even debunking the world-wide threats to nature. The view is normally heard from the right-wing in politics, those who believe in 'market forces' and first became popular with the rise of the Green party in Britain which is opposed to such things as new motorways and the Channel Tunnel. It was here in Hat Yai, just after learning about the disastrous floods, that I read for the first time a full-blown attack on the very philosophy of the conservationists and in particular their preservation of trees. It appeared as an article in the *Spectator* in which an accompanying illustration depicted a tree with green branches but red roots over the caption: 'James Bowman finds the true roots of environmentalism. Red to green.' Just in case we had missed the point, the first page of the article has another drawing of a tree whose gnarled branches cast a hammer-and-sickle shadow, under a heading: 'Green Grows the Rousseau-O! James Bowman argues that the new environmentalism bears a disturbing family resemblance to a tyranny from which we were only just escaping.'

In his long article, Mr Bowman sets out to prove the point made by the drawings, that those who can no longer believe in Marxism have turned to the Greens for a secular creed. He says that the Green programme is 'about far more than tidying up after ourselves, which is an old and not intrinsically very interesting problem'. To prove this, he quotes from some daft and pretentious Green writers that I had never heard of and certainly would not read, to suggest that conservationists are as doctrinaire and fanatical as other extreme believers, like fundamentalist Christians and Muslims. However, he makes the distinction that while those religions and even Marxism rose from historical events, 'Greenery just growed'.

He then sets out to show that environmentalists and socialists both have their origins in the eighteenth-century theories of men such as Jean-Jacques Rousseau. Both view the world as static rather than dynamic. As the socialists believe that there is only a fixed amount of wealth to be shared, so the Greens believe in a fixed amount of oxygen or food for the population. Both ideologies, Mr Bowman contends, require planners and technocrats and therefore appeal to intellectuals. Both believe in a pre-industrial moral order, threatened by profiteers or polluters. Both believe in the mystique of the 'soil', and think agrarian life superior to urban.

James Bowman scoffs at what he calls Wordsworth's sentimentality about nature, backing his arguments from an essay by
Aldous Huxley called 'Wordsworth in the Tropics', where nature
is 'an unconquered, unconquerable, ceaselessly active enemy'.
From this Mr Bowman goes on to suggest that to destroy tropical
nature may be a positive virtue: 'It is just possible that it is something more than greed and perversity which makes the Brazilians
hack down their rain forests.' He reminds us of Gladstone's favourite pastime which, he says, sprang from 'the old tradition that to
cut down trees was to strike a blow for progress'. He ends with a
catalogue of those he considers the forerunners of 'Greenery', from
Rousseau, Wordsworth and Blake to Freud, the Nazis, Le Corbusier
and D. H. Lawrence.

This article, which I read in a city whose very survival is
threatened by deforestation and other threats to nature, struck me
as muddled, odd and at times almost mad. It should have been
based on the awareness that we are *not* tidying up after ourselves,
which is an interesting and also a very old problem.

Ancient China, India, Egypt, Persia and Greece were all in their
time concerned about deforestation and soil erosion. Even today,
the Greeks mark the birth of a child by planting trees. Throughout
the Balkans, they say that 'no grass grew where the Turk trod', so
that when you move from the Serb to the more recently Turkish
part of Yugoslavia, you notice at once that the mountains are
bald. The Venetians, everywhere in the eastern Mediterranean, cut
down forest to build their ships. Greenery did not 'just grow'. In
Thailand, as everywhere, it is a natural response to threat.

Environmentalism in Britain goes back far beyond the eighteenth
century, which Mr Bowman chooses because it also gave rise to
socialism. The arch conservationists were the Normans, who jeal-
ously guarded the deer forests against the intrusion of farmers and
wood-cutters. The Sheriff of Nottingham, rather than Robin Hood,
was a Green; his failure is shown by the present absence of trees in
Sherwood Forest. Later kings guarded the forests to keep a supply
of timber for shipbuilding. The landowner who cut down his trees
to pay off his gambling debts was looked upon as a cad in the
eighteenth century, even by people who had not heard of Rousseau. Gladstone cut down only the timber that needed felling; so
great was his love of trees that after a storm swept England,
similar to the one of 1987, the Gladstone estate used giant cranes
to replant the fallen trees rather than use them for firewood.

How can Mr Bowman think that socialists and environmentalists both view the world as static? Marxism is based on the idea of a dialectic and violent change, ending in proletarian revolution. Environmentalists, if one has to use that word, believe in the natural cycle. While socialism needs planners and technocrats, the conservationists are by their nature opposed to social engineering. Theirs is a negative or defensive stance. How is it possible to contend that the Marxists, like environmentalists, believe in the 'sanctity of the soil'? Karl Marx himself spoke of 'the imbecility of rural life'; Lenin modelled himself on Henry Ford; while Stalin achieved the elimination and murder of tens of millions of peasants.

Aldous Huxley may have regarded tropical nature as hostile. Those who live in the tropics do not regard it so. Why invoke Huxley, a now almost forgotten pedant, against a poet as great as Wordsworth? Huxley's own understanding of nature is summed up by the fact that he spent the end of his life in California, the ultimate modern hellhole, where no birds sing. As to Mr Bowman's list of the forerunners of 'Greenery' it has to be pointed out that Blake and Wordsworth detested Rousseau. I can think of nothing in common between Freud, the Nazis, Le Corbusier and D. H. Lawrence, except that I find them repellent, and that they all derive from Rousseau. Apart from a touch of pride in my role as the Jean-Jacques Rousseau of Bougainville, I loathe this man as the source of all our modern ruin, with its preposterous isms and ocracies, and bogus religions, including the cult of progress that Mr Bowman follows.

Conservation, which I would call the defence of nature, is quite opposed to all modern ideas like progress and Marxism. There may be loonies and boobies among the Greens but they are by nature conservative, like the monks of Thailand. The people who used to believe in Marxism have indeed found another cause but it is not conservation. It is feminism, multi-racialism, the Third World; not socialism but sociology. The vain desire to abolish the difference between the classes has given way to a still more vain desire to abolish the difference between the sexes and races and nations. Those who wanted to bring down capitalism now want to bring down South Africa. The set of views that used to be called by the shorthand of *Guardian* Women's Page, now hold sway in most of the Press, TV and the bench of bishops.

There is one more twist to the story. It is just in these 'Third

World' countries, beloved of the loonies and boobies, that 'First World' countries like Britain, the United States and Japan are wrecking the rainforests and other creations of nature. Former colonial countries, run by incompetent politicians, are selling off their resources to pay for their profligacy. Brazil, in debt to international bankers, cuts down the Amazon jungle. Ferdinand and Imelda Marcos razed whole islands for sugar to pay for their real estate in San Francisco and New York. Corrupt and paralytic regimes in Kenya and Tanzania allow the poachers to kill off the elephant herds, whereas in South Africa, the herds are on the increase.

In authoritarian countries like Laos, Burma and Malaysia, the felling of trees continues apace, to the advantage either of socialism or 'free market', progressive capitalism. Thailand, almost uniquely in the Third World, enjoys a government which, though often corrupt and misguided, is nevertheless responsible to the people, the monarchy and monks. All three are in the best sense Green.

CHAPTER FIFTEEN

Messing about with Boat People

From Hat Yai, I went on the minibus to Songkhla, a fishing port on a northward-pointing peninsula between a saltwater lake and the South China Sea. Songkhla, or Singora as it was called by the Europeans, has quite a history, as I found in the charming, small museum in the old Governor's Palace. A black-stone Vishnu and Siva lingam serve to remind of the Indian as well as the Chinese presence in Indo-China. Archaeologists think that civilization flourished here as long ago as the eighth century. The town on the old site probably dates to the early Ayutthaya period, the fifteenth century. Modern Songkhla started about 150 years ago under a Chinese merchant, whose family held an almost hereditary governorship. They got birds' nests, for soup, from Cat and Rat Islands a few miles offshore, also exporting rubber and tin to China. Some of the treasures of Governor Yieng Hoa and his descendants are found in the Songkhla Museum, including some finely carved doors and screens, lacquered furniture, with mother-of-pearl inlay, and also King Mongkut's bed, which must have been sturdy to have survived the shaking of so much procreation. The Songkhla Museum is a welcome change from the often grotesque and garish monuments of Bangkok and some other towns of Thailand.

About two or three blocks from the harbour, your nose starts to tell you that Songkhla is mainly a fishing town, the Grimsby or Peterhead of Thailand. Most of the fishermen are Malays, dark-skinned with a frowning countenance, no doubt from haggling with Chinese fish merchants. Among the go-downs, foodstalls and primitive cafés of Songkhla, I was surprised to find a computer centre, in which a dozen teenage boys were crouched in front of the video screens, playing computer games. I should think that the proprietor of the computer centre will make his fortune before very many of the Songkhla children have bullied their parents into buying a home video.

The architect of the Queen Hotel has somehow contrived to build a number of windowless rooms, which means that during the day you not only need the air-conditioning, because there is no natural breeze, but electric light as well. The grandly-named Holland House, in fact a bed-and-breakfast place run by a Dutchman, was full. The beach hotel was too expensive. Nightlife in Songkhla consists of an outdoor café where you can drink your beer in the company of two white rabbits, that nuzzle each other in loving fashion, a corpulent dog and a great many rats that climb up a tree and occasionally try to jump into one of the cooking pots. During the day, you can take a tuk-tuk, or walk across the peninsula to Samila Beach, and sit in a deckchair and look out at Cat and Rat Islands. At one of the seafood restaurants, famous for excellence even in Thailand, I treated myself to shark's fin soup and wondered how long it will be before the shark is declared an 'endangered species', and we have to endure the Year of the Shark and read prose poems about the fish by Heathcote Williams.

Unknown to most of the tourists here, Songkhla is also a nest of pirates, who prey especially on the Boat People, driven here from Vietnam. In his novel, *The Rescue*, set in this part of the world, Conrad describes how an English yacht is wrecked on 'the shore of refuge', a bitter joke, for the people who live there are warrior Malays, with spears and muskets, who plunder the ships coming too near their savage kingdom. The pirates of Songkhla have never enjoyed such easy pickings as during the last ten or fifteen years.

In 1979, when the Boat People were coming in large numbers, a US official in Songkhla told me: 'They couldn't have come to a worse shore in the world. It's the current that brings them, since some of them tried to head eastwards, to get to the Philippines.' He said that Thai naval vessels and planes kept constant patrol to spot the Boat People but most were discovered first by fishermen:

> The refugees are robbed, raped or rescued, or all three, according to how negotiations go. Most of them have some money, an old ten-

dollar bill in a shoe or a trouser cuff. The Vietnamese government shakes them down but generally leaves them something but some arrive with nothing, and that's what the fishermen can't believe. Sometimes the refugees come in naked. They jump out as soon as they land, and fall flat on their faces with exhaustion . . . and then they burn the boat to stop the Thais towing them out to sea again.

At that time, 1979, the plight of the Boat People caused great anguish and guilty conscience. Although the refugees who arrived at Songkhla had probably suffered no worse than those who came through the minefields of western Cambodia, the agony of the Vietnamese was more dramatic and telegenic. Everyone blamed everyone else for the Boat People. The Vietnamese accused the Chinese of scaring people into leaving. The Thais said that the Vietnamese were swamping the country, preparatory to an invasion. The West blamed the Thais for turning away the Boat People, and the Thais turned round and said, 'Why don't you pick them up by ship, and let them settle in your countries?'

To make matters more complicated, most of the Boat People were ethnic Chinese, from Cho Lon, the Saigon Chinatown, or from some of the towns in the Mekong Delta. This prompted the Western friends of Hanoi to suggest that most of the Boat People were war profiteers, dope dealers and brothel keepers, the same smear aimed at the Jews under Hitler. The truth is that there was at the same time a still greater exodus from North Vietnam of ethnic Chinese fishermen, dockers and miners, heading for Communist China.

Most of the Boat People certainly came in part for financial reasons. They wanted to better themselves, as well as to live in a free society. I whole-heartedly sympathize, and yet I thought at the time and still think, that the West was hypocritical in condemning the Vietnamese who had not behaved as badly as other communists. They did not erect the coastal equivalent of the Iron Curtain to stop the Boat People leaving. Although they occasionally shot escaping Boat People, they more often allowed them to leave, and sometimes even obliged them to leave. They allowed them to take some possessions and valuables. Compare this with Solzhenitsyn's account of how Stalin arrested anybody who might have gold: dental technicians, jewellers, watch repairmen and even draymen: 'The prisoners got salty food to eat but no water, but some people still refused to disclose their hoard, or had no hoard to disclose. These last were beaten, burned or steamed to the point of death before their interrogators believed them.'

The Vietnamese who, in 1979, were virtual rulers of Laos and Cambodia, did not try to prevent the anti-communists leaving those countries, as hundreds of thousands did. The Vietnamese had permitted tens of thousands of ethnic Chinese to cross overland into China. But from South Vietnam, there is no way to get to the West except by water. Apart from Canada and the United States, most Western countries were very reluctant to take even those Boat People who made it to safety.

At the time I was here in 1979, a senior Songkhla official announced the arrest of 300 fishermen, not for robbing or killing the Boat People, but for helping them to get ashore. 'Too many people have boat licences,' he added grumpily, 'especially since the Gulf of Siam is almost fished out'. A foreigner here explained to me: 'It's very difficult for the immigration officials. If they're hard on the refugees, they get the outside world coming down on them. If they're lenient, they get their own ministry coming down on them. The atmosphere has soured badly during the last few months.'

This was made clear to me at a camp for the Vietnamese where a surly immigration man said that I could not talk to the Boat People without two permits, neither of which had been necessary in the past. To be honest, I was not sorry. It was sad enough just to look through the wire at the Boat People and think that they might be towed out to sea again, and probably death by starvation, drowning or pirates. Moreover, I knew from old experience that when you interview refugees and ask for their names and experiences, nothing you say will make them believe you are only a journalist and not some kind of a British Consul, offering them an escape from their plight. That is a high price to pay for another harrowing story that all the world knows by now.

At that time, 1979, the West still clung to the Domino Theory on Southeast Asia but with a difference. It was no longer Communist China that threatened to topple the pieces, starting with Vietnam; for China and Vietnam had recently fought each other. Vietnam was now getting arms and support from the Soviet Union, in return for naval bases. Now it was Brezhnev, the Russian dictator, who wanted to conquer Southeast Asia. There was even a school of thought among the Americans that Vietnam herself was a new imperial power, hell-bent on conquest. An American diplomat here in Songkhla, told me during my visit:

I have a theory, I offer it to you, that Vietnam is not really a nation, it's an army. Fighting is the thing they really like and are really good at. Do you know why the Chinese didn't put any planes up over Vietnam in January? They'd have been shot down. The Vietnamese have the latest MIGs and the Chinese planes are twenty years old. The Chinese got a rude surprise trying to invade Vietnam. And those Americans who want to play the Chinese Card are on a loser. China isn't an ace, it isn't even a face card. It's nearer a deuce. Vietnam is the card to play in this part of the world, as the Russians know. When Vietnam went into Cambodia, there were Americans who said they'd bitten off more than they could chew. They took out the maps – Americans in this part of the world love maps – and they pointed to the Mekong River. No army could cross the Mekong, they said, It took the Vietnamese an afternoon to cross the Mekong. All it needed was lots and lots of bamboo . . . And this sending out of refugees was a stroke of genius. They couldn't have thought of anything that would so destabilize Southeast Asia and make all these countries quarrel with the United States and other Western powers.

Ten years ago, the Thais, the Americans and even the British seemed to endorse that diplomat's theory. Today it appears a bit thin. Most people would now think it was China rather than Vietnam which threatened this part of the world. While the Vietnamese have withdrawn from Cambodia, the Chinese are still supporting the Khmer Rouge. The Chinese suppression of dissidents in 1989 dismayed the West, especially Britain, which had agreed to hand back Hong Kong. At the time of writing, Britain was threatening to return to Vietnam many thousands of Boat People who had escaped to Hong Kong and were living in squalid camps. An opinion poll in the colony showed that 85 per cent thought that the Boat People should not even have the right to land in Hong Kong as a first point of call.

On the other hand, thousands of overseas Vietnamese, including former Boat People, are now returning to Saigon, armed with Western passports and money. A lady who had been a young girl in the camp here in Songkhla in 1979, is now the manageress of a Vietnamese restaurant in Soho, and hopes to revisit Vietnam. The very success of those Boat People who made it, encourages those who remain to take a similar risk. For in Saigon, at any rate, there is now no longer much political persecution; just the poverty and corruption that follow a socialist economic system.

So the Boat People are still coming and some of them have the misfortune to sail or follow the current to Songkhla, this 'shore of refuge'. But now there is no refugee camp, no sign of a Vietnamese face and no more talk of the plight of the Boat People. They still come in their hundreds or even thousands, but only a handful get to shore. I learned of them only from fragments of news in the Bangkok papers.

Three Songkhla fishermen are awaiting trial for an alleged act of piracy in March 1989, when they are said to have sunk a boat and broken the arms and legs of the Vietnamese with cutlasses, so that they could not swim to land: also the blood attracts sharks.

According to *The Nation*, about 150 Vietnamese were massacred in an attack in June 1989. The sole survivor, a seventeen-year-old girl called Phom Hong Cuc, says that eight Thai fishermen rammed their two trawlers into the boat, sinking it and drowning everyone but herself and fourteen other women. They were taken on to the trawlers and raped by the fishermen for a week. On the eighth day, as the trawlers were coming near land, the fishermen threw the women into the sea, where all but Cuc were drowned. She survived by holding on to an oil drum, thrown by a fishing vessel that spotted her but would not pick her up. After two days in the water, she was rescued by another fishing boat which took her to Songkhla. Here she told her experiences to the Marine Police.

After the publication of Cuc's story, a spokesman for the Thai Supreme Command, Lieutenant General Naruedol Detoradiyuth, denied that pirates were preying on Vietnamese in the Gulf of Thailand. He said these attacks took place outside Thai waters. 'There are no pirates in Thai waters', he told *The Nation*. General Naruedol also said that Vietnamese who survived pirate attacks tended to exaggerate their ordeals in order to gain sympathy. He added that stories of piracy harmed Thailand's reputation. 'The country's image is very bad as far as sea travels are concerned,' General Naruedol stated. As for Cuc, she remained in custody, awaiting deportation to Vietnam. 'The fact that she was raped does not make her a political refugee,' a Thai official explained.

CHAPTER SIXTEEN

Border Incident

The 'shore of refuge', which over the last fifteen years has taken the lives of so many Boat People, was also the starting point for one of the major campaigns of the Second World War. The Japanese drive down the western side of the Malay Peninsula, and the subsequent capture of Singapore, began with landings at Songkhla and Patani in Thailand and Kota Bahru in eastern Malaysia. As southern Thailand and northern Malaysia were jointly involved in resisting the Japanese, so, after the Second World War, they were jointly involved in resisting insurgency by the communists. So at this point my travels take me up to and even across the border into the only one of the neighbouring countries with which Thailand has good relations. There are many ethnic Malays in southern Thailand, and many Malaysians come north to shop and have fun in a less puritanical country. Malaysia was also the scene of the disappearance in mysterious circumstances of Jim Thompson, the silk millionaire and one of the most famous people in Thailand.

But let us begin with the Japanese *blitzkrieg*. After the fall of Singapore, the shocked and bewildered British, having recently underrated the Japanese, now looked on them as a military master race, who had executed a plan of genius. In fact, the invasion was neither as well planned nor as well performed as the British imagined; it relied partly on luck and British incompetence.

The Japanese timed the attack on Thailand and eastern Malaya to coincide with the raid on the US fleet at Pearl Harbour, on 6 December 1941. Secrecy was all-important. The invasion fleet had assembled in Vietnam, which Japan had occupied with the unwilling consent of Vichy France. The ships that set out from the Saigon River were lucky to have the protection of cloud from reconnaissance planes, and even when one pilot spotted the fleet and reported it, the British took no action. The landing craft putting ashore at Songkhla, Patani and Kota Bahru were almost defeated by heavy seas.

The Japanese hoped to avoid fighting in Thailand, or Siam as it then was. Hours before the invasion, they asked the government in Bangkok for free passage of troops and a military pact, to which the Thais at last agreed. Until that agreement, the Thais fought hard. The Japanese had installed an intelligence officer in their consulate at Songkhla whose job was to signal in the landing craft and enable the troops to take the town and the army barracks before dawn. This agent got drunk the previous evening and over-slept. As the Japanese roamed Songkhla in the dark, they encountered Thai troops and militia who opened fire and engaged them in battle.

All this we know from the memoirs of Colonel Masanabu Tsuji, who served on the Japanese staff throughout the campaign in Malaya and Singapore. He gives the lie to the story that Japanese troops were specially trained in jungle warfare. Most of them had battle experience during the war in China but none had fought or trained in jungle conditions. The men of the 18th Division were coalminers from Kyushu Island. The Japanese were battle-hardened and had the advantage for jungle warfare of being on the attack for, in dense vegetation, when the defenders cannot see or hear the enemy coming, the attackers have the chance of sur-prise.

The Japanese wore light uniforms. They lived off pickles and rice. Their light machine guns were more effective than Lee-Enfield rifles, whose accuracy was useless in terrain where the field of fire was generally less than fifty yards. The Japanese bought or com-mandeered bicycles with which to speed down the fine metalled roads the British had built. The British later portrayed this as some kind of fiendish Japanese trick but there was nothing to stop the British using bicycles, most of which had been made in Birm-ingham. The British had also had months to train in jungle con-ditions.

The dread inspired by the Japanese was all the greater because we had underrated them. It was an axiom of the British staff that the Japanese fought badly in China – which had not stopped them conquering most of that huge country. The Japanese were supposed to be useless pilots because of their poor eyesight and also the vertigo caused by having been swung to and fro on their mothers' backs in childhood. Japanese pilots disproved these theories by sinking the battleships *Prince of Wales* and *Repulse*, off eastern Malaya.

Certain journalists proved to have been more correct than the military men. The American Theodore White, who had been in China, wrote in July 1941, in *Life* magazine, that in the event of war, the Japanese Navy would try to sink the American fleet at Pearl Harbour, while Japanese troops would land on the east of the Malay Peninsula, cross at the narrowest point and push down the west coast; which is just what they did. The British staff officers, early in 1941, had worked out a plan, code-named 'Matador', to repulse such an attack. It involved reinforcing Kota Bahru and entering Thailand to occupy Songkhla and Patani and then hold the defensive position, known as 'the Ledge', which runs through both countries. But in early December, the British Minister in Bangkok begged the military not to breach Thailand's neutrality. If the British held back, he assured them, Thailand would enter the war on Britain's side. In fact, Thailand soon entered the war on Japan's side; by which time it was too late to hold the Ledge.

When the Japanese started their quick advance down the west coast, the British, Australian and Indian defenders seemed to lose heart. The Japanese made a bombing, machine-gunning raid on the crowded streets of Penang, inspiring still more terror. A few days later, Sir Alfred Duff Cooper, the resident Cabinet Minister for Far East Affairs, went on the radio in Singapore to announce that 'the population of Penang had been evacuated'. He meant the white population. The Chinese and Indians of Penang, fearing the rape of their womenfolk, clubbed together to hire a number of prostitutes to assuage the lust of the conquerors. The Japanese stormed on down the peninsula, enjoying control of the air but always greatly outnumbered by the defenders. The present capital of Malaysia, Kuala Lumpur, fell without a shot having been fired within thirty miles. On 31 January 1942, 30,000 British troops crossed over the causeway to Singapore. That too fell on 15 February.

During their occupation, the Japanese favoured the Malay majority over the Chinese who, then as now, were about a third of the population. In southern Thailand as well, the Chinese had more to fear than the ethnic Thais or Malays. Some of the Chinese in Thailand as well as Malaya, joined the Communist party and went to fight in the jungle, where they were trained and supplied by the

British. Their leader, Chin Peng, was given the OBE and marched in the Victory Parade in London in 1945. Then, in June 1948, Chin Peng ordered attacks on the British tin mines and rubber plantations, in a revolt that came to be called the Emergency. (The insurance companies would not have paid on death or damage in 'war'.)

Englishmen who are now entering old age, fought as young National Servicemen in Malaya. Leslie Thomas's novel and film about his experiences, *The Virgin Soldiers*, now has a period charm. Malaysia became independent in 1957 but British troops remained to help in dealing with the Emergency, which formally came to an end in 1960. But thirty years later and almost fifty years since he started his struggle, Chin Peng was still leading his rebel band in the jungle, truly the Rip Van Winkle of communism.

Back in the 1950s, the communists lost their sanctuaries in southern and most of central Malaysia but found a new haven round the border with Thailand, where they joined up with the local Thai communists. As long ago as 1952, the British Vice-Consul in Songkhla reported that Chin Peng's people were smuggling arms over the border. However, the Thai Police Chief, General Pao, who had stage-managed the trial of the three accused of murdering King Ananda, had little stomach for jungle warfare. By the 1960s, Chin Peng was said to be spending more of his time in Thailand than in Malaysia. The Thai communists near this border announced the intention of starting a 'Long March' to Bangkok, which never in fact advanced more than a few hundred yards. But they sometimes ambushed and plundered the trains. In July 1968, a senior Thai official, during a visit to Malaysia, announced that the insurrection in southern Thailand was led by the former Prime Minister, Pridi, who had been overthrown and exiled after the death of King Ananda.

In that same year, 1968, I went to Malaysia to write a retrospective article on Chin Peng and the Emergency. It was not altogether retrospective, for I read in the papers that Thailand had joined Malaysia in launching a new campaign against the communists round the border. I met Mr C. C. Too, the Chinese policeman and psychological warfare expert who had done so much to defeat the communists in the 1940s and 1950s. He was now cautiously optimistic. But still Chin Peng remained in the border country, jovial and friendly with those who found their way to his jungle fastness. When I went to southern Thailand in 1982, Chin Peng's guerrillas had just blown up a railway train and plundered and looted the passengers. My own journey from Hat Yai down to the border at Sungai Kolok was like a retreat in time, except that it made me feel thirty years older rather than younger. For as far as people remember anything about the Emergency, it is the frequent ambush of trains, which also produces the climax of *The Virgin Soldiers*.

The train I joined was third-class only and seemed to be used for freight as much as passengers. Hens clucked in their boxes up on the luggage racks, there were sacks of vegetables in the corridor and the two seats in front of me were piled with great bunches of jasmine and frangipani. The Muslims of southern Thailand are well known as bandits as well as pirates. Two swarthy young fellows stared greedily at my luggage. Another young man with what used to be called in thrillers 'an indescribably evil face', kept peering along the train, for reasons I could not at first discern. When he saw the ticket collector approaching, the young man slipped off his sandals, climbed out of the window, and hauled himself on to the roof, which must have taken some nerve for the train was going apace. Later he climbed back, sneering at us dopes who had bought our tickets.

After five hours on the train, when it was quite dark, we eventually arrived at Sungai Kolok which lies on the Thai side of the Kolok River. The river was flooded and so I spent the night in Thailand and learned the politics of the place. Security on the road was the main problem, I discovered from two Chinese brothers in business there. It was better than last year but still not nearly as good as in Malaysia. However, almost everything is cheaper here on the Thai side, so Malaysian shoppers have made Sungai Kolok a boom town for all kinds of wares. There is also much smuggling, which gives the place that shady and slightly villainous atmosphere that often hangs round border towns.

Another eight years later, in February 1990, I read in the *Bangkok Post* that Chin Peng and his army were about to surrender their weapons to the Thai and Malaysian forces. More than a thousand troops of the Communist Party of Malaysia (CPM) would witness the ceremonial burial and then blowing up of 1,161 rifles, 457 artillery shells, thirteen mortar cannons, 318 hand grenades and 85,529 rounds of ammunition. Chin Peng himself would take part in this moment of history in the two southernmost provinces of Thailand. Greatly excited by this news, I got a berth on the sleeper to Yala, through which I had passed on the train eight years earlier. I took with me the latest issue of *Asiaweek* magazine, which carried a series of photographs of the CPM's 12th Regiment, up in the mountains by the Malaysian border. These included heroic shots of a soldier on sentry duty overlooking a wooded ravine; a beautiful and starry-eyed girl soldier doing her rifle practice; and a parade in which a twelve-year-old stood next to a pot-bellied veteran in his fifties.

The report in the *Bangkok Post* said that the Thai Army wanted the Press to witness the blowing up of the weapons, and so I addressed myself to the general commanding the troops at Yala. He proved very hard to find. I spoke to a colonel, first at the Sirinthorn army base and later that night in the coffee shop of the Yala Rama Hotel. He too was evasive. It seems that Chin Peng had refused to authorize photographs of the destruction of his weaponry, which might be interpreted as surrender and therefore a loss of face. Later, I heard that he wanted to keep up the price of the rare and exclusive photographs like those I had seen in *Asiaweek*. In southern Thailand, they say that Chin Peng has a strong entrepreneurial streak.

From Yala, 'the cleanest city in Thailand' but also one of the dullest, I took a place in a share-taxi to Betong, on the Malaysian border, and near to the camp of the CPM 12th Regiment, with its radiant Amazon warriors. The Thai town of Betong is a rum place to conclude a war that began almost fifty years earlier in the British Colony of Malaya. Apart from rubber planting, Betong's main occupation is entertaining Malaysian tourists who come here for shopping and girls. For some reason, the Betong brothels go under the guise of barbers' shops, the red-and-white poles acquiring a new significance outside the Pink Lady Barber, the Cleopatra Barber and Casanova Barber.

This southern province of Yala is also famous for songbirds which are kept in cages in front of the house or hanging from tall poles. A week after destroying the communist weapons, the Province was host to an 'All-Asia Dove-Cooing Contest'. However, the same poster said that this would be followed by cultural shows and 'sheep-fighting'. This is not, I hasten to add, a local version of Spanish bullfighting, for it involves a contest between two angry rams. The Thais also sponsor and bet on fights between cocks, tropical fish and even buffaloes. The sheep and goats which you find in southern Thailand were introduced by the Muslims as a substitute for pigs.

The Thais endeavour to get on well with their Muslim, Malay fellow-countrymen. Thailand, India and South Africa were the only non-Muslim countries to ban Salman Rushdie's *Satanic Verses*. A Swiss who lives in southern Thailand said that the Thais, like the Thai-Chinese, are careful not to cook pork if there are Muslims around. However, in Southern Thailand, as in Malaysia, there is a rising Islamic militancy. An aggressive new government in Malaysia during the late 1970s, stepped up the discrimination against the Chinese, and tightened Koranic law. The Malaysian Special Branch pulled in Malaysian Chinese who came too often here to Betong, suspecting them of connections with the CPM. A group of Islamic militants shot dead seven Thais at the border here, after which tourism in Betong fell by two-thirds, and did not recover again until last year. Here in Yala Province, the Thais and Thai-Chinese outnumber the Muslim Malays, but not in some of the neighbouring provinces. The Muslims in Patani Province have started a separatist movement and when the wife of one of their leaders was jailed, they kidnapped a Thai woman schoolteacher.

If the Thais and Chinese in towns like Betong are apprehensive of Muslim power, it does not mean that they favoured the communists. Quite apart from the ambushes and banditry, the CPM have for years run a protection racket; Chin Peng and his two chief henchmen are known in Betong as the Godfathers. A local businessman, Bunchong Wong, said that for years he had paid out hundreds of pounds on his rubber trees and the Cathay Hotel. 'We had to,' he told me. 'If you didn't pay they would burn your shop or shoot your rubber workers.'

Many people resent the methods used in ending the war with the CPM. The Thai Government, meaning in practice the Thai Army, has learned from the British experience in the Emergency, that large sums in cash and a future in business can 'turn round' even the most doctrinaire CPM member. Chin Peng, who is said to be a multi-millionaire in his own right, has promised each of his soldiers, man, woman or child, young or old, a demobilization payment of £2,000. In addition the Thai Army has promised to each guerrilla or family, five acres of farmland and, what is more, freedom to clear the forest to plant rubber.

It is this concession that really upsets the Thais, especially those in the south, where 350 people were drowned in 1988. Even before the Armistice had been agreed, the CPM had started to fell the mighty trees that once gave them protection, in order to plant rubber. On this visit to Betong, more than a year after the logging ban, I saw trucks laden with timber heading north. Deforestation is, maybe correctly, blamed for unusually torrid weather in Betong though, not having been here before, it seemed no hotter than anywhere else in Thailand.

Many policemen and soldiers, who do not stand to profit from deals with Chin Peng and his band, are bitter over the settlement. 'Those whose friends have been killed or lost limbs fighting the communists, ask why give them this money and land', was one comment I heard. Some fifty CPM soldiers who tried to go back to civilian life in Thailand, have already been murdered.

The Cathay Hotel manager, Mr Bunchong summed up his feelings about the CPM: 'This destruction of weapons has two sides. This year, for the first time, we don't have to pay money to the Godfathers. But now we may be ruled by the Muslims.'

If you have come to Thailand armed with a multi-entry visa, you may be tempted to cross the border and visit the pleasant town of Penang, or get a change from the heat in the cool Cameron Highlands. This was the place where Jim Thompson disappeared in 1967. As I have mentioned, Thompson was famous throughout East Asia as a silk entrepreneur, antique collector and what we would now call a conservationist. But even before his disappearance, some believed that Thompson was rather more than that. He had served during and after the war in the OSS, the American secret service, and mixed in the sometimes murderous business of Thai politics. Certain legends about him could have come from a Sherlock Holmes story. His collection of art in Bangkok was said to contain stone heads taken from secret caves in the jungle, or statues of Buddhas, whose disappearance had earned him the curse of the monks.

After he vanished, various soothsayers and spiritualists (the votaries of a practice followed by Holmes's creator, Conan Doyle), offered their version of what had happened to Thompson: that he had been abducted by communists, or fled to China or Cambodia; that he had fallen prey to a leopard, tiger or python; or more prosaically, died without trace in the jungle.

The Malaysian police, who throughout the affair were cast in the blundering role of Scotland Yard in the Sherlock Holmes stories, followed up every lead and suggestion, however grotesque. For a time the trail moved to Pennsylvania, the scene of the Holmes story *The Valley of Fear*, where Thompson's sister was murdered in peculiar circumstances, including the fact that her guard dogs did not bark – another reminder of Holmes. The mystery of Jim Thompson had all the ingredients of a Sherlock Holmes story except that there was no Holmes, no Watson, no body, no clue and finally no solution. More than twenty years after the disappearance of Thompson in March 1967, nobody is a penny the wiser.

With the United States involvement in Vietnam already amounting to 200,000 troops, and 30,000 US airmen in Thailand, Thompson stood for everything that was admirable in America. He had come to Thailand to free it from Japanese occupation. He had stayed to build up its tourist trade and then to create, or recreate, a business in Thai silk, which not only gave work to thousands of weavers but helped to give Thailand a pride in her art and traditions. He built up an unrivalled collection of Thai and other oriental sculptures, paintings and ceramics. A trained architect, he had helped to conserve and even to popularize traditional Thai building in wood, against the proliferation of glass and cement. Although Thompson had a few enemies in the business, art and political worlds, he had still more friends in every walk of society. His house by the klong was the undisputed social centre of Bangkok and Southeast Asia.

It was, in short, a famous man who set off on Thursday, 23 March 1967, for a weekend holiday in Malaysia before going to Singapore to advise an American businessman on starting a textile firm. He was to spend the Easter weekend at Moonlight Cottage in the Cameron Highlands hill resort as the guest of Dr and Mrs T. G. Ling, a Singapore couple, he Chinese and she American. As the Cameron Highlands are cool, they have always attracted visitors since British colonial days, and the Lings were among the wealthy Singaporean, Thai and Malaysian people who kept a cottage there, while other visitors stay at hotels or guest houses. The place where I lodged had sporting prints, fake oak beams, copper warming pans and an open fireplace.

On this, as on two previous occasions, Thompson had been invited along with a Thai English lady, Mrs Mangskau, a fifty-nine-year-old widow who ran an antique business in Bangkok. She and Thompson were old friends but nothing more. Since his wartime marriage came to divorce, Thompson had not been known to have a romantic attachment with any of his woman friends; nor his men friends, though there were rumours along those lines after his disappearance.

Thompson and Mrs Mangskau flew first to Penang Island, off western Malaysia. They did the sights then took a taxi down to the Cameron Highlands. There were two incidents in the journey that later were made to sound suspicious. Before leaving Penang, their driver got out of his taxi, ran to a nearby building and came back with another man whom he introduced as the new driver. Later in the journey, at Tapah, the driver complained of engine trouble and asked Thompson and Mrs Mangskau to switch to another taxi, already occupied by two Chinese passengers. They declined to share because they had paid for a car to themselves. The two Chinese got out and the journey continued without any further surprises. Anyone who has travelled by long-distance taxi in Asia will see nothing extraordinary in either incident, much the same happened to me between Penang and the Cameron Highlands, but later, these incidents were portrayed as preparations for kidnap.

Thompson and Mrs Mangskau arrived in the late afternoon at Moonlight Cottage, the Ling home, which lies at the north of the straggling village of Cameron Highlands. It is a pseudo Alpine chalet of a design common enough in Surrey but it was later credited with a sinister reputation. In the Emergency the communists sometimes raided the Cameron Highlands and it is said that Moonlight Cottage was once their headquarters and that they had murdered prisoners in the garden. It is not clear whether this legend existed before the disappearance of Thompson.

The Lings and their weekend guests from Bangkok took dinner together on Friday, then had an early night. Next morning, Easter Saturday, Jim Thompson said he had had his best sleep for ages. According to Mrs Mangskau, he looked rested and in excellent spirits. These details are to be found in William Warren's *Jim Thompson: The Legendary American of Thailand*, originally published by Houghton Mifflin and now reprinted by Jim Thompson Thai Silk Co., in Bangkok. It is on sale at the Jim Thompson House and Museum, and therefore can be regarded as an account of events approved by Thompson's family and friends.

On that Saturday morning, the ladies from Moonlight Cottage drove to the village, while Thompson and Dr Ling decided to walk on a trail through the forest, which here is dangerous and forbidding. The towering trees, dense vegetation and broken terrain of hills and ravines reduce visibility to only a few feet and make it almost impossible to recognize landmarks. Except for the aboriginal tribes, few people have managed to live for long in this jungle. The

Japanese did not venture there but the guerrillas fared little better. In the Emergency, the Chinese communists started in the more easy terrain round the rubber plantations and tin mines and, only when they were hard pressed, took to the dense jungle of central Malaysia.

Although in the ten square miles of the Cameron Highlands resort there are well-kept trails, literally beaten tracks through the forest, the tourist authorities warn hikers to never walk alone; to always carry a water bottle, a box of matches, compass, torch, knife and a little food. They printed instructions on what to do and what not to do when lost, and a sketch map showing the numbered routes. All these things, Thompson knew, for he was no stranger to jungles. During the war he had taken a two-month course in Ceylon on jungle survival. He had frequently been in dense terrain, if not strictly jungle, in Thailand. Moreover, he had already been twice to the Cameron Highlands, had walked through the forest and had, on one occasion, barely escaped from difficulty after meeting a swarm of hornets.

This Saturday morning, the eve of his disappearance, Thompson had one more reminder of danger. Dr Ling said he had found a trail leading from near Moonlight Cottage down the hill to the golf course. Walking from Moonlight Cottage along the road to the golf course takes twenty minutes. He and Thompson started off on their walk before ten in the morning, having arranged to meet the ladies at the golf club at eleven. They did not arrive until nearly one p.m. Apparently, soon after leaving Moonlight Cottage, they had got lost in the undergrowth; furthermore, Dr Ling had tripped over a root and sprained a ligament. Thompson had got them to safety by keeping the course of a stream. Nevertheless, the two men had been delayed two hours on a trail that Dr Ling had walked before. It showed that Thompson knew the risk of even the smallest venture away from the metal road.

The next morning, Easter Sunday, the Lings and their guests went to the little Anglican Church at Tanah Rata, then drove for a picnic to a plateau a few miles away. Thompson had favoured lunch in the garden at Moonlight Cottage and after the picnic was keen to pack up his things and get back. But at the time, no one saw anything odd in his behaviour. They may have thought he was tired and wanted to rest as did the Lings and Mrs Mangskau who retired to their rooms in Moonlight Cottage. They left Thompson in the sitting room; he said that he too would be going to bed. It was the last time they saw him.

In their bedroom, the Lings heard the sound of an aluminium deck-chair placed on the verandah, and shortly afterwards heard the sound of footsteps on the gravel footpath to the road. Mrs Ling said she was sure they were the footsteps of a European, not of an Asian. They heard no voices, nothing untoward, nothing in fact that might have caused them to get off the bed and look out of the window. They simply imagined that Thompson had gone for a stroll, which is probably what he did.

An hour or so later, or shortly before four p.m., Mrs Mangskau got up and did some packing as they were planning an early start next day for the drive to Singapore. At about four-thirty, she went to the living room where she found Dr Ling reading. He mentioned that he had heard Jim Thompson leave for a walk at about three. They noticed that Thompson's jacket was hanging on the back of a chair and that he had also left his cigarettes and lighter. Since he was always a heavy smoker, this suggested that he had gone out only briefly. Later it was discovered that he had left in his bedroom the pills he took against gallstone pains.

At about five o'clock the Lings and Mrs Mangskau took some tea. Around six o'clock, when sunset begins and the air turns quite suddenly cool, the three of them started to wonder what had happened to Thompson. Dr Ling thought he must have walked to the golf club and drove to fetch him. He came back to say that Thompson had not been seen. Then Mrs Ling telephoned a local hotel where some of their friends were staying, including Thompson's doctor from Bangkok, but once again no one had seen him.

By about seven-thirty p.m., when it was quite dark, unease had turned to alarm. Dr Ling recalled the mishap of the previous day, in daylight. At night-time one cannot venture a step in the jungle. Moreover, at this altitude, about 5,000 feet, the temperature drops to the forties Fahrenheit, and Thompson had left in his shirt sleeves.

At this point Dr Ling called up the rental agent for Moonlight Cottage, a Dutchman who knew the area well; and also the Tanah Rata Police Station. The police said they would notify people in the vicinity and begin a full-scale search at dawn, if Thompson had not appeared. The Dutch rental agent arrived with a guest, a British Major, who happened to have a cocker spaniel which he said was trained in hunting, although retrieving sounds more likely. They all went to the place where Thompson had met the hornets but came back at midnight with no news. They had shone their torches and shouted his name, and the dog had presumably sniffed around, but all to no purpose.

Apparently on this first night and for some days afterwards, nobody thought of the weird and sinister explanations of Jim Thompson's disappearance that would come later. The Lings and Mrs Mangskau thought he had lost his way, or had had some kind of attack, perhaps from his gallstone trouble, or had had a fall and could not move. Anxiety had turned into alarm but not yet horror. That was to come when news of the disappearance spread from the Cameron Highlands into newspapers all over the world, where Thompson was a celebrity. His story partook of the glamour and mystery of the East.

Thompson's maternal grandfather, a Civil War General called James Harrison Wilson, had gone out to China, exploring the possibility of a railway, and later wrote a popular book, *Travels in the Middle Kingdom*. He became a friend of the future King Rama VI of Siam. In Jim Thompson's house, which is now a museum, you can see a dining table formed from a pair of gaming tables, made for the palace of King Chulalongkorn. In spite of his grandfather's career, Thompson had no early hankering for the East. He was born in Delaware on 21 March 1906, the youngest of five children, to wealthy, though not plutocratic, parents. His father ran a finishing works for cotton and later rayon fabrics which may have inspired Thompson's later interest in Thai silks. He learned French, went to boarding school and Princeton University and although failing to qualify as an architect, he made a career in that profession in New York during the 1930s.

The first odd departure in Thompson's career came when he chucked his job and joined the army in 1940, more than a year before the United States entered the war. By the time of Pearl Harbour, Thompson was an NCO and then got a commission in the artillery. In 1942 he joined the newly-formed Office of Strategic Services, and partly because of his knowledge of French, was assigned to North Africa and then with the invading army to Italy and France. He did not discuss the war, so we do not know whether he did routine intelligence work or something of a clandestine 'cloak and dagger' nature. Nor do we know whether he later kept his connection with OSS, or its successor the CIA.

When the war ended in Europe, Thompson volunteered to serve in the Pacific. He had spent only six months with his beautiful wife, Pat, whom he married in 1942 but he showed little eagerness to resume the marriage which later was dissolved.

Although pushing forty, Thompson survived a course in jungle survival and parachuting. By the time he was ready to jump into Thailand, Japan had surrendered, so Thompson arrived in a military plane at Bangkok airport. He and the other OSS men took up residence in one of the royal palaces and were in effect the military government of the country. Within a few weeks, Thompson was station chief and, in effect, the power in the land. Even after the Allies made formal peace and re-established their embassies in Bangkok, Thompson remained the political advisor to the Americans.

Thompson became a friend of Pridi, the Regent and later Prime Minister, apparently sharing his aspirations. As a French-speaker, Thompson also got to know and supported the nationalist and anti-French politicians from Vietnam, Cambodia and Laos. He spent much time in the north-east where the OSS was in conflict both with the French and the British, as described in an earlier chapter. At about this time, Thompson decided to make his home in Thailand. His marriage had broken up in 1946, so he had no more ties with America and he had also fallen under the spell of what was still a delightful country. In the Bangkok of 1946, the klongs had not been paved over for roads; the cool teak houses had not been replaced by air-conditioned cement boxes; the tricycle taxis or samlors had not given way to motor cars.

Although Thompson was never embarrassed for money, and later came into a family fortune, he needed work as an outlet for his energy. He joined in relaunching the Oriental Hotel, also designing a new extension. He became interested in the Thai silk he found in antique shops. Like most East Asian countries, Thailand had always been a producer of silk and there were mulberry trees in the north-east to support the silk-worms; but mass-produced clothes had undercut the traditional fabric whose colours tended to fade in the wash. However, Thompson liked the texture of the material, what he called its 'lumps and bumps', also its colour combinations. He investigated what remained of the Thai silk industry and found a village of weavers, most of them Muslims, in the Bangkrua district of the capital. He had some pieces made and took them to New York where they were publicized by *Vogue* magazine. In 1948, the Thai Silk Company Ltd came into existence.

From the start of the enterprise, Thompson was always its best salesman. He would stand in the lobby of the Oriental Hotel with pieces of silk over his arm and wait (never long) before some woman tourist would make inquiries. With his Ivy League manners and excellent sense of colour, he found it easy to persuade each customer which fabric suited her. More and more magazines and famous people enthused over Thompson's silk which also received a boost from the film *The King and I*. By the end of the 1950s, the success of Thompson's enterprise was measurable by its imitators, as much as by the famous people who came to see him.

Contrary to some rumours, Thompson was not the sole owner of his company, but he held shares and accepted a salary. Most of his earnings went on works of art, which were not hard to find then in Thailand. His hoard grew so big that Thompson decided to build the house, which is now a museum, across the klong from the village of weavers.

Some said that the Thompson house was too crammed with works of art and therefore unfit to live in. Certainly, it is not a place to hold a riotous party, or to bring up children, but as a setting for some remarkable paintings, sculpture and furniture, it is a triumph. One Buddha, especially, is breathtaking. To be a guest at dinner was a privilege, though one that Thompson freely awarded for he enjoyed entertaining. The house won the approval even of Somerset Maugham, the crotchety old Asia hand, who went there to dinner during a voyage in 1959. 'You have not only beautiful things,' wrote the old iguana, 'but what is rare, you have arranged them with faultless style.'

His art collection also contributed to a certain ill-feeling between Jim Thompson and the authorities in Thailand. The politician he had admired, the left-wing Pridi, was deposed in 1947, to be replaced by Pibun, the wartime dictator. When Pridi had gone into exile in China, police terror followed in Thailand and several of Thompson's friends were murdered or jailed. To make matters worse, Sarit Thanarat's wife set up in business as a competitor, or imitator of Thompson's silk. Very probably it was Sarit who inspired an investigation of Thompson on the suspicion that he had stolen five sculptured heads of Buddha and Bodhisattva from a cave near a temple in Petchaboon province. As it happened, Thompson had bought the heads from a dealer and only afterwards found the caves from which they might have been taken. Since he had no intention of abducting any Thai art works and had already willed his collection to the nation, Thompson was understandably furious. He nearly decided to leave an ungrateful country, until a sense of proportion returned.

This unpleasantness was already almost forgotten when Thompson went to the Cameron Highlands. But he was tired and his health had been troubling him. He was getting a little grumpy sometimes with crass or importunate visitors. However, old friends thought there was not much wrong with Thompson at Easter, 1967, when he vanished.

The official search for Jim Thompson started at first light on Monday 27 March, fifteen hours after his disappearance. The police led a search party amounting to one hundred people, including some British soldiers on convalescent leave and a number of guests from hotels. Quite apart from the impenetrability of the jungle, the chief problem facing the searchers was not knowing where to start looking. There are jungle trails officially marked and periodically cleared all round the area loosely known as the Cameron Highlands, between two concentrations of housing at Tanah Rata and Brinchang. Moonlight Cottage stands at the dead end of a road leading up from the main road that rings the golf course. If Thompson had got on this main road he might have walked miles before turning off on to a jungle track. If he had entered the jungle near Moonlight Cottage, he could not have gone far, because nobody could go far in that jungle. But nobody did remember seeing the elderly and distinguished-looking American walking alone on that Sunday afternoon.

Although more than a hundred people joined in the search for three full days, and many more during the following week, it was not a thorough operation. No specialized trackers were employed, nor the aboriginal tribespeople, nor any tracker dogs apart from an elderly and obese bloodhound. Even so it is fairly certain that had Jim Thompson been alive and conscious, out in the jungle, he would at some point have heard and answered one of the search parties. No vultures gathered at any point. He could have died from a natural cause, like heart attack, or fallen into one of the animal traps dug by the tribespeople, or been attacked by a tiger, leopard or python. But the fact is that of the hundreds of thousands of people who visit the Cameron Highlands, none either before or since Jim Thompson has died or disappeared in the jungle.

On the Tuesday after his disappearance, Jim Thompson's company in Bangkok offered a large reward for information about his whereabouts. At the same time, all sorts of people in Malaysia,

Thailand and soon the rest of the world came up with explanations of what had happened. A con-man from Singapore offered to lead people to Thompson if he was offered 'expenses'. A *bomoh* or medicine man in the Cameron Highlands said that Thompson had fallen prey to a forest spirit. An English music-hall mind reader, Al Koran, who was then performing in Bangkok, disclosed that Thompson had gone into the jungle to die, like an elephant. The *New York Times* was one of the first newspapers to voice the suggestion that Thompson may not have gone into the jungle; it emphasized that he had left behind his cigarettes and medical tablets; also the failure of vultures or dogs to trace the body. Other journalists dwelt on oddities in the days preceding the disappearance, especially the switch in taxi drivers. Malaysia has seen many kidnaps involving Chinese secret societies and there were also communists in the jungle, seven years after the formal ending of the Emergency.

Soon the papers started to talk about Thompson's wartime role with the OSS and hinted that he was working now for the CIA. Another school of conspiracy theorists harped on his sympathy with the Viet Minh and other communist forces in French Indo-China, and also his friendship with Pridi, the Thai politician in exile in Peking. Was Thompson a secret communist? The various strands of conspiracy theory were brought together and publicized by a most extraordinary person called Peter Hurkos, a Dutch-born, self-styled mystic, whose psychic powers were much regarded in California, especially after he claimed to have solved the case of the Boston Strangler. In fact, Hurkos had not found the killer, but had greatly impressed the Boston police. When a detective turned up late for a meeting, saying his car had broken down, Hurkos said in his broad Dutch accent, 'You no late because of car, you late because you get fucked'. He went on to describe in accurate detail how the detective had been detained by his girlfriend, a pretty divorcee of twenty-seven or twenty-eight: 'She say, "Before you leave, honey, you have a cup of coffee." You go into kitchen with her, she bend down to get coffee pot in cabinet, you grab her, you push her on kitchen table and you fuck her. Then you come here. That's why you late. Right?' Right.

With these credentials, Hurkos arrived in Hong Kong, with his secretary and assistant, Stephany Farb. 'Hurkos wished to avoid the Press and also to check out the border between Red China and Hong Kong,' Miss Farb explained. In Bangkok, Hurkos visited

Thompson's house where he got impressions and vibrations. He also heard some of the stories concerning Pridi. He felt at this time that Thompson had been abducted by kidnappers and might be held just north of the Thai-Malaysian border.

Arriving at Cameron Highlands, Hurkos visited Moonlight Cottage, went into a trance and started to utter a number of revelations. The transcript recorded by Miss Farb, starts with the words:

> He was sitting in the chair . . . right there . . . he was not sitting in the house . . . the chair was on the verandah . . . ag, Prebi, oogh . . . Thompson . . . Prebi, Pridi . . . fourteen people . . . fourteen people captured him . . . Prebe or Bebe . . . or a blonde Bebe . . . he is not in the jungle . . . I want to follow the route where they picked him up . . .

The revelations continued, exhausting Hurkos. Later, as he was drinking coffee in Moonlight Cottage, Hurkos suddenly felt inspired to disclose where Thompson was. He leaped to his feet, pointed his finger at a map and exclaimed, 'There! That's where he is now! Cambodia! That's where he is, I'd give my neck on it!'

This revelation produced big headlines over the whole world; also a diplomatic problem. Cambodia, under the happy rule of Prince Norodom Sihanouk, had no relations with the United States and would not allow in Hurkos. Yet it shows his influence that the State Department in Washington made an approach to Cambodia, through a third party, asking for help in the search for Thompson. Long afterwards, Sihanouk said he knew nothing about the matter, as did Pridi.

Then a more serious witness lent his authority to the belief that Thompson had not disappeared in the jungle. This was Richard Noone, an Englishman who had served in Malaysia through the Emergency as an advisor on aboriginal tribespeople, forming a regiment of these men to fight the communists. Apart from his elder brother Pat, who had fought with the same aboriginals against the Japanese, nobody knew the Cameron Highlands better than Richard Noone. He went to the Cameron Highlands, stayed at Moonlight Cottage, and went into the jungle with a border scout and an aboriginal bomoh. On his return he said: 'I am fully convinced that Mr Thompson is not lost in the jungle'.

More than twenty years after Thompson's disappearance, we still are no nearer an explanation. The kidnap theory seemed less probable every week that went by without a ransom demand. It is possible that, as suggested by Al Koran, Thompson went into the jungle to die. But death by thirst and exposure is not an easy way to go and we have no reason to think that Thompson was suicidal. He had just attended a church which teaches that suicide is a sin. He was a gentleman who would not have wished to bring anguish to old friends like the Lings and Mrs Mangskau. The laws of probability suggest that Thompson got lost, or took ill or had an accident in the jungle. And yet . . .

As I strolled from the golf course up the hill to Moonlight Cottage, whose garden is still well-tended and trim, it seemed inconceivable that anyone could get himself killed among the innocuous-looking ferns and rhododendrons lining the road. Nobody else has vanished here. We are asked to believe that the only peacetime victim of this attractive hill station was one who had trained in jungle survival, a former secret service agent who still was perhaps engaged in the lethal politics of Southeast Asia. For once, I find myself among the conspiracy theorists.

Epilogue

Returning to Thailand in August 1990, I found the usual serenity and the usual reports of impending disaster. The authorities at Koh Samui were proposing to give a compulsory blood test for AIDS to all foreign tourists setting foot on the paradise island. Yet another foreign TV company has made a documentary on Pattaya and the sex industry. When two young British women were apprehended at Bangkok airport with several kilos of heroin, journalists from the London tabloid newspapers came in droves to report on the horror of Bangkok's women's prison, only to find that the girls were kept in a model establishment. Bangkok's usual warnings of late summer floods were this year compounded by talk of an imminent earthquake, leading to comparison with the doomed cities of Sodom and Gomorrah.

As I have tried to explain in this book, the ill repute of Thailand in countries like Britain is largely due to the anti-American, pro-Vietnamese beliefs of the liberal establishment in the Press and the television companies. This attitude dates from the time of the Vietnam War and the efforts to stop the spread of communism in Southeast Asia. But even before the end of the Vietnam War, Thailand had dropped its alliance with the United States, made friends with Communist China and closed the American air force bases. This attitude is still more out of date since it looks as though Vietnam is rapidly going the way of the communist countries of eastern Europe.

Pattaya beach and the Patpong Road began as brothels for US servicemen on 'R & R' from the Vietnam War; but R & R ended eighteen years ago. In both places, these days Americans are outnumbered ten or twenty to one by Europeans and Australasians. The only enduring legacy of the United States is AIDS.

The disease began with the liberalization of laws and attitudes relating to drug abuse and homosexual behaviour. Both these practices are rampant today in Patpong Road and Pattaya, which specializes in prostitution of young boys. The astonishing number of murders in Pattaya sometimes involve homosexuals but more often heroin users or dealers.

It was not the American politicians and generals but advocates of the Permissive Society who have in the end depraved and corrupted Thailand. Paradoxically, those who still advocate the Permissive Society tend to be those who still support Vietnam. Those who railed against the prostitution of Thai girls by American servicemen, do not complain of the prostitution of Thai boys by West European tourists. Indeed, the liberal establishment in Europe and the United States refuses to recognize that homosexual behaviour is one of the two prime means of spreading AIDS.

The same hypocrisy obscures the question of drugs. The campaign to legalize first marijuana then all harmful drugs was a popular liberal cause in the 1960s. When this led to an epidemic of heroin, cocaine and now crack abuse, the liberals would not admit they had been mistaken and called instead for a programme to cure, or rehabilitate drug users. At the same time, society turned its wrath on those who supplied the drugs, especially the opium growers of Southeast Asia and the coca growers of South America. The US Drug Enforcement Agency has mounted costly campaigns and even military operations against poor peasant producers of drugs rather than taking action against the consumers in the United States.

Meanwhile the liberalization of attitudes towards drug abuse has spread from the United States and Europe to countries like Thailand where there are more than 100,000 heroin addicts. They are dying of AIDS even on Koh Samui, the former paradise island. Yet when the Thais arrested the two British girls carrying several kilos of pure heroin, the British Press portrayed this as an act of injustice. The outrage was partly based on a rubbishy TV serial 'Bangkok Hilton', in which a foreign girl is jailed and eventually executed in Thailand.

The remorseless campaign against Thailand will no doubt continue as long as the communists hold power in the neighbouring countries of Laos, Cambodia and Vietnam. The foreign friends of those countries cannot forgive Thailand for having remained peaceful, prosperous and happy. Long may she remain so.

Bibliography

Boontawee, Kampoon, translated by Susan Fulop Kepner, *A Child of the North-east* (Bangkok, 1988)

Botan, translated by Susan Fulop Kepner, *Letters from Thailand* (Bangkok, 1965)

Collis, Maurice, *Siamese White* (London, 1936)

Conrad, Joseph, *The Rescue* (London, 0000)

Crawfurd, John, *A Journal of an Embassy* (London, 1828)

Fitzpatrick, Sir Percy, *Jock of the Bushveld* (Cape Town, 1987)

Kemp, Peter, *The Thorns of Memory* (London, 1990)

Kruger, Rayne, *The Devil's Discus* (London, 1954)

Kusy, Frank and Capel, Frances, *Thailand & Burma* (London, 1988)

Leonowens, Anna, *The English Governess at the Siamese Court* (Boston, 1870)

Marsden-Smedley, Philip and Klinke, Jeffrey (eds), *Views From Abroad* (London, 1988)

McCoy, Alfred W., *The Politics of Heroin in Southeast Asia* (???)

Neville, Richard and Clarke, Julie, *The Life and Crimes of Charles Sobhraj* (Jonathan Cape, 1979)

Praagh, David van, *Alone on the Sharp Edge* (Bangkok, 1989)

Pramoj, Kukrit, *Four Reigns* (2 vols) (Bangkok, 1981)

Sadam, Pira, *Siamese Drama* (Bangkok, 1983)

Sadam, Pira *People of Esarn* (Bangkok, 1987)

Saul, John Ralston, *Paradise Eater* (London, 1988)

Warren, William, *Jim Thompson* (Bangkok, 1983)

Williams, J. H., *Elephant Bill* (London, 1946)

Wilson, David A., *Politics in Thailand* (London, 1982)

Index

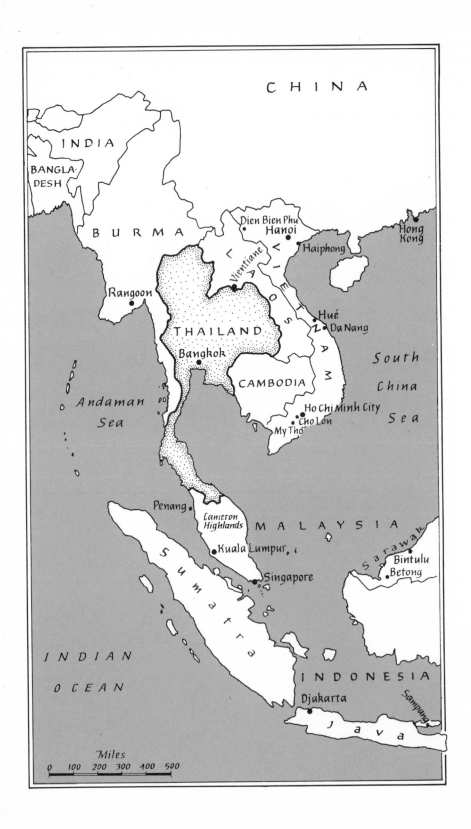